Sandra Chait

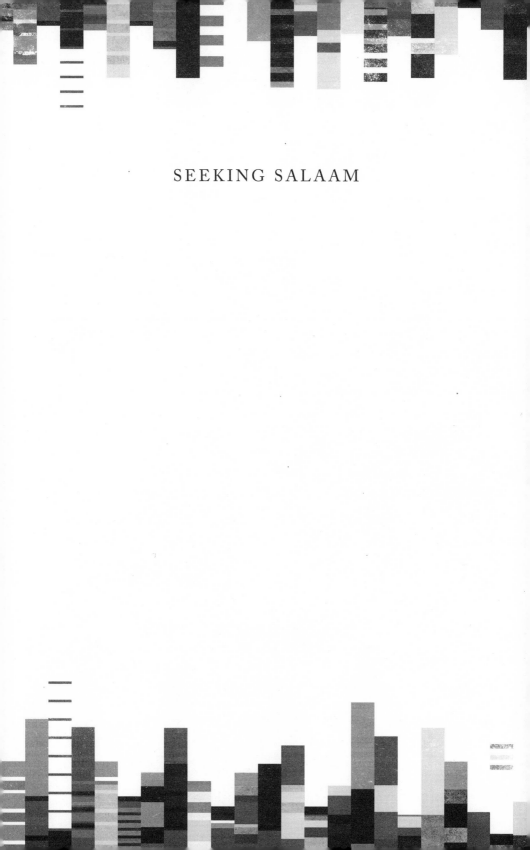

SEEKING SALAAM

SEEKING SALAAM

Ethiopians, Eritreans, *and* Somalis
in the Pacific Northwest

SANDRA M. CHAIT

A Samuel and Althea Stroum Book

UNIVERSITY OF WASHINGTON PRESS *Seattle and London*

This book is published with the assistance of a grant from the Samuel and Althea Stroum Endowed Book Fund.

UNIVERSITY OF WASHINGTON PRESS
PO Box 50096, Seattle, WA 98145, USA
www.washington.edu/uwpress

LIBRARY OF CONGRESS CATALOGING-IN-PUBLICATION DATA
Chait, Sandra M.
Seeking salaam : Ethiopians, Eritreans, and Somalis
in the Pacific Northwest / Sandra M. Chait.
p. cm.
Includes bibliographical references and index.
ISBN 978-0-295-99143-6 (cloth : alk. paper)
1. Ethiopians—Northwest, Pacific—Social conditions.
2. Ethiopians—Northwest, Pacific—Ethnic identity.
3. Eritreans—Northwest, Pacific—Social conditions.
4. Eritreans—Northwest, Pacific—Ethnic identity.
5. Somalis—Northwest, Pacific—Social conditions.
6. Somalis—Northwest, Pacific—Ethnic identity.
7. Pacific, Northwest—Ethnic relations.
8. Group identity—Northwest, Pacific. I. Title.
F855.2.E74C53 2011
305.8009795—dc22   2011016698

The paper used in this publication meets the minimum requirements
of American National Standard for Information Sciences—
Permanence of Paper for Printed Library Materials, ANSI Z39.48–1984.∞

CONTENTS

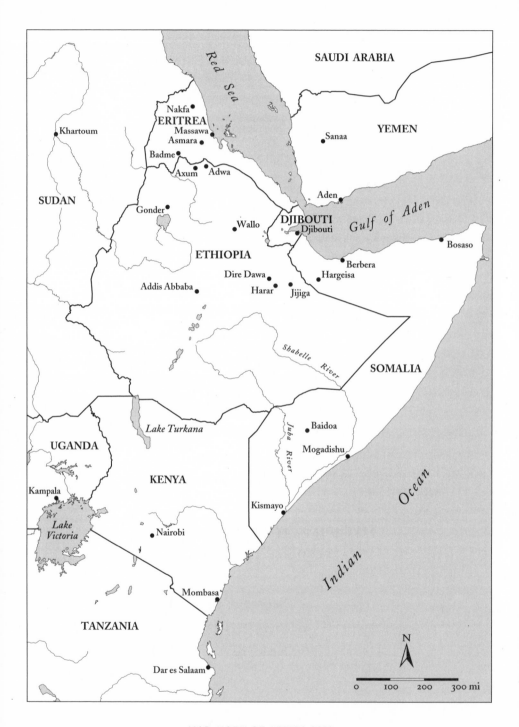

MAP HORN OF AFRICA 2010

ACRONYMS

ARS	Alliance for the Re-liberation of Somalia
EDA	Eritrean Democratic Alliance
EDU	Ethiopian Democratic Union
EIJ	Eritrean Islamic Jihad
EIS	Eritrean Islamic Salvation
ELF	Eritrean Liberation Front
EPLF	Eritrean People's Liberation Front
EPDM	Ethiopian People's Democratic Movement
EPRDF	Ethiopian People's Revolutionary Democratic Front
EPRP	Ethiopian People's Revolutionary Party
ESDL	Ethiopian Somali Democratic League
FGM	female genital mutilation
HOAS	Horn of Africa Services
ICU	Islamic Courts Union
IRC	International Rescue Committee
IRCO	Immigrant and Refugee Community Organization
NUEW	National Union of Eritrean Women
OAU	Organization of African Unity
OCOSMA	Oromo Community Organization of the Seattle Metropolitan Area
OLF	Oromo Liberation Front
OPDO	Oromo People's Democratic Organization

ONLF	Ogaden National Liberation Front
PFDJ	People's Front for Democracy and Justice
PSJTTF	Puget Sound Joint Terrorism Task Force
SBCSW	Somali Bantu Community Services of Washington
SNF	Somali National Front
SNM	Somali National Movement
SRN	Somali Rights Network
SSDF	Somali Salvation Democratic Front
SSF	Somalia Salvation Front
SWDO	Somali Women's Democratic Organization
TPLF	Tigray People's Liberation Front
TFG	Transitional Federal Government
TNG	Transitional National Government (prior to 2004)
UNHCR	United Nations High Commissioner for Refugees
UNMEE	United Nations Mission in Ethiopia and Eritrea

PREFACE

History is a story that is never wholly told,
never entirely true, but always
at least partially true,
always true at least in its parts.

—HAROLD SCHEUB, *STORY*

THE ABOVE quote has stayed with me ever since 1998, when I read Harold Scheub's wonderful book about storytellers in southern Africa. I had spent my childhood in apartheid-era South Africa, so his words held special resonance for me. They reaffirmed the complexity of history I had observed in my home country and reminded me that while dominant voices try to control the national myths, they can never fully marginalize or suppress those other voices that challenge theirs. Alternate stories have a way of floating to the surface and disrupting the status quo, and once again we find history undergoing reconfiguration. No single account of events can ever explain the past in its entirety, and each new or recovered narrative adds its own slice of truth to the multi-storied history of a country.

Given my background, it was no surprise to me therefore when, in the course of teaching African literature and advising students at the University of Washington in Seattle, I came upon contradictory accounts of Horn of Africa history narrated by local Ethiopians, Eritreans, and Somalis. I felt tremendous sympathy for these storytellers who wanted their particular versions of history witnessed and, as importantly, their own lives acknowledged. They spoke with great passion and integrity when they told me their stories, and they often moved me to tears with their tragic tales of flight and loss. For most of them, there could be only one true version of events, and they objected vociferously to alternate scenarios offered by their "enemies," who were of other Horn nationalities, ethnicities, or clans. They were convinced these others had lied to me.

The more I got to know these communities, the more fascinated I became with their conflicting stories. My interest took me to Eritrea in 2001 with two Eritrean friends, Hidaat Ephrem and Yosieph Tekie, plus UW colleagues Gretchen Kalonji and Richard Anderson. The visit led to academic connections with the University of Asmara, including an online course on life stories that brought me and my students into direct contact with young Eritreans in that country. At the same time, members of the local Ethiopian and Somali communities started attending talks I'd organized on campus, and soon they, too, were dropping by my office to discuss relevant issues and inviting me to join them in celebrating their communal events.

It became obvious that jobs, homes, and schools were not the only challenges facing these immigrants in the Pacific Northwest. In addition to such basic struggles, they needed, as a matter of dignity, to persuade their American neighbors of the truth of their particular versions of Horn history. In order to satisfy their sense of themselves as communities, they needed to be able to say with pride, "This is who we are." Unfortunately, their Horn rivals living down the road were equally adamant about putting their stamp on that same history. To make matters worse, the Internet brought further divisive developments from back home. With a simple click of a mouse, online diatribes could inflame the diaspora communities and turn one against another. In no time, the Internet became an influential but also destructive tool in the struggle for control of the word. The power of the diaspora communities to orchestrate change in their home countries also played into local cultural competition, complicating the picture and creating yet other stories to be either promoted or undermined.

The Pacific Northwest thus became the site of competing stories, some of which I decided to record as a way of marking a particular time and place in the history of these three communities in Seattle and Portland, from 2004 to 2010. With conditions in the Horn of Africa changing constantly, and with them the views of the local communities, I realized that details of these early immigrant days of contradiction and controversy would most likely be lost as new agendas wielded more selective narratives. While I harbored no wish to reinforce the divisive issues that now split these local communities into distinct social, economic, and political entities, I did want to capture them so that readers could appreciate the hold that events in the home countries maintain on those in the diaspora. The country of origin continues to manipulate emotions, and its politics, both past and present, add to the immigrant challenges these exiles already face. What is more, the continuing enmity further complicates the process of post-conflict reconciliation that has been part and parcel of the passage to citizenship of virtually every immigrant group in the United States. Living alongside one's enemies has never been easy, and I count Americans' ability to do so as one of the country's most laudable achievements.

Seeking Salaam focuses on the personal stories and viewpoints of forty-one Horn Africans whom I interviewed in Seattle and Portland and whose thoughtful and sometimes provocative words provide glimpses into the little-understood entanglements of these three communities. Most importantly, the book also brings attention to their frequently expressed desire for peaceful accommodation with their neighbors. What's the point, many asked me, in passing on to the next generation an inheritance of hate? Why poison our children's minds? Let us educate them in their cultures, yes, but let us also teach them tolerance and understanding.

Their stories ranged widely, and few were the topics overlooked. Interspersed with accounts of harrowing flights from war zones were expressions of hope both for themselves and for their communities in the United States. They wanted to make it in this country and to live the American Dream, and so they spoke often of jobs, homes, schools, and the difficulties of the immigrant life. They spoke, too, of love and of family dynamics and enthused proudly about their cultures' food and clothes, their music, dance, and art. Yet, whatever the topics raised and however focused the subjects under discussion, the narrators' stories inevitably veered toward their motherlands' ongoing struggles with neighboring countries, whose citizens now share their new neighborhoods in the diaspora and air their own versions of events back home. The home country remained a battleground, and many local Eritreans, Ethiopians, and Somalis, their loyalty wedded to those family members still living in their countries of birth as well as to those who had perished in the wars and civil unrest, grappled with the challenges posed by their longtime enemies. In the United States, all had a democratic right to express their own versions of history.

Their stories thus center on the issues that both divide the three communities from one another and cause tensions *within* each of them. The arguments of scholars, journalists, and institutional agents, but also the novels and poems of internationally acclaimed Horn writers such as Nega Mezlekia and Nuruddin Farah, provide context for these stories. Quotes from other Horn memoirs and inspirational works also contribute to the conversation, as do some anonymous conversations picked up on the street or in restaurants or taxicabs. This veritable cacophony of voices testifies to the divergence of opinions on the issues that divide the peoples of the Horn as they seek their spot in America's cultural marketplace.

The book is organized into seven chapters, each dealing with the competing narratives that shape and color the identity of these three Horn of Africa peoples. Chapter 1 introduces the communities and their oft-intertwined histories and, in providing a brief overview of the underlying tensions, begins to build an interconnecting story-tapestry. Chapter 2 brings in other narratives of identity that have been imposed on these communities by their host country in accord with its strategic interests. Chapter 3 discusses the cultural assets and handicaps the exiles bring from home, which they must balance as they compete to establish their cultural credentials in the Pacific Northwest. In chapters 4 and 5, we follow them as they enter the fray with their competing stories; these two chapters focus in detail on the issues that sour relationships *between* one community and another. Chapters 6 and 7 center on those stories that cause tensions *within* each community. Speaking words whetted on the sharp edges of intercommunal and intracommunal disagreements, these Pacific Northwest voices discuss the roles played by clan, ethnic, and religious rivalries and their related economic interests in the Horn of Africa wars and then address the issue of gender in each country.

Despite the disagreements found throughout, a persistent cooperative thread runs through each chapter. While each national group continues to jealously protect its own stories from home, some members of all three groups aspire to negotiate greater opportunities for all within the host country. They have come together to create new combined northeast African, rather than national or ethnic, narratives and, in some cases, the institutions necessary to uphold their efficacy. *Seeking Salaam* concludes with the stories of these interviewees, with whom lie not only the possibility of achieving the American Dream but the hope of peaceful coexistence and productive relationships with their fellow Africans.

Since those who tell their stories here want their histories to be known far and wide, I have chosen to angle the text toward a general audience. For that reason, I have minimized notes and citations and, unless quoting directly, have cited only sources that contribute material that seemed unique at the time of writing. Readers who want to research the material further should check out the bibliography. I have also chosen not to review the various scholarly developments in recording and writing life stories for the same reason, as I wanted the stories themselves to predominate. Further, although life-story writing crosses a number of disciplines, this book draws from my field, literature, and is not intended to be a work of ethnography, anthropology, or any of the other life-story-writing disciplines. My interest lies in the content of the stories and in their construction. What fascinates me is that in telling them, the interviewees construct themselves and their culture, and they do so in the context of negotiating with the state and the American people. How they shape their stories to find meaning and coherence, why they organize them in the particular ways they do, what is left out and why are the questions that form the backdrop to the content of the stories.

In terms of methodology, I have approached this qualitative study of narratives with an open mind, accepting the coexistence of contradictory truths and each person's right to the truth of his or her own story. Obviously, pursuit of accurate knowledge remains of utmost importance if justice is to be served and untruths should not be perpetuated indefinitely, but I hope to show that, given the same knowledge, individuals can perceive their own particular truths and understand that knowledge differently. Also, since I wanted to present as broad a spectrum of views as possible, I sought participation from a variety of age groups, ethnicities, religions, levels of education, and political persuasions. For that reason, too, I went against polite protocol and asked interviewees about their ethnicity or clan membership. Most willingly told me to which groups they belonged, but many also emphasized ethnicity's irrelevance to them. In selecting such a range of people to interview, I relied on introductions, recommendations, and friendships as well as literally going up to strangers on the street. The interviews, both individual and group, took place over six years and wherever convenient for the interviewees, thus conducted mostly in coffee bars, homes, and offices but also in a shopping mall, in a taxicab, and at both the University of Washington and Portland State University. The interviews lasted from one to four hours, and I followed up most with further interviews, phone calls, and e-mail correspondence. Whether the storytellers were recent refugees or immigrants of longer standing, all were amazingly gracious and generous with their time, for which I am extremely grateful.

Needless to say, I have my own personal views on each community's case, and such views inevitably colored my words even as I tried to be even-handed. In order to limit my influence on their words, I kept the conversations open and free-flowing, and while asking questions on specific topics, I did my best to avoid soliciting negotiated memory, namely, getting interviewees to remember what I wanted them to tell me in the context of my book. No doubt this happened in some cases, but I just as frequently followed where interviewees led, all of us going off on tangents of discovery that broadened and enriched our joint endeavor. Still, my voice in the interview context adds yet another vocal strand to the multi-voiced narrative of this book.

In telling their stories to a U.S. audience, these East African refugees and immigrants took risks. They were speaking not from the safety of the outside but from within the United States itself, where they must negotiate for their own and their communities' status and well-being in the cultural marketplace. Inevitably, some followed the mythico-historical path, projecting themselves as morally superior vis-à-vis their Horn neighbors, but most merely stated what they or their families had experienced. In doing so, they entered a narrative game in which the United States constantly changes the rates of exchange and the level of the marketing field to suit its foreign policy, domestic needs, or covert arrangements. It decides which "facts" to highlight or downplay depending on its strategic interests and frequently fuels divisive and competitive jostling for positions and funds among the Pacific Northwest communities. Since the terrorist attacks of September 11, 2001, for example, the stories of Ethiopian, Eritrean, and Somali Muslims have been disadvantaged, their narratives made suspect, their chances for employment, funding, and housing lessened. Somalia has become the new front in the fight against Islamic terrorism, and Somalis in Seattle and Portland have to contend with being seen by some as unreliable narrators. Given this American context, one wonders how local Muslims can ever speak their minds. I was genuinely surprised and immensely grateful that they did.

Before completing the manuscript, I gave all interviewees the chance to see how I had quoted them and in what context. Thus, they were able to edit their words, choose to be quoted anonymously or under a pseudonym, or else refuse permission completely. On the one hand, since events had taken a turn for the worse in all three countries after the interviews, many grabbed thankfully at that opportunity out of fear of endangering their families back home, inciting Horn relations here, or upsetting their American hosts. On the other hand, others denied nothing, saying, "I stand squarely behind everything I've said." To protect interviewees further, I also relocated some conversations to different, impersonal settings and made them anonymous. In addition, during interviews, I chose not to repeat to any one person what another might have said. I have no wish to further tensions within the communities and air the more general disagreements only in the hope that those who participated will see them in the context of others' hopes and dreams as well as their own.

Given the volatility of events in the Horn and its related effects in these communities, I feel honored to have been entrusted with these stories. Telling some of them, I realize, must have felt like reopening scabs, often painfully, and I am in awe of the storytellers' willingness to speak out in spite of it. Whatever their reasons for doing so, whether to set the record straight, pay tribute to those lost in war, or testify to the marginalization or suppression of an ethnic group, their honesty and willingness to stand behind their words have impressed and touched me. I hope I have done their words justice by quoting them accurately. I apologize in advance for any mistakes I may have made and take full responsibility if my own blinkers prevented me from seeing what seemed most obvious to them. I realize, too, that each group would have preferred that I push its viewpoint over and above those of the others, but that was not my purpose, as I made clear from the start; instead, I sought to allow each person to express his or her opinions on their own merits. Since Ethiopia appears as the Goliath in many of these narratives, it might seem that the text favors the other two countries, but that picture simply reflects the relative power divisions that exist in the Horn and the way these color the words of those interviewed.

I hope that in attempting to capture the struggles for identity of these forty-one Ethiopians, Eritreans, and Somalis as they sought to find their cultural, social, and economic balance in their new American home, I have given other Americans a glimpse into another aspect of the immigrant passage and into the intertwined lives and cultures of the people with whom they now share their neighborhoods, schools, and offices. My sincere wish is that this glimpse will promote appreciation of these most recent newcomers and their successful integration into American life.

ACKNOWLEDGMENTS

MY GRATITUDE goes to the Ethiopians, Eritreans, and Somalis I interviewed for this book and who gave so unstintingly of their time. Although *Seeking Salaam* recounts only a fraction of all they told me, I hope that what appears in this book will please them. I would like to express my appreciation in particular to Hidaat Ephrem and Yosieph Tekie, who first introduced me to Eritrea, and to Gretchen Kalonji whose support made my trip to the Horn of Africa possible. A number of other people deserve my thanks not only for sticking by me during the lengthy process of getting the manuscript ready for publication, but also for biting their tongues rather than express doubt as to whether the book would ever see the light of day. I owe a debt of gratitude to my Tuesday and Thursday morning walking partner, Carol; my Tuesday Happy Hour pals, Isabel and Anne; my long-time bookclub aficionados; and my friends from the last Monday of the month philanthropy group. Thank you all for keeping me sane. Thanks, too, to Kip and Marianne for helpful conversations; to Linda, a careful and astute reader; and to my editor son, Mark, who always tactfully advised his mother along the way. I am indebted to the Gideonses and Lipmans for housing me in Portland while I conducted interviews, and to Robert

Hamilton who facilitated some of the interviews and patiently redirected me around the city whenever I got lost. My gratitude also goes to my two peer reviewers, whose sound advice definitely improved the book. To my editors at University of Washington Press, Beth Fuget, whose editorial skill and market knowledge I sincerely appreciated, and Marilyn Trueblood, who expertly guided the book through the publishing process, thank you. I would also like to thank Press designers, Ashley Saleeba and Lola Migas, who captured the colors and vibrancy of the three countries in their striking cover; Barry Levely, who produced the informative map of the Horn; my old friend, Alice Herbig, who with the help of Phoebe Daniels, marketed the book; and finally Director Pat Soden, who first saw promise in the subject and encouraged me. To the Samuel and Althea Stroum Endowed Book Fund, I am indebted. Their support made the book possible. To all of you, and to my husband and family, a heartfelt thanks.

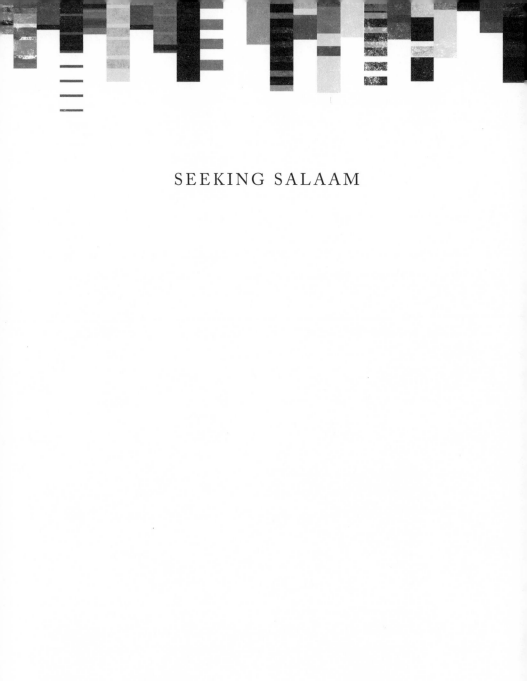

SEEKING SALAAM

ONE

AT "HOME" IN THE
PACIFIC NORTHWEST

Yes, we have different views on politics, religion,
and ethnicity. But we have far more things in
common, and these get obscured by the
differences that paralyze collective actions.

—HADDIS TADESSE, SEATTLE, 2005

T HE METRO bus slows down at the intersection of East Cherry
and Martin Luther King Jr. Way South in Seattle. When it
stops, an Eritrean woman carrying a blue plaited basket in one
hand carefully steps down to the sidewalk. As the bus pulls off, she
adjusts her white *netsela* so that the muslin covering drapes her head and
splays delicately across her neck and shoulders. Thus cowled and covered,
she squares her shoulders and looks around. Although the shadows under
her eyes and her sagging cheeks peg her as elderly, once she has properly
arranged her Tigrinya shawl, she takes off with the brisk stride of a young
woman of purpose. Beneath her white skirt, her black rubber sandals hit
the sidewalk and lend spirit to her gait.

At the Ethiopian restaurant on the northwest side of MLK Boulevard,
men in jackets or with their shirtsleeves fashionably rolled drink small
cups of dark black coffee. They sit framed in the curtained windows and
bring their cups to their lips with smooth, unhurried movements. Every
so often, they check to see if their SUVs and Hondas are still parked
outside. The men's conversation, though low, sparks with the guttural
sounds of Amharic. At the far window, a man taps the table for emphasis
in mid-sentence while another leans forward on his elbows, the thumb

3

and fingers of his right hand poised in an enclosing motion as if he were about to make his own point. Or perhaps simply eat.

A few blocks down, on East Union, Somali-driven taxis converge on a dilapidated storefront mosque. The car doors open and lanky men unfold themselves from their seats and greet one another in Somali. Each carries a cell phone, and the air resonates with the pitches of different ringtones, like so many birdsongs. "Land of Hope and Glory" spills from one of the phones, conjuring up images of past graduation ceremonies, or perhaps future ones, before the sound is cut and the men go inside.

This is the Central District in Seattle, where many Ethiopians, Eritreans, and Somalis live, work, or worship. Although they are all Africans from the Horn who share similarities in looks, culture, and history, seldom does a word pass from a member of one community to a member of another. While they *almost* rub shoulders in their workaday lives, with few exceptions they remain strictly separate, each a discrete people. Such scenes of detached coexistence can be found in other parts of Seattle and in Portland as well. In both cities, Ethiopians, Eritreans, and Somalis live alongside one another in apartments, townhouses, or, if financially secure, in leafy suburbs where they interact with other Americans who frequently see them simply as East Africans or people from the Horn and do not distinguish one community from the other. In American public schools, their children play soccer with the sons and daughters of their erstwhile enemies, while they look on tremulously and admonish their kids to remember their identities. As newly arrived exiles in the Pacific Northwest, these Somalis, Eritreans, and Ethiopians cling to their own histories, and even as they aspire to the American Dream and pluralistic democracy, they worry the political, economic, and emotional wounds inflicted on them by their Horn brothers. They have so many stories to tell, some bitter and resentful, some merely sad. The violence of war hurts everyone, victims and perpetrators alike, present generations and future ones.

America as the home of huddled masses yearning to be free has long dealt with outbreaks of hostilities brought from fatherlands and relocated to its cities and towns. Earlier immigrant groups such as Jews and Poles, Hutus and Tutsis, Irish and English, Japanese and Korean—indeed, the list runs to virtually every immigrant group that has arrived on these shores—all suffered the trauma of dealing in their host country with the devils they thought they'd escaped, only to find as the years wore on that they had to forge some kind of reconciliation so that the enmity would not extend into the future of younger generations. Because the three communities share the same problems of joblessness, illiteracy, and family pressures, many of the interviewees aspire to go beyond the recriminations and hatreds that hinder their progress to try to work together for the common good of all of them.

Even as they stand poised at that point of cooperation and collaboration, however, they want to ensure that their particular stories are known by Americans. Having been nurtured in the bosom of their communities by stories imbibed with gunpowder and mother's milk, they are determined to tell *their* versions of historical events before others displace their stories with their own. For they understand that if they hope to promote the welfare of their communities here in the Pacific Northwest and affect the direction of political and economic affairs back home, their narratives must compete in the American cultural marketplace.

Take Yegizaw Michael and his wife, Mehret Mehanzel, for example. While these young Seattleites practice peace and cooperation in their own lives and with friends in the other communities, they also speak out strongly on behalf of their people, the Eritreans. Although Yegizaw was born in Addis Ababa, Ethiopia, his Eritrean parents brought him up as a Tigrinya-speaking Eritrean, and although Mehret has been in the States for almost fourteen years, her Eritrean American identity, she says, remains "a vibrant part of [her] and continues to grow."

I met Yegizaw and Mehret when they first fell in love and was delighted when, later, Mehret produced their pretty little daughter, Bilen, whose first word, *adey*, meaning "mother," they proudly told me, she spoke in Tigrinya. The family lived in a bright, airy house in the Central District, with an East African store close by. When I arrived at the house on a visit, Bilen's toys festooned the living room. Her parents sat with friends and, over Eritrean coffee, discussed the political situation back home. Outside, a small neat yard lay ready for a time when Bilen would be old enough to play there with her own friends.

Like other Eritreans, Yegizaw and Mehret resent the "lies" told by their rivals in their new country. However, they also appreciate that American democracy protects their freedom of speech as well as that of their neighbors. Both have the right to say what they want, and for that they are grateful. "Look," Yegizaw says, leaning across the table, his dreadlocks swinging, "I'd rather be here than anywhere else. If people in Seattle don't like what I say, they can just turn away. They don't have to listen to me or agree with me if they don't want to. It's not like back home, where I would have been stoned for the things I say here, especially things concerning sensitive issues such as religion."

Fortunately, no one can stone him in Seattle. Nor can anyone officially muzzle him or any other person, for that matter, though, needless to say, communal pressure and fear certainly influence the conversation. "The propaganda gets to us," another Eritrean, Abraha Alemseged, says wearily, asking me to use this pseudonym rather than his given name. "It is psychological warfare," the middle-aged man explains. With each group trying to break the other's spirit, it is wearying. Even so, he and most Horn Africans do speak out. They want to be heard. Still, their inability to fix language permanently and moor its truth to their advantage bothers many of those I interviewed. Indeed, this incapacity to ensure that *their* truths rule the day and make it into the history books for future generations lines the immigrant passage to the American Dream with yet another uncertainty. Besides contending with housing and employment challenges, which Yegizaw claims Eritreans have had the strength to do because their experience of struggle taught them to stand on their own feet, they must live at risk of others overlooking or even erasing the very histories that have given them identity and status.

HISTORICAL SOURCES OF DIFFERENCE

The stories that underlie the hostilities among the three communities in the Pacific Northwest revolve around a number of major historical events. Grandparents have propagated their versions of these events through the generations, passing them down in straightforward us-them stories that have become indelibly imprinted in the minds of their offspring in Seattle and Portland. When new developments, like by-products of the original conflicts, occur at home, they entrench the diaspora views further. Advocates and challengers dig in and erect barriers, and communication among the groups ceases.

Eritreans

To Eritreans like Abraha, for example, the Eritrean stories are quite simple. They reflect the irrevocable belief that Ethiopia's ruler Menelik II betrayed them—even sold them—by ceding Eritrea to the Italians in 1889 in return for his own sovereignty and freedom from colonial occupation. Then, they say, when their area thrived in the post–World War II years through Eritrean education and Italian investment, and the city of Asmara became one of the most modern conurbations on the continent, the Ethiopians wanted it back. From the Eritrean perspective, the area's wealth and particularly its busy seaports drew the envy and hostility of Ethiopia's emperor Haile Selassie. Thus, when the United Nations General Assembly passed a resolution in 1952 calling for a loose federation of Eritrea with Ethiopia that specified internal self-government for Eritrea, Selassie went on to annex the country instead. He claimed its businesses for Ethiopia, removed the Eritrean flag, replaced Tigrinya with Amharic as the official language, and had himself declared Patriarch of the Coptic Church, where Eritrean Christians worshipped.

"We Eritreans saw this development as tantamount to colonization by another African country," Abraha says, voicing his government's later wartime rhetoric. Abraha wears his nationality with pride and holds himself with a dignity I've noticed often on Eritrean men and women when they talk about home. "We organized ourselves into guerrilla groups—first the Eritrean Liberation Front and later the Eritrean People's Liberation Front—to stop Ethiopia's dismantling of freedoms in our country. But when we expressed our wish for independence . . . you know what? The Ethiopian government sent out troops."

No Eritrean I interviewed could speak of the subsequent war between the Ethiopians and Eritreans without revealing some emotion, even if merely by a tightening of the lips. The war lasted for thirty years, from 1961 to 1991, and left indelible scars on Eritrean souls and minds. Some of these scars bear testimony to the bloody rivalry that broke out along religious lines between the two liberation groups in the war's early phases during the 1970s. The devastating split occurred when the predominantly Christian Eritrean People's Liberation Front (EPLF) broke off from the original revolutionary movement, the predominantly Muslim Eritrean Liberation Front (ELF) that had formed on September 1, 1961. Not surprisingly, most of the local interviewees who spoke of it asked not to be quoted. Nevertheless, in talking to EPLF supporters, it became clear that they believed the ELF to have had different ideological goals, namely, that it sought pan-Arabist hegemony. When internal divisions led to conflict and, according to the EPLF, some Christian members of ELF were murdered and Christian villages attacked, the EPLF emerged as a separate group with a different ideology, namely, socialism. The two groups fought a bitter two-year civil war in which thousands died before calling an uneasy truce in 1974.

Another Eritrean, Yosieph Tekie, remembers well the period that followed. By 1975, Haile Selassie had been overthrown and Mengistu Haile Mariam's Derg forces ruled both Ethiopia and Eritrea. In no time, the situation for young men in Eritrea had become terrifying. "Secret police would go around Asmara and pick you up off the street," Yosieph says. When he tells me this, we are sitting with his wife, Almaz Bahre, and their son, Abraham, who plays peek-a-boo with me from behind his mother's chair in their home overlooking Lake Washington in Renton. Unlike the majority of local Eritrean immigrants, Yosieph and Almaz live middle-class lives. Yosieph, a Microsoft team manager, travels regularly to Eritrea to visit his relatives and has spearheaded a number of projects there to educate schoolchildren in the latest technology. "I want to make Asmara the Bangalore of Africa," he used to tell me, referring to India's information technology hub. Here in Seattle, he is proud of his home. On a wall in the dining room hangs one of Yegizaw's striking paintings, and on the dining-room table between us is a traditional Eritrean meal. I recognize from my trip to Eritrea the *tsebhi* (stew), *shiro* (ground chickpeas), and *hamli* (greens), which we scoop up with *injera*, the spongy bread made from teff, an indigenous cereal grown back home. Yosieph had been just a teenager during the Derg's rule, and his family home in Asmara, which he showed me in 2001, bordered an infamous Ethiopian prison. He describes his life there:

> The rock walls of the prison and our house were next to each other, and
> my home . . . it was like a fort to prevent Derg forces coming in and

surprising us. Sometimes at night, we would hear the screams of prisoners from across the yard, and it would send chills through us as we lay in our beds listening. . . . When we were still kids though, and it was a predominantly Italian area, we used to jump over the wall and pick peaches from the trees. It was like heaven for us children to play in that yard. But now . . . well, now . . . you know, it's known as a place where a lot of Eritreans suffered.

Yosieph hung around Asmara, keeping out of sight of the Derg and learning how to run the farm, but in the end, it was too dangerous to be there, and so, together with lots of other young people, he fled to Sudan.

The thirty-year war of liberation, Yosieph reminds me, pitted 70 million Ethiopians against only 3 million Eritreans. Despite the latter being short of military hardware as well as funds, their desire for self-determination enabled them to persevere against the Ethiopians. By 1977, the ELF and EPLF, working in tandem, had gained control over most of Eritrea, but when the Soviet Union brought its support to the side of the Ethiopian government, ELF forces were destroyed. The EPLF then removed itself to its regional center in the northern mountains near the border with Sudan and ultimately became the main force in the struggle. Some ELF members joined the EPLF, while others fled to refugee camps in Sudan or went abroad.

Mehret's father belonged to the ELF. She chooses not to explain further but says that during her childhood, even though she was very young, she knew what was going on and was aware of the danger. "I was also aware of the loneliness of my mother," she adds, "who was left alone to care for so many children." It was a difficult time for her family, and Mehret carries the memories of those days with her. "One thing I remember especially," she recounts, "was when our school building was destroyed and my brothers had to leave home. When we said good-bye, it was 1980, and we were standing in my vegetable garden." Only in 1990, when she came to the States from Sudan, did Mehret meet up again with her older sibling, Esayas.

To return to the general history as Eritreans see it, the EPLF, with the support of the Tigray People's Liberation Front (TPLF), which was also fighting the Ethiopian government, finally prevailed. In May 1991 it marched victoriously into Asmara, and two years later, Eritrea declared itself independent.

The legacy of the ELF-EPLF struggle produces fault lines in the diaspora. Makonnen (Michael) Damtew, who now runs a distribution company for coin-operated machines in Portland, explains to me how that legacy complicated the composition of the local groups in Seattle. A self-assured and eloquent speaker, Michael is also a history buff whose own life follows yet another historical trajectory. Born in Ethiopia of a Falasha Jewish Ethiopian father and an Eritrean Orthodox Christian mother, he came to the United States in 1974 to study when Emperor Haile Selassie shut down the universities back home because of demonstrations against his policies. After Selassie's overthrow, when Mengistu Haile Mariam's regime resorted to terror, Michael, who was living in Seattle at the time, joined an urban intellectual group of leftists. From exile, he says, they provided "whatever support [they] could to the Eritrean armed struggle." Thus, he was here when the first wave of Eritrean refugees thronged into the city in 1981 and well remembers how the two groups dug ever deeper into their divisions. "Since the EPLF was the one that finally brought independence to Eritrea," he tells me, "its supporters in Seattle were mostly homogeneous Tigrinya Coptic Christians. They became the preferred group in Seattle, guys who went around talking of '*my* government' and '*my* country.' You see," he explains, "since the government at home was also Tigrinya and received money from that group in the diaspora for its war effort, it tended to nurture those members."

By 1981, the two groups had already become alienated. Thus, when local Tigrinya EPLF supporters "started asking uncomfortable questions that were sensitive for the ELF members to answer," Michael explains, the latter retreated for refuge to their own.

The Tigrinya Christians continue to dominate Seattle's and Portland's Eritrean communities, their internal squabbles often preventing them from organizing themselves to challenge the stories of the Ethiopians, which have become even more complicated since the thirty-year war. Whereas the Eritreans waged that war against mostly Amhara and Oromo Ethiopian troops, since the establishment of an independent Eritrea in 1993, they found themselves fighting the Tigray Ethiopians who had helped them win independence and looked very much like themselves.[1] In fact, the

Tigrayans of Ethiopia and the Tigrinya of Eritrea both derive from the people of the great trading Axum civilization of 500 B.C.E. and are linked with each other through their common history, language, and religion. They lived as highland neighbors on either side of the river Mereb for centuries, but when the TPLF, which had fought alongside the Tigrinya-dominated EPLF for the freedom of Eritrea and Tigray, took control not just of Tigray but the whole of Ethiopia, disagreements between the liberation groups led to stand-offs. The two related governments—the Tigray-led Ethiopian People's Revolutionary Democratic Front (EPRDF) and the Tigrinya-controlled People's Front for Democracy and Justice (PFDJ)—became locked in ill will and economic rivalry. The resulting tension led to renewed conflict over the borders between the two countries, and in 1998, as Eritreans see it, Ethiopia refused to accept the demarcation of the 1902 Italian-Ethiopian treaty and began hostilities. The war lasted for two years, and the tensions remain.

Today, this common background is one of the factors that complicate the competition with Ethiopia and divide the local communities. Brothers in blood and comrades in battle (EPLF and TPLF), some Eritrean Tigrinyas and Ethiopian Tigrayans still yearn for a Greater Tigray. Since the Tigrayans dominate Ethiopia at this time, such a partnership would, in effect, mean a combined Ethiopia-Eritrea. Others in the local communities, however, are committed to their Eritrean and Ethiopian identities and want no further political connection. Eritrean wisdom has it that Ethiopia is still an imperial power that covets Eritrean land and seaports and continues to maneuver for advantage in the region. Eritreans see their homeland as a small nation ignored by the countries of the rest of the world that look to Ethiopia as the more powerful ally for their strategic interests.

Ethiopians

In Seattle, Ethiopians see their relationship with Eritrea quite differently. They talk about it in their Central District restaurants on East Union, East Cherry, and East Jefferson, but not half as much as Eritreans discuss that same relationship in theirs. Still, the Ethiopian restaurants, like men's clubs, become hubs for political discussion, places where patrons can exchange the latest news from home even as they dip into spicy communal platters and lick their lips. While some of the restaurants cater mostly to their own specific groups, others aspire to a multiethnic, multi-religious policy and open their doors wide in the hope that Eritreans might enter as well. Sometimes, when I drive by, I wonder how each one makes a living, as they rarely appear full and new Ethiopian restaurants continue to pop up, adding to the competition. That they persevere I count as a gift to the neighborhood and especially to the Amhara, Tigray, Gonder, and Oromo peoples who live both there and farther south on Rainier Avenue. For in the end, the presence of so many of these brightly painted homes-away-from-home, albeit with ubiquitous burglar bars covering the windows, satisfies so much more than just hunger.

What the Ethiopians say about their relationship with their Horn neighbors raises suspicion among the Eritreans. Tigrayans claim common descent with the Tigrinya Eritreans, considering the latter brothers whom they want to bring back into the fold, while the Amhara say they want to make Eritreans part of Ethiopia's long, noble heritage. Since the Amhara purport to be descendants of the royal son born of the union of the Queen of Sheba and King Solomon, they pride themselves on their lineage. Also, as the only African nation not colonized for any length of time by Europeans, the Ethiopians consider themselves the continent's heroes, a view constantly reinforced by Western powers as well as many black people, the Rastafarians in particular. In 1896 Ethiopia defeated Italy at the Battle of Adwa, one of the few victories of an African nation over a European colonial power.

"Ethiopians take great pride in their uncolonized status," Haddis Tadesse enthuses. "It was something that was taught to us early, both at school and at home." At the time of this interview in 2005, Haddis is a senior policy adviser to Seattle mayor Greg Nickels. When we meet at his downtown Seattle office, I am fascinated by this young man's open yet diplomatic take on our conversation. He sits at a large conference table looking confident and at ease, an example himself of what that status means to Ethiopians. Unlike many Ethiopians, he does not identify himself by ethnicity, noting, "I am a product of a multiethnic family and grew up in Addis, which is a multiethnic city." What is more, he states up front that he will not talk about his family because he feels that he still hasn't fully internalized their stories. Again, I am struck by how people are defined by the choices they make about their stories. What he does tell me, however, is that Moscow, where his parents were sent as students, is his birthplace. From there, he moved to Addis at the age of two, later attending private school in the city, before heading off to the States on his own in 1989, age fourteen, to further his studies.

Most of the Ethiopians I interviewed share Haddis's pride in their nationality and see the loss of Eritrea as regrettable. Although Ethiopia retained its independence, it lost Eritrea to the Italians. Nevertheless, Haile Selassie's increasingly important standing in the international arena allowed him to reclaim the area Ethiopia perceived as one of its provinces by annexing it in 1962. Although Eritrea subsequently fought for and won its independence in 1991, the country is understood by Ethiopians to be a colonial construction and to have no real future on its own. It is Eritrean arrogance, they say, that drives them to separate themselves from their brothers; they identify too much with white Italian culture and consider themselves more advanced than the Tigrayans. From the Ethiopian perspective, Eritrea is far worse off now than when it was part of the homeland.

Such beliefs underlie the tensions between the two peoples and leave them sensitive to any perceived slight or encroachment on their power. Thus, when Eritrea attempted to move in on Ethiopian land at the border, Ethiopians say, they responded militarily. They attacked Eritrean forces on the ground in 1998 because they believed that the latter were trying to seize territory on the Ethiopian side of the border at Badme in the Tigray region. "The government claims that the Badmeans . . . or at least the ones in the areas Ethiopia controlled administratively," David Makonnen tells me, "consider themselves Ethiopians. Forcing them to become Eritrean citizens," he says, trying to explain the government's reasoning after the Eritrea-Ethiopia Boundary Commission at The Hague awarded Badme to Eritrea in 2002, "will lead to their prosecution by the Eritrean government for being loyal to the Ethiopian government during the war." Being of mixed Ethiopian-Eritrean heritage and being married to an Eritrean help David see combative situations from both sides. Neither group benefits, he says, "from fostering perpetual instability in the region," which is what happens if you don't take into account the practical reality on the ground.

David has worked hard to bring the leaders of all three Seattle communities to the table to talk. Like some of the other Horn Africans quoted in this chapter, he is middle class, an M.B.A. graduate who works as a senior development manager at Microsoft. For that reason, perhaps, he is less intransigent when it comes to ethico-political stances than are refugees who have not been exposed to other worldviews. For that reason, too, he has the resources to pursue social justice, which he considers "his first love."

During the bitter border war of 1998–2000, ignited by the Badme skirmish, more than seventy thousand Ethiopians and Eritreans were killed before the declaration of a ceasefire and the signing in Algiers of the Agreement on Cessation of Hostilities. According to the agreement, both sides were to abide by the findings of the Eritrea-Ethiopia Boundary Commission, but to this day, the demarcations related to Badme and other disputed areas along the Ethiopian-Eritrean border continue to provoke conflict.

As becomes obvious from accounts of history as seen by Eritreans and Ethiopians respectively and summarized above, each views the community's historical relationship in decidedly different ways. Even as further developments occur in the home countries, each group continues to perceive the other's actions through the same lens as in the past. To complicate matters further, their enmity spills over their borders into Somalia, the third corner of the triangular relationship that now plays itself out in the Pacific Northwest.

Somalis

Ethiopian involvement in Somali politics is not anything new. Land struggles in the Ogaden have fueled tensions between the two ever since Ethiopia occupied the Ogaden in 1887. For centuries, ethnic Somalis have lived on that sloping plain that runs from the Harar Plateau in the north of Ethiopia to the Somali/Ethiopian border in the east and south and the Shabelle River in the west. So when Britain ceded part of the territory to the Ethiopians in 1954, the Somalis objected vociferously. And when the British later included the northeastern part of the Ogaden known as the Haud and the Reserve Area, which had belonged to Somali clans and been administered along with Somaliland by Britain, they were furious. Like most of their mainland brothers at the time, they considered the area to be Somalia's western province and the center of Somali culture and heritage. Today, Ogadenia, which is the name Ogadeni Somalis call the area where they live, plus the Haud and the Reserve Area make up one of the nine ethnically based administrative areas of Ethiopia, the Somali region, or *kilil*. The Ogadeni are fighting with the Ethiopians for their right to self-determination.

The Haud is the birthplace of Jamal Gabobe, a Somali poet and Ph.D. student in Comparative Literature at the University of Washington. His maternal grandmother, also a poet, came from the Ogaden in the Somali region of Ethiopia. During his childhood, Jamal's father, a livestock trader, moved the family from the Haud to Aden. Then from 1975 to 1977, Jamal lived in Abu Dhabi in the Arab Emirates before coming to the United States to study. The Haud, however, still retains a certain hold on him, and he tells me that its transfer by Britain to Ethiopia was seen by Somalis as a betrayal. "The British felt so bad about doing this, they tried to wiggle out of it and even offered money to Ethiopia as compensation, but the Ethiopians refused to give the Haud back." He tells me all this in a matter-of-fact way, although the subject is emotional. "Did you know the U.S. had something to do with this decision?" He leans forward, his smile knowing. I nod, apologetic on behalf of my country, now his, too. After World War II, Haile Selassie used American influence to put pressure on Britain to give this land to Ethiopia.

"It was in this British betrayal," Jamal explains, "that the genesis of Somali nationalism arose." For a moment, he looks at me to see if it's sinking in. We've known each other for a number of years, ever since I invited him to read his Somali work-in-progress at an African literary series I was running.

"So that is why, when President Siyad Barre came to power in 1969," I say, "he was able to revive Somali aspirations for a Greater Somalia?"

"One that would include land lost not only to Ethiopia but also to Kenya and Djibouti."

This renewal of pan-Somali irredentist policies exacerbated relations with Ethiopia, and the Ogaden became the scene of a series of Ethiopian-Somali struggles, including the destructive Ogaden War of 1977–78.

Although Somalia and Ethiopia signed an agreement in 1988, committing to respect each other's borders, Mogadishu ultimately refused to abandon its claim to the Ogaden, and the struggle between the two claimants continues.

Clan rivalry has complicated Somali relations with Ethiopia in that at various times Ethiopia has supported one clan or another for its own strategic purposes. In the 1980s, for example, the Siyad Barre government settled Ogaden refugees among the Isaq clan of Somaliland. Barre then used the Ogadeni to spy on and control the Isaq, unleashing a massacre that sent Isaqs fleeing across the Ethiopian border to make their homes in the Haud, thus increasing the Muslim population of Ethiopia and threatening the Coptic Christians' sense of security.

Clan rivalry, however, touches every group, not just the Isaq and Ogadeni. At the housing project in Portland's southwestern suburb of Tigard, for example, young Somali widows of different clans struggle to make ends meet. Many of those living here are victims of clan rivalry, exacerbated in large part by men for economic reasons. Generally, women have no say in clan business, yet it is they and their children who suffer most from its fallout. Even so, the women carry on heroically with their lives. Arriving at the complex, you could imagine you have just come upon Little Mogadishu. Around the inner streets of the complex, seven-year-old Somali girls wearing headscarves and blue jeans bicycle with their friends, while a younger brother nags them in high-pitched Maaha and tries to tag along. Tall, thin women in long colorful robes peer from doorways, checking on the children and shouting loudly to one another about the domestic problems of the day.

Between 1988 and 1991, various clan-based resistance groups tried to bring down the government of Siyad Barre. Although he struggled to hold on, Ethiopian-Somali tensions together with clan rivalry and widespread starvation caused by the disruption of food supplies eventually led to his defeat in 1991. In the absence of any central authority, the northerners in what had been British Somalia then declared independence for their area and called it Somaliland. They thrived economically and held democratic elections that, they claim, proved they could overcome clan rivalry. The Somalilanders thus withdrew from the problems of the south, where warlords competed for control and clan violence sent Somalis fleeing.

In 2004 the fragile Transitional Federal Government (TFG) under the presidency of Abdullahi Yusuf Ahmed ruled the country but was unable to rein in the warlords or bring order to the area. A semblance of peace was restored in September 2006, however, when the Islamic Courts Union (ICU) took control of Mogadishu and other cities and set the economy going once again. Although many Somalis welcomed its control, the Christian-dominated Ethiopian government, fearful of Islamic influence among its own Muslim Somali population in the Ogaden and elsewhere, continued its military support of the government, while Eritrea, in order to encourage just such destabilization in the border area, provided aid to the Courts.

In December 2006, with the help of Ethiopian forces and tacit support from the United States, the TFG's army regained Mogadishu and the rest of the south. The Ethiopians, however, proved unpopular in Somalia, and by the time their forces withdrew from the country in January 2009, they had lost ground to the insurgents and the TFG had become largely ineffective. The government, left with few options, negotiated a power-sharing deal with an ICU splinter group, the Alliance for the Re-liberation of Somalia (ARS), whose leader, Sheikh Sharif Ahmed, was then elected TFG president. Another ICU group, however, the more radical al-Shabaab (Youth), rejected Sharif Ahmed's peace deal and continues to fight the government and its supporters. In 2010 the civil war still flares, Somali pirates attack ships in the Red Sea, and the area remains in a state of chaos.

Although events overtake me even as I write, the summaries above provide the framework within which the interviewees take their stances.

IDENTITY POLITICS AND STORIES

Beneath much of the conflict and stimulating the arguments that fester among and within these groups lies a far-reaching question of identity: What defines identity? What is it that makes you who you are? Ethiopians and Eritreans spent thirty years fighting a war that would allow Eritreans to call themselves Eritreans and not Ethiopians, and they still fight over their borders today. In Ethiopia's Somali regions, there is a similar crisis of identity. In the novel *Maps*, by Somalia's Nuruddin Farah, the protagonist Askar asks his uncle, "Who is Askar?"[2] Born of a Somali mother in disputed territory in the Ogaden and raised by an Ethiopian "mother," Misra, whom he loves, Askar does not know how to identify himself. Is he Somali or Ethiopian? He wonders what it is that establishes who you are. Does the particular side of the border on which you live define identity? But what if those borders are open, as they were between Somalia and Ethiopia at the time? Perhaps then, he thinks, identity refers just to appearance, how you look. But his Uncle Hilaal shakes his head. "It's not what one looks like," his uncle says. "For all we know there is no ethnic difference which sets apart the Somali from the Ethiopian." No, a "Somali is a man, woman or child whose mother tongue is Somali. . . . The Somali are a homogeneous people: they are homogeneous culturally speaking and speak the same language wherever they may be found."[3]

As will become clear, Somalis are not homogeneous and language is not necessarily the linchpin of identity. So then, what does make *Somalinimo*? What constitutes Somali-ness? Ethiopian-ness? Eritrean-ness?

What distinguishes one person from another cannot be reduced to just language or looks alone. While both play a part in providing clues to identity, the stories that people choose to tell about themselves ultimately must identify them. A man says to the world "This is who I am" by selecting and shaping the histories with which he identifies, the ones that express best what is important to him about his individual life and the lives of his family. Perhaps he does so within specific groupings such as ethnicity, clan, religion, or nation, but whatever he focuses on, he inevitably emphasizes those aspects of his narrative DNA that are meaningful to him in his current context. Though history has frequently denied humans self-determination, it is their prerogative to choose their own, individual identities.

"People shouldn't tell me who I am," Yegizaw insists. His brother-in-law, Esayas Mehanzel, concurs. "Identity is knowing yourself and where you come from. It's what you have in your heart." Yegizaw's and Esayas's stories, like those of the other contributors in this book, convey to those around them how they wish to be seen and understood. It is their right.

Mowliid Abdullahi and I meet for coffee in a northeast Seattle coffee bar where he has agreed to tell me his story. Like many of the Muslims I interviewed, Mowliid does not drink with me because he cannot be sure the coffee has been prepared by a Muslim. In this way, he chooses to express one aspect of his identity. Other identities, he tells me, are his professional class (he is a doctor, but since he fled Somalia without papers, he cannot prove his credentials) and his clan (Biyomaal, which also cannot be confirmed). The dictator Siyad Barre forced the Biyomaal to carry out his violent purposes against other clans, and as a result they were considered collaborators by Barre's enemies and persecuted as such. That's why Mowliid had to flee his home, he explains, and why he cannot go back.

Having offered me these stories as background, he leans forward on the table and fills me in on his escape to the United States, via Yemen and Mexico. It is an escape that involves a hired Yemeni smuggler who brought him a passport and ordered him to keep quiet. "I was like scared to death," he says, "and when he told me in Arabic that we had arrived, I said, 'Are you sure?' And he said, 'Yes, that is the border between Mexico and the U.S.' And then I started crying." For a few seconds, Mowliid stays silent as the emotion wells up. Then he shakes it off and continues:

Luckily, I said, "Which state?" Because I have schooling, I knew the geography of the states. He said "California," so I said, "Can we go to L.A., because I have friends there?" And he said, "Yes. But do you know their phone number?" But I didn't have it because he said that I wasn't to take anything except only a small bag that held two trousers, two shirts, and a toothbrush. Nothing else. So I said, "If you can take me to any Somali, I'll be OK." So he asked the guy who brought us, but he didn't know any Somali, but he did know an Ethiopian restaurant in L.A. So I said that's OK, too, because I was so scared of everybody, of being caught, because I had nothing. Anyway, with $10 given to me by the smuggler, to that restaurant I went, and I ordered a coffee. I could speak English, so I could not get lost. After I'd relaxed a bit, I asked if there were any other Somalis around. "Are you from Somalia?" the owner said. "I thought you were Ethiopian. Are you new here?" And then he said, "I know a Somali— let me make a phone call." And do you know whom he called? [*He smiles broadly at the impossibility of such a coincidence.*] My friend! He said to him on the phone, "There's this Somali guy here, he's from New York and he doesn't know anyone, so can you please . . ." And then he said to me, "Can he ask you something?" And when I spoke into the phone, the Somali said, "I recognize that voice. Who are you? What's your name?" When I heard, I couldn't even speak. I became tongue-tied [*his eyes mist over*]. And then after some time, the Somali said, "Hello? Hello?" I said, "Come and pick me up, it's Mowliid." And then he was like, "Oh, oh, I thought you were dead, I didn't know what had happened to you." I said, "Come right now," and he said, "I'll be there immediately." And then he came, he picked me up, and here I am.

Mowliid's story, like so many I heard from Somalis, is incredibly moving, and it is difficult not to be in awe of men and women, some of them youngsters, who have undertaken such dangerous and epic journeys, which one day they will tell to their grandchildren. Mowliid's story, however, also tells us a great deal about the identity he wants to convey and adds a number of details to what he has already said—for example, that he is not anti-Ethiopian at a personal level and in fact could be mistaken for one by looks, he speaks English and knows the geography of the United States, and he is enterprising and daring. Together with details he provides later in this book, his account offers a picture of Mowliid as an individual. We can only guess at his reasons for stressing certain aspects of his story. What is more, we have no idea of yet other features he might have skipped over or even dispersed to the story cemetery. He has chosen how he wants to be seen, as is his prerogative.

Ethnicity, Language, Religion

If each of the three communities were homogeneous, the issue of identity might be simpler. Perhaps then the story lines and hence the battle lines could more easily be drawn. But each community consists of a number of ethnic or clan groups, each looking to establish its credentials in the Pacific Northwest. The Eritreans of Seattle and Portland, for example, derive predominantly from the Tigrinya people, who speak Tigrinya, a Semitic language derived from classical Ge'ez, which, like Latin, is now mostly a liturgical language used in hymns. By and large, they adhere to Coptic Orthodox Christianity, although there are some exceptions. A small number of Tigrinya are Muslims known as Jiberti; others are

Catholic. Yosieph, for instance, attended private Catholic school in Asmara and identifies as Catholic. "My parents were Catholic," he says, "but before that, they practiced the Eastern form of the religion, Coptic Christianity, with its Ge'ez rites and practices. It's not clear to me exactly how their conversions came about, but at some stage, I don't know when, something happened that triggered them. In fact, many other people from the same village and area from which my family came turned Catholic. To tell the truth," he confides, "there's not really a lot of difference between Catholicism and Coptic Christianity. My aunt's husband is a Coptic priest, so on my mother's side, all of them are Coptic Christians."

Most other Eritreans in the Pacific Northwest belong to the Tigre, Bilen, or Beni-Amir ethnic groups and practice Islam, although there are Christians among them as well. All of them speak Tigre, a language closely related to Tigrinya.

Given these different groupings, it is not difficult to imagine the tensions that attend intercommunal and also intracommunal conversations. Divisions break along a number of fault lines, none of them neatly.

In the Ethiopian communities of Seattle and Portland, which have their own fault lines, the Semitic-speaking Amhara and Tigray dominate, as they do at home. Most Amhara I interviewed chose to downplay their ethnic identity and definitely appeared more entrenched in the Pacific Northwest world outside of their group. The more numerous Cushitic-speaking Oromos, whether Christian or Muslim, bear deep bitterness toward the Amhara and Tigray for what they perceive as their exploitation at the hands of both groups. Oromo immigrant Tesfaye Kumera argues that the Tigray "are only interested in impoverishing and disempowering the Oromo so they can never challenge Tigray hegemony in Ethiopia."

With resentment, grudges, and hostilities from home playing out in the Pacific Northwest, no one seems surprised that the Ethiopians, like the Eritreans, divide along political, religious, and ethnic lines. Such splits translate into separate community centers, separate places of worship, and, ultimately, separate lives.

"The part that is discouraging to me is our inability to work together on the things we agree on," comments Haddis Tadesse, discussing the divisions with me. "Yes, we have different views on politics, religion, and ethnicity. But we have far more things in common, and these get obscured by the differences that paralyze collective actions."

Like the Ethiopian community, the largely clan-based Somali one, the third-largest in the United States, also fractures into lineage-based institutions, and few Somalis above the age of twenty mix with Somalis outside their related clan families. Only the Mogadishu Somalis, accustomed to a diverse, urban population, continue to interact relatively freely.

"Actually, it was my generation that had ideas about mixing together," Abdihakim Hassan tells me with some pride. He was born and raised in Mogadishu when Somalia still had a government and city life encouraged mixing. "We were a younger generation who grew up here, with Web sites, so we were thinking more broadly than most Somalis. Know what I mean? Even if you were tribal, you would never use clan identity against your friends."

On the whole, however, each clan in Seattle and Portland sticks to its own. The Darod, Hawiye, and Isaq predominate in the Pacific Northwest, with numerous other subclans making themselves felt. All speak the Somali language, and for this reason, scholars in the past have described Somalis as a homogeneous ethnolinguistic group. In 2004–5, however, a virtually unknown subgroup of Somalis turned up in Seattle and Portland, with its own distinct ethnic identity. These recent immigrants to the area, collectively known as the Somali Bantu, subvert the notion of Somali homogeneity. Treated as second-class citizens by the clan-based Somalis, the Somali Bantu keep a low profile both in Somalia and in the Pacific Northwest and do not bring attention to their status. Their presence creates a further division within the already clan-driven Somali community.

Behind the tensions in Seattle and Portland lies the long-standing discriminatory structure of the Somali lineage system, which divides Somalis into two main lineage lines: the *Samale*, or "noble" Somalis, mostly nomadic northerners like the Isaq, Dir, Darod, and Hawiye, who speak Maaha (also known as Af-Maxaa) Somali, and beneath them the *sab*, or "commoners," which includes some of the occupational castes, who resemble the *Samale* in looks but do not share their claimed lineal purity. Lumped together with the *sab* are the slave descendants (*sheegad*), who are mostly farming southerners like the Bantu and speak Maay (Af-Maay, or Maay Maay).[4] The inferior status imposed on the occupational castes through this lineage structure, and which allowed for their economic exploitation by the *Samale* at home in Somalia, is being perpetuated in the diaspora. The continuation of this unjust system ultimately delays the healing process as Somalis find it harder and harder to trust one another.

THE AMERICAN DREAM

Abraha Alemseged is an opinionated and outspoken man who, for many years, has been a loyal supporter of Isaias Afwerki's liberation movement–turned–government. He grieves for his relatives back home who must bear the brunt of the violence and poverty, which he sees as the direct result of Ethiopia's power-hungry intransigence. But Abraha is also a sentimental man and a loving husband. So when his wife asks him to find her a new basket for their *injera*, one that she hasn't been able to find at Eritrean stores in their neighborhood, he puts aside his reservations and enters an Ethiopian shop in the Central District.

"Ethiopians are gracious people," he admits to me later, "and the store owner, knowing that I was Eritrean, couldn't have been more friendly and helpful. He was showing me the baskets and discussing their various attributes, and after I had decided on one and paid, he came out from behind the counter and said, 'Here's a gift for you.'"

"That was a nice gesture," I say with a smile, and Abraha nods his gray head. He is a tall, angular man and avoids my eyes now by bending down over his long legs to loosen the buckle on his left sandal.

"It was a kind gesture, but . . ." He slowly straightens up, then admits reluctantly that he didn't know how to respond. "I couldn't appreciate his generosity fully because all I wanted was to get out of there as quickly as I could. I realized he was reaching out to me, partly as a customer—he's a businessman, after all—but also because of all the bad blood between us." He shakes his head slowly, amazed himself at how deeply seated his antagonisms are.

Given the violence generated by the many divisions, it comes as no surprise that people like Abraha hold onto their grievances against their "enemies." Even as they aspire to reach out for the sake of future generations, some find themselves unable to make that stretch and expose vulnerable feelings. Their children, however, skip blithely from culture to culture. They share classrooms and lunches with friends who, in their parents' eyes, bear the same ethnic features as their foes. Sometimes they speak the identical language. This new generation, beneficiaries of their parents' flight from bloody struggles at home, simply leapfrogs ahead. Like all young people, they are eager to fit in with their peers even if, as they move between home and school, their two worlds frequently collide. In the confusion, sameness and difference vie for precedence, but these young people persevere, engaged in the greater struggle to make it in yet another more urgent narrative, the American Dream.

Like other immigrant groups, East Africans interviewed for this book want to do well in America. Even if going home remains part of their dreams, all want to succeed in the economic and social realms that constitute the good life in the Pacific Northwest. Their versions of the American Dream assume as many different forms as there are dreamers, but in one particular respect most share a common aspiration, namely to lift up the entire community so that all may participate in success. Unlike others in the United States who articulate making it in terms of individual accomplishments, independence, and autonomy, these immigrants generally see themselves and their communities as inextricably linked, their health, wealth, and well-being interconnected in a marriage of reciprocal responsibilities and loyalties that play out over the duration of their lives. This means that the personal dream is conjoined with the communal one, the individual with the group, and both depend on the other for their success. The connective lines to success radiate out from the individual to the family, to the clan, the ethnic group, the national entity, and, beyond that, to the religious community. Thus we find that Somalis, for example, are expected to care for and provide economic help to members of their clan whether they know them or not, an obligation that more than one of the Somalis I interviewed resented. Nevertheless, they may still fulfill their obligations. That those who have should assist those who have not constitutes a hard-core belief among the three communities.

Like individual dreams, those of communities are equally varied, but all picture a place in the sun, a position of standing and status among those other groups who make up the American landscape. In a land of ethnic diversity and huddled masses, the American Dream for a community means being a political, economic, and social player whose views and actions contribute to not only the betterment of its own members, but that of the country as a whole. Living the American Dream signifies that a community matters and that it elicits respect from its new compatriots.

That their adopted country should inspire such aspirations is a measure of America's own constructions of identity. Its master narrative of rags-to-riches success and its projection of itself on the world stage as a global powerhouse have made it a simulacrum that invites emulation. Despite the fact that the "real" America struggles under the burden of its own reputation with inflation, debt, and crime, its larger-than-life image evokes envy and that primordial urge to side with success. Immigrant neighborhoods are notoriously badly served in terms of education, housing, and health services, and only some newcomers achieve success in the face of poverty and discrimination. Yet, immigrant groups believe in the stories and aspire to make it in America. "You know America through stories," the Eritrean-Ethiopian narrator in *Of Beetles and Angels* imagines the truck taking them away from the refugee camp to the United States saying. "You know it to be paradise. But beware! Rumors are malignant tumors. Snakes lurk even in paradise. And the advice of mothers does not always ward off evil."[5]

Seated at my dining-room table in Seattle, Mehret Mehanzel and an Eritrean friend, Yodit Tekle, talk about the stories and myths that shape their fellow Eritreans' notions of the United States back home. Yodit attended both elementary and high school here, plus business college, and like other Americans her age, she has a slightly cynical attitude. "All Eritreans know about this country is the value of money," she says. "They have no idea. Someone will come here and do janitorial work at a hospital and send a picture of himself in hospital uniform to his family, so they think he's a doctor. Then the family back home will ask for more and more money. Why? Because the person this side is saying he's doing well, when in actuality he struggles to pay rent and to look after his children and spouse." She shakes her head. "He won't admit to his family back home that he's not making it in this land of plenty."

Mehret nods. She has been in the States for fourteen years and hopes to get her master's degree in social work soon. She has seen the unrealistic expectations of America at close hand and understands. "Because they feel that coming to America is such a great opportunity, they don't realize that being here also has its problems, that it will challenge their culture and that they will struggle with communications."

Racism, too, will create problems. As open-minded as Seattleites and Portlanders like to think themselves, racism continues to undercut the best efforts of the immigrants. In the eyes of those who are prejudiced against black people, only the skin color may register. The neo-Nazi skinheads who murdered Ethiopian Mulugeta Seraw in Portland on November 12, 1988, the gang that goes by the name of East Side White Pride, never asked him whether he was Ethiopian or African American, or whether he derived from freeman or slave ancestors, before one of them, Ken Mieske, brought his bat down on Mulugeta's head.

Still, the American narrative with its authority and longevity exerts its pull. Not only can the power of narratives win funding and assistance for the communities in Seattle and Portland, but they also can bring military, financial, and medical aid to their countries of origin. Working as Americans in conjunction with the U.S. government or other institutions, such communities can effect change and make a difference in their homelands. What is more, and most important, the successful community can ensure a place for its historical narratives in the history books of the world. And this is the ultimate success, to control the word and, in turn, one's community's past and present. The future is anyone's guess.

ACCULTURATION THROUGH STORIES

Just as Eritreans, Ethiopians, and Somalis know America through stories, so, too, does America know its immigrants through their cultural histories, myths, and legends. Thus the stories that interviewees *choose* to tell (and not tell) play an important role in the immigrants' process. Their ability to be the subject of their own stories rather than merely objects in the stories of others allows them to control how Americans see them as well as their communities. Their rights to their own stories therefore are extremely important to them and ultimately influence their ability to integrate themselves into the United States and to make it in their new home. Refugees and immigrants instinctively know this and for that reason willingly compete to be the defining voices in establishing their community profiles. The greater the impact of their individual image, the better that of the community, and vice versa, the two irrevocably entwined.

Although much has been written about the cultural marketplace in the United States, the Horn Africans' experiences are relatively recent, and little scholarship on their U.S. acculturation through story exists. Indeed, scholars' explorations of Ethiopian, Eritrean, and Somali narratives in *other* countries suggest that, rather than being helped in their acculturation by recalling their stories, Horn Africans become stuck, stymied, and prevented from finding their American feet. In Atsuko Karin Matsuoka's and John Sorenson's insightful writing about Ethiopians and their Eritrean and Oromo challengers in Toronto, for example, they claim that the East Africans' space of exile is a "haunted" one, where stories from home, like ghosts, trouble and disturb them and intrude into their present lives.[6] Past Amhara power over Eritreans and Oromos, the Canadian researchers say, binds the members of the diaspora communities in tenacious strands of violent memories and desires from which they cannot escape. Thus they cannot move forward with their lives and instead remain in a kind of limbo, a foot in each country, and continue to measure actions here by the tape of the past. Defining themselves in positive terms against the negative moral values of the other, they create even more impenetrable barriers and further inequities that knot the strands further.

Nuruddin Farah, in his *Yesterday, Tomorrow*, discusses Somali exiles in Kenya, Sweden, Switzerland, Italy, and England and writes of haunting stories, too. However, whereas Matsuoka and Sorenson look to continuing Ethiopian expansionism to explain Eritrean and Oromo fixations, Farah blames his fellow Somali exiles themselves for their inability to move on and create new diaspora identities. Stuck with their anger and sorrow, they cannot quiet the past narratives in their heads or push aside the spectral cobwebs that get in the way of even their best intentions.[7] Despite his obvious sorrow at their situation, Farah writes that they are "blamocrats par excellence" who pass the buck and cite "circumstantial generalizations about the culpability of the other." Even taking refuge in notions of clan identities, he argues, is merely a way of subsuming their individual identities in the larger unit and thus avoiding their share of the censure. Farah makes a point of not mentioning any clan names, no doubt as a matter of principle, because he sees the "clan as malady" idea as a smokescreen for the real problem, which he understands as individual Somalis' inability to acknowledge their share of the blame.[8] Yet, for all the American reader knows, Farah's interpretations could be based on interviews of a single clan's members alone. He doesn't say. What is more, his own fame ensures that everyone he interviews is aware of *his* clan identity which has the potential to discourage other clan members from freely expressing their opinions.

Farah's interviews were published in 2000, before 9/11 complicated the picture and made it difficult to separate what he describes as lack of responsibility from the effects on the Siyad generation of anti-Islam narratives, both verbal and written. While it remains true that many local Somali men are not integrated into U.S. culture and remain unemployed or in menial jobs, the current climate of intimidation and intolerance accounts for at least some of their apparent lack of success in pursuing the American Dream. Rima Berns McGown, in her study of Somali communities in London and Toronto, argues that the host country's political culture in large part determines whether or not Somalis move on and create new diaspora identities. Their success at acculturation depends on the responsiveness of the host country's institutions to Somali cultural and religious practices, what she calls "external integration." But it also depends on "internal integration," namely, the ongoing process of "cultural weaving" that layers together the experiences and meanings of the immigrants' birth and adopted cultures so they make a meaningful whole.[9]

Perhaps I was lucky in my choice of Somali interviewees, in that those to whom I spoke impressed me with their ambition and their desire to transcend clan differences. For example, Ubax Gardheere, together with Awale Farah and Mohamud Esmail, set up Somali Rights Network (SRN), which aims to bring to justice Somali warlords accused of crimes against humanity. "Not just warlords belonging to the clan that caused *our* flight," she explains, "but warlords of all clans. We want Somali Rights Network to be inclusive of everybody, so the organization has no clan affiliation." Ubax is a tall, striking, and vivacious young woman who turns the heads of all the young men we pass. As the daughter of Abdullahi Mohamed, who was exiled to Kenya in 1977 during the Siyad Barre regime, she tells me, she tried to stay away from politics, but, she admits, she just couldn't "hide her passion." She is an activist. So, while studying computer information systems at Washington State University in 2005, she started building SRN. One would think this smart young woman could make anything she wanted happen, but she admits that despite her best intentions, she was not able to get people from different clans to join SRN. "So we're trying to focus now more on students who haven't been affected as much," she says, explaining how much harder it is to interest older people who suffered during the civil war. "Their minds are too full of what other clans did to them."

Despite the aspirations of Ubax and those like her who try to transcend clan tensions, few are the Somalis who have succeeded in achieving all-inclusive organizations. Even within the universities, Ubax tells me, when I meet with her again in 2010, clannishness has increased. Clan loyalty is alive and well and inevitably plays a part in the inability of so many Somalis here to work together for their mutual benefit. For them, the clan rather than the Somali community benefits when individual members achieve a modicum of the American Dream.

To return to the notion of haunting, however, certainly Somalis, Eritreans, and Ethiopians in Seattle and Portland also carry a shadowy mix of anger, resentment, and loyalty from the past. Whether religious, regional, ethnic, political, or ideological, such emotions *do* haunt each intercommunity and intracommunity group. They result in competition for control of the narrative and a babble of competing voices all vying to be heard. Those who have experienced downward mobility, for example, keep the ghostly specters alive, because their hope for the future lies in a transformed utopian homeland, an "imagined community," where once again they can reestablish their status. In the Pacific Northwest, far from the bloodier and more frightening reality on the ground, "home" thus elicits emotional encomiums and nostalgic yearning, even as the bitterness and hatred spawned there are reinforced and played out in different patterns in the new place of sojourn.

Sometimes, the degree to which an immigrant may be haunted depends on his time of arrival in the States. Thus, he may remain fixated on the status quo and discourses at the time of his flight even when the situation changes at home. So internalized can such haunting become that members of the older generation are seldom aware of their slanted perspectives and will deny any prejudice. Slightly later arrivals may be even more overt in their animosities, especially if they have suffered firsthand. Often, they continue to lash out at the descendants of those responsible for their situation. Outsiders may shake their heads at the futility of such self-defeating behavior, but it is also understandable. In the immigration process, victims and perpetrators seeking asylum at different times may end up living or working alongside each other, as Edgegayehu Taye discovered when she took a job in an Atlanta hotel and, on entering a service elevator, found herself face-to-face with her torturer.[10]

While haunting voices certainly exist in the three Horn of Africa communities in Seattle and Portland, in this book, they make up only part of the cacophony of voices that shape the communities at any one time, for such voices compete with others who also have their say and who struggle likewise to make over the community here in their own image. These are the voices, first, of the young, whose friendships with "the enemy" slowly begin to erode the fixed hatreds of those living in the past, and, second, the voices of the large pool of local East Africans of mixed ethnicity and nationality who do not want to take sides. Distrusting and bad-mouthing the other does not work for them, and they look for ways of collaborating and cooperating, seeing in this line of action a more promising path to the future for themselves and their communities. Alongside these two groups is a third constituency for progress, namely, wealthier, educated, and integrated middle-aged exiles. Ethiopian Ezra Teshome, for example, sees in ethnic divisions the seeds of discord. "Ethnicity is the way rulers divide us, and it works even here because people use it for the wrong purpose." When I talk to him of the benefits of belonging to an advantaged ethnic group, the Amhara, he qualifies my words by saying that it is "a sort of fake advantage, a fake good" and, from across his desk at his insurance office just off Madison, explains to me that people should be united. "In fact," he adds, "I would be daring enough to say that the whole of East Africa could be one country. I mean, the people are very similar in culture and tradition. They just need to learn to respect each other and to survive."

Eritreans and Somalis may not agree with Ezra's daring suggestion, especially if the one country in which they are to be united is Ethiopia. Nevertheless, many of those I interviewed do understand that ethnic and clan specters can impede progress and that they therefore need to interact with them in a new way. What becomes immediately clear on talking to them is that they look forward rather than back. Although the past remains always with them, the future lies in their adopted country. Thus, even as they speak with nostalgia of the utopian sites of their youth, they are ultimately much more concerned with their here and now in the United States.

"My life is here," says Abraha. "This is my country now, and how we live here should take precedence over what's happening back home." But it's not always that easy. "When people are heated with anger, they don't always see this," he explains. "So I try to find the elements that work for all of us rather than the elements that send us on our separate ways. I say to people, 'Listen, we're here, we've got to live here, we've got to live by the rules here, and we've got to aspire by the rules here.'"

Acculturation works hand in hand with attaining the American Dream, but for Muslims, fitting in is easier said than done. While some of the Somalis to whom I spoke represent various degrees of integration, few were confident of their standing in the two cities and most had drawn closer to Islam since leaving their homes in the Horn. In effect, most communities practice a kind of pragmatism when it comes to acculturation. None wants to attain success by forfeiting its cultural differences, which include the narratives from which its members derive their strength. Even assimilated, so-called model minorities like Chinese Americans and Jewish Americans retain great stores of cultural narratives and nurture their links with China, Hong Kong, Taiwan, and Israel. Pragmatism is inevitable. Somalis, Ethiopians, and Eritreans, like immigrants before them, are both the same and different from one another and from the majority culture. As they adjust to their new country and draw on their pasts in order to negotiate the present, they are both self and other, both insider and outsider.

"WHO WE ARE"

Cultural competition is fierce, and the Ethiopians, Eritreans, and Somalis whose voices provide the competing conversations at the center of this book have quickly learned how to make themselves heard. Needless to say, numbers play an important role in getting out their words, but numbers for these three communities remain inconclusive because no single body of data, not even that of the U.S. Census, provides appropriate and up-to-date demographic profiles. Not surprisingly, aggrandizing mythostats are common among all three groups, who rightly understand that numerical size plays a role in the competition for communal resources. With each group giving its own estimate of itself, the figures for the Greater Seattle area are Ethiopians, 25,000–30,000, Eritreans, 8,000–10,000, and Somalis, 30,000–35,000; in the Greater Portland area, the numbers are Ethiopians, 3,000–4,000, Eritreans, 2,000–3,000, and Somalis, 3,000–4,000.

In addition to families, newcomers include unaccompanied young women who have been widowed or have lost their families, teenage boys sent to safety abroad by their parents, and elderly men who were once the local leaders of their villages. They came to the Pacific Northwest mostly as victims or else as students who later found themselves unable to return for fear of persecution or simply because they saw no economic future for themselves back home. As such, they fit into three of the five immigration categories delineated by Robin Cohen in *Global Diasporas*. She bases the categories on the circumstances that initiated the move from homeland to diaspora, namely, victim, culture, trade, labor, and empire.[11] Ahmed Samatar identifies Somali forms of departure similarly. The *qaxootin* he describes as a desperate exodus to escape violence, persecution, and hunger and the *tacabbir* as a temporary adventure to improve one's material life through education and work experience, which then equips one to return to Somalia with a new worldliness.[12]

By and large, those who fled did so following traumatic upheavals or persecution in their home countries. They left in waves to escape the violence, fleeing first to refugee camps elsewhere and then to the diaspora, where they hoped to make new lives. Robert Johnson, regional director of the Seattle office of the International Rescue Committee (IRC), who has been involved with members of all three Horn communities, says that the first to flee are usually the more educated, the professionals, and those with better jobs. "Government officials, that sort of thing." And then, gradually, other groups start to move out, particularly the minority groups that suffer discrimination. "Of course," he adds in an aside to me, "sometimes people just leave because others are leaving." Not surprisingly, people do not want to be left behind without their kin and community. Later waves usually bring close family who tend to be less educated, followed by extended family members, some of whom, he says, have no education at all.

Their flights correspond with six major dates or periods in the history of the Horn: 1974, the fall of Ethiopian emperor Haile Selassie; 1977–78, the disastrous Ogaden War and the Red Terror launched by Mengistu Haile Mariam; the 1980s, Ethiopian forced conscription into Mengistu's armies; 1991, the implosion of Somalia; 1998–2000, the two-year border war between Ethiopia and Eritrea; and 2003, the breakdown of the Somali food system and competition for fertile riverine lands.

Now, as they put down roots in the Pacific Northwest, these immigrants and refugees begin their new lives as Americans. Like other immigrants and refugees before them, many settle in areas where federally subsidized rentals offer them relative comfort and space, if not always security. For example, in West Seattle, some Ethiopians live in High Point and focus their community life around the Islamic Center and the Masjid Al-Tawheed in the area. For most Eritreans and Ethiopians, however, the Central District and South Seattle, including Rainier Valley, Yesler Terrace, and Holly Park, represent home. It is in these neighborhoods that you will find the mercato where the Horn locals buy their *injera*, the beauty salons where women have their hair braided in the particular fashion of the Tigrinya, and the community centers where the second generation studies the languages of its ancestors. Tigray and Tigrinya inscriptions above the entrances add a dash of elegance to the buildings. Even when the words are painted on nothing more than a piece of cardboard, the sinuous lines of the script appear so much more beautiful than the square roman letters found on American stores.

The Central District and Rainier Valley also house some Somalis. Upstairs, at the King Plaza strip mall on MLK Boulevard, for example, young Somali men learn how to solder components onto circuit boards in a class run by the Refugee Federation Service Center. Alongside them, but separate, Ethiopians also practice assembling electronics in the hope of finding employment once they are trained. In an odd juxtaposition of history, both groups have experienced frequent sightings of Absolute, an elderly dreadlocked Rastafarian runner who jogs along MLK with an Ethiopian flag sewn on his cape.

The highest concentration of Somalis, however, is in Tukwila and Sea-Tac, where the Masjid As Salam attracts Somalis from all of the clans. It is in these neighborhoods, too, that you will find service centers as well as stores and restaurants owned by different clans. A strip mall in Tukwila, just off Pacific Highway South, boasts a number of halal establishments and brings together numerous Somalis from the neighborhood. Taxicabs fill the parking lot, and the whole area functions as a kind of marketplace where Somalis meet to trade stories and catch up on the latest news. While the women gather at the grocery, where they purchase turmeric and goat meat, the men make their way to the Marwa restaurant next door, where they catch up on news from Al Jazeera on a large flat-screen TV.

As individuals from each group move up the ladder of success, they relocate to neighborhoods such as North Seattle and Ballard or, if they work at Microsoft or Boeing, to Redmond, Bellevue, and Kent. Slowly but surely, Horn merchants follow, and soon, stores and restaurants pop up to service the relocated brothers.

In the Greater Portland area, Eritreans and Ethiopians have concentrated in the north and northeast of Portland, in Beaverton, and in Vancouver, Washington. Along Martin Luther King Jr. Boulevard, for example, one finds Orthodox and evangelical churches as well as community centers and restaurants. Abe Demisse is the president of the Ethiopian community center on Northeast Russell Street and complains that it is only 250 square feet in size. "We need a proper center that will be a hub for many, many things," he says, "a place that will accommodate cultural activities, business, teaching, career counseling, psychological counseling, women's organizations, a senior association." The list goes on and on. Unfortunately, he says, there is no money to hire anyone.

Westside Beaverton is also home to Somalis. In a street around the corner from the mosque, Somali men in shirtsleeves shoot the breeze over the open hood of a stalled blue Chevy. One wears an embroidered cap, or *koofi*, on his head and bends over to turn the ignition switch. When it fails to catch, he twists his open hand in a gesture signifying "Nothing." Somali Bantu were placed in Beaverton, too, when they arrived in Portland, but their discomfort amid members of Somali clans who had treated them as inferior led to their relocation to the Gateway District in northeast Portland. In southwest areas such as Tigard, new subsidized housing locates Somalis close to the local mosque and Islamic school as well as the Somali community center and halal meat market. At one time, the U.S. government wanted to place Somalis on subsidized farms. It thought Somali women in particular would feel more at home and productive if they were planting things in the soil. So they made long-term plans to build farms in west Olympia, Washington, only to discover that the women had no wish to work the soil; they preferred the city.

These then are the three communities of the Pacific Northwest: their numbers, their general flight history, and the areas in and around Seattle and Portland where they reside. While the Horn Africans whose voices fill this book do not speak *for* these communities, in the process of agreeing with or contradicting the stories told about them, they contribute to their emerging and evolving images. In effect, they participate in the creation of a network of stories that, in their dialogical chafing and jostling of one another, create a picture of communal identity-shaping in action.

The interviewees have all come a long way from the trauma of flight and loss. Against the odds, they have secured jobs and housing and attended to the health care and education of their children. As they begin to interact with their American neighbors, they form friendships across cultural differences, adapting a little here, adjusting a little there, even as their neighbors step beyond their own habits to taste *injera* for the first time or try to understand a few words of a foreign language, perhaps greeting these new Americans with a gentle "*Salaam.*" It is in this kind of exchange and in the telling of their stories that Eritreans, Somalis, and Ethiopians slowly but surely begin to influence American attitudes toward the Horn people and their communities in the Pacific Northwest. Through stories shared in the workplace, tales told to the neighbor in the next-door apartment, and anecdotes contributed at school, the Horn communities say, "This is who we are, a strong and proud people."

TWO

WITHIN THE
AMERICAN GAZE

We Somali, Ethiopian, and Eritrean exiles are like guests in
somebody else's house. We each live in separate rooms and have
little to do with one another. Out of respect for the host family,
we are polite and try to keep our antagonisms out of sight.

—ABDIHAKIM HASSAN, SEATTLE, 2006

WE ARRANGE to meet at a Columbia City coffee shop in Seattle.
I arrive a few minutes early and, in preparation for our interview,
set up the recorder with date, time, and place. I have not met
Asia Mohamed Egal before, so every time the door opens,
I look up hopefully. Through the large window, I have a good view of
Rainier Avenue and every so often, among the United Nations–like
passers-by, I recognize Somali women going about their business. Up the
road, Horn refugees from the nearby Rainier Vista housing development
feed their longing for home at a small grocery store that displays Ethiopian,
Eritrean, and Somali videos, while around the corner, workers at an
Ethiopian restaurant start preparing for the evening meal. By the time Asia
arrives, I've already drained the last foam bubbles from the bottom of my
latte. Asia (pronounced Asha) is a tall, imposing young woman. Her eyes
sweep the room and linger on the notepad and recorder on my table. She
breaks into a smile. Her gums are purplish black in the Somali fashion and
accentuate the whiteness of her teeth.

"Sandra?" As I rise and smile back in greeting, she strides toward
me, holding out her hand. We shake, and I offer to get her something to
drink, but she refuses. Her head is covered, but below her neck, American-

style sweater and pants complete the picture. Once the greetings and my explanations about the manuscript are over, Asia and I settle down to talk. Amid the steaming hisses of the espresso machine and the strains of Norah Jones's distinctive voice flowing from the ceiling speakers, Asia begins to tell her story. A vital and lively young woman with the confidence of someone of privilege, she constantly interrupts herself to greet and hug Somalis who enter the cafe. She seems to know everyone. She is a member of the elite Egal family, the Italian-educated daughter of Mohamed Egal, a former colonel in the Somali military whom, she says, Siyad Barre appointed governor of Bosaso in 1990.

Just before "everything hit the roof big time," she tells me now, talking of the 1991 civil war in Mogadishu, her mother had gone to Kenya and her father to Bosaso, while she went to stay with her grandmother in Mogadishu. Since nobody thought there would be a civil war at that time, she says, her grandmother flew off to Saudi Arabia and left her with Omar, the butler, plus two other ladies related to her grandmother. What she goes on to recount horrifies me, yet her storytelling remains nonchalant, and she frequently breaks into laughter, astonished at her own experience:

> So, anyway, right before New Year's Day, it really got frightening. The electricity went out, so Omar went to find the generator. And then the next thing I know [*she alternates between past and present tense*], bombs are flying everywhere. I wanted to scream, but I couldn't scream. So I was, "OK, you're dreaming. Just stay calm." And then I started hearing gunshots. You know, I wasn't sure if they were actual gunshots [*laughs*] or if it was just firecrackers. That's how dumb I was! So, I don't know, but somehow I ended up being under a bed. And it's like daylight outside even though it was about nine or ten at night. So I thought, OK. I guess I fell asleep eventually. I don't know what happened, but I got up about six the next morning because I could hear the animals making a noise, and . . . I come out and there's no Omar and no ladies and blood everywhere. Half the house is gone. So, I'm like, "O . . . K." And I go back and I brush my teeth—it was weird. I brushed my teeth, put on my tennis shoes. I was wearing jeans, but I said to myself, "If you go out in jeans, you're going to get killed." So I put on this black dress covering, an *abeaa* that a lot of

women wear. And as I was walking, it was a very beautiful day, and I started to see bodies. I mean, I couldn't scream, I couldn't cry. I was just numb. And I saw more bodies and I just kept walking. And walking. And as I walked, you know, it was just b-b-b-blood, lots of blood and bodies, that I became so numb that I started . . . Every time I came to an obstacle and I went this way, and I couldn't, and I went that way, and I couldn't . . . [*she makes zigzagging movements with her hands*]. So I started walking on the cadavers. And I was like, "You're going to wake up, you're going to wake up." I was at that time fourteen. It was half a week to my fifteenth birthday. But I think the worst . . . I walked and walked and as soon as I came to the guard . . . that was the first time I got scared. I did not know if they were militia or what they were doing. But that's when I first felt something. The rest of it, it wasn't real. So, anyway, the militia comes up and they say, "Oh, did you see the job we did?" And I kinda was like . . . [*laughs, shakes her head*]. And I just kept walking. And he looked and he was like, "Maybe she's one of them." I did not run because I did not have energy to run. I'm walking. And another one says, "Oh, she couldn't be. These Darod don't have the guts to walk the way she's doing." It was just fear though. I remember that I have never been so scared in my entire life.

For a moment, we sit in silence. I cannot think of anything to say that doesn't sound trite in the face of Asia's experience. In the months to come, I would interview other Somalis as well as Ethiopians and Eritreans who also had wrenching stories to relate, but the horror of their traumas never ceased to render me speechless, the more so for the storytellers' ability to speak of themselves dispassionately as if in the third person.

What became clear to me, too, in the process of listening to the various accounts, was that even though there were common threads in the refugees' stories of their flights from the violence of their countries, no flight replicated another exactly. Similarly, no two refugees experienced Seattle and Portland in an identical fashion, nor did they recover their emotional stability at an equal pace. That each person's story was unique and that each person's story belonged to him or her alone would seem an obvious conclusion, something we would take for granted. And yet . . . Here, in the United States, we lump everyone together and in describing them use associated adjectives as if they were essential characteristics, like the epithets of oral verse. For example, we speak thoughtlessly of "refugees" as "poor" and "uneducated," and immigrants as "illegal" as if neither could exist in any other state. Likewise, we unthinkingly pair "radical" and "Muslim" and "Islamic" and "terrorist," casting *all* Muslims in a damaging light, as many of them confided. It is human nature, of course, to categorize people and perceive them all through the same lens. It provides a kind of shorthand to which people resort so that they can deal with large numbers and act and make decisions. Nevertheless, it is difference that creates identity and difference that constitutes the yardstick by which we legitimize our selves and represent our selves in our stories.

Long before people like Asia arrive in Portland and Seattle with their stories, Americans have formed their own notions about people like her. And about their countries. Before the speaking subjects have even opened their mouths in their host land, U.S. television programs, movies, and newspaper articles have categorized and stereotyped them in the particular ways that serve the interests of U.S. involvement in those countries. To many Americans, the Somalis, Ethiopians, and Eritreans do not signify as autonomous players with their own strategic needs but instead appear as by-products of the United States' own politico-economic narrative, meaningful mainly to the extent that they impinge on or contribute to the interests of the United States. The United States has involved itself in Horn of Africa affairs ever since World War II and the Italian invasions of the area and today still ventures purposefully into the struggles and conflicts of all three countries. Two major ideological narratives—the Cold War and the war on terrorism—have governed the way the United States relates to the countries of the Horn.

AMERICAN FOREIGN POLICY IN THE HORN

"America has been good to me," Yosieph tells me as we talk about the latest machinations of U.S. foreign policy. He always smiles when he talks, and his enthusiasm and sincerity are infectious. While he was still in Sudan, he explains now, his brother in the United States arranged a scholarship for him at Inglewood High School in Wisconsin. "A professor at the University of Wisconsin, David Johnson, sponsored me, and I lived with him and his wife, Marjorie, for three whole years." When I ask him what the Johnsons were like, he starts to tell me about every single little thing they did for him and then concludes, "They were just these really good people. They possessed something that I call 'American spirit.'" Then he adds, "But it wasn't just them. Even the students at the high school possessed that spirit. When I told them about my two sisters who had also escaped the violence in Eritrea and were living alone in Sudan, they set up Yosieph's Fund to bring them out. Within three to five days, they had raised a thousand dollars, and almost twenty families came forward to sponsor my sisters!" He smiles as if to say, "Can you believe it?" "The school even gave my younger sister a scholarship. American people do this kind of thing, you know. It's all about people's relationships." When I nod, he confirms, "That's how people make a difference in other people's lives."

Yosieph is a delightful and endlessly optimistic man who talks of the painful events that overtook Eritrea during his childhood without rancor or notions of revenge. Yet both he and I know that Eritrea, like Somalia and Ethiopia, was often a pawn in the chess game played by the two superpowers of the time. The Cold War mind-set divided the world into pro-Communist and anti-Communist countries and led the United States to support the former and sabotage the latter whenever it felt that developments in a particular part of the world affected its politico-economic goals. Oscillating between being "friends" of the United States in some periods and "enemies" in others, the Horn countries were placed in unstable and untenable positions as the superpowers played them off one against the other. Since the Red Sea basin's strategic position provides access to the oil-producing countries as well as to the hot spots of the Middle East, the United States needed to ally itself with the countries that bordered the Red Sea and thus soon become embroiled in the area's politics.

In 1943 the U.S. military found it could eavesdrop on half the world from Eritrea's capital, Asmara. So it set up an intelligence station there, which ten years later came to be known as Kagnew, after the Kagnew Battalion sent by Haile Selassie to fight alongside the Americans in Korea. Yosieph attended school next door to the military base. He was a child at the time, but he would see "all these American guys striding around and calling back and forth to one another." They were the Kagnew personnel, and Yosieph would watch their sons and daughters going to their own school in a bright yellow school bus. "We kids would stare at them to see what clothes they wore and what they looked like." Then, once a year, the Americans would open the base to the locals, and Yosieph and his friends would go inside and play baseball and various other games. "All these things were at the base station," he recalls, "plus, of course, lots of music. So I grew up listening to American music. In fact, before I even started speaking English, I was singing in it, memorizing lines to such songs as Tom Jones's 'She's a Lady' and also 'In the Summertime.'"

This listening post became so indispensable to the United States in its Cold War game with the Soviet Union that Washington was prepared to promise Ethiopia anything, including Eritrea, for the right to maintain its position there. Since it feared that an independent Eritrea would not be able to resist Communist offers of financial and military support, the United States preferred Ethiopia, its ally, to control the highlands. Thus it allowed the United Nations to impose an Ethiopian federation in 1950, in spite of Eritrea's desire for self-determination and the moral qualms of President Dwight D. Eisenhower's own secretary of state, John Foster Dulles. Twelve years later, on November 14, 1962, as I am reminded by Yosieph, Ethiopia "forcefully annexed" Eritrea as its fourteenth province. Only Yosieph's use of the word "forcefully" suggests what he really feels.

The Americans, however, soon found themselves outsmarted by Ethiopia's emperor Haile Selassie, who had become adept at the Cold War game and learned to play them off against the Soviets. On June 6, 1954, Selassie visited Seattle and was whisked off to Boeing and Bremerton to preview what he might need. Whenever the United States refused to supply him with military hardware to protect his country from the Eritrean guerrillas who now organized to oppose the annexation, he would turn to the Soviet Union, and through such blackmail was able to persuade the Americans to build schools and hospitals in Ethiopia and buy its coffee. In the 1960s, after a failed coup attempt on Selassie, the U.S. government signed a secret agreement to train, equip, and modernize forty thousand Ethiopian forces and was directly involved in the suppression of Eritrean nationalists in 1964 and 1966.

Ezra Teshome, one of Seattle's favorite sons, is a mover and shaker on behalf of the Ethiopian people. Through partnerships with the Rotary Club, he has built libraries and homes in Ethiopia, shipped computers and books to students, brought clean water to villages, and helped with the eradication of polio in his homeland. Despite his achievements, he is a modest man who continues to help Ethiopians fleeing to the States. He has brought numerous Ethiopians to Seattle and regularly opens his home to those in need. He originally came to the city to study in 1971 because Ethiopian students were demonstrating against Selassie's land policies and the colleges had been closed down. "There were only a dozen of us Ethiopians in the entire Washington State then," Ezra remembers, "and we would meet to discuss the political situation back home. We all knew each other, had good connections, and intended to go back. But when the military junta overthrew Haile Selassie in 1974, my parents, friends, and family said, 'Don't bother to return. Anybody coming from the West with a lot of Western ideas, there are two places they'll end up: in jail or dead.'"

His parents were right. Yet, despite Mengistu Haile Mariam's terrorizing of the population through the actions of a council of military officers who called themselves the Derg (Committee), the United States continued to supply him with weapons. At the time, the Derg seemed only moderately socialist in its rhetoric, and, in any case, Ethiopia was a Christian country and the Americans perceived it as a bulwark and ally beset by the Muslim countries surrounding it. They saw Eritrea, in contrast, furthering pan-Arabic expansion and feared that its nationalism could encourage other Ethiopian groups to secede and thus disturb the status quo that served American interests so well.

By 1977, satellite technology had made Kagnew less important to the United States, and the Americans became aware that the weapons they gave Ethiopia to protect itself from Somalia were being used instead against the Eritrean Liberation Front and Eritrean People's Liberation Front and also against Eritrean citizens, who now blamed Americans for the situation. At the same time, dissatisfaction with Derg rule in Ethiopia led to the formation of organized resistance, which Mengistu attempted to wipe out in a bloody purge known as the Red Terror.[1] Having massacred his opponents in the Derg as well as in the Ethiopian People's Revolutionary Party (EPRP) and the All-Ethiopia Socialist

Movement, or Meison, Mengistu cleared the way for his totalitarian rule. When the United States tried to renegotiate its arms deal with him, he refused and instead turned to the Soviets for aid. Marxist-Leninist Ethiopia now changed sides, accepting Soviet weaponry and demanding U.S. withdrawal from Kagnew.

When the Soviet Union began arming the Ethiopians, the Somalis found themselves at a loss to understand how the Soviets could play both sides. That same year, the Soviets had supported Somalia's attempt to regain the disputed Ogaden territories by invading Ethiopia. Now, at the height of Somalia's success, they switched sides. When huge Soviet arms deliveries to Ethiopia, together with Cuban troops, ensured Ethiopia's military success, Somalia withdrew its troops, abandoned its Socialist ideology, and turned to the United States for help. The U.S. government promptly switched the object of its affections, reopened the U.S. Agency for International Development mission in Somalia, and two years later concluded an agreement that gave U.S. forces access to military facilities at the port of Berbera in northwestern Somalia. In return, the United States helped defend Somalia, which, in the context of the Cold War, became its partner. Washington never quite gave up on Ethiopia, however, and, in the hope of a rapprochement later, avoided supporting Eritreans or Somali clans in the Ogaden.[2]

The capitalist/Communist lens of the Cold War era confused Eritrea, too. The EPLF was also a Marxist group, but in the 1970s and 1980s, it was put in the awkward position of fighting for liberation from another Marxist country. Its Soviet hosts saw no sense in breaking up the region, which it intended to bring under Soviet dominion anyway. Thus, the Soviet Union continued to arm the Mengistu regime and help it suppress the Eritrean nationalists. During Mengistu's rule, the Soviets were granted Red Sea access, and thousands of Ethiopians—Haddis Tadesse's parents among them—were sent to study at Soviet universities. Soon after Mikhail Gorbachev came to power, however, the Soviet president started criticizing Ethiopia for its constant warring. At the same time, various humanitarian organizations in Somalia began planting red flags to warn the United States of the danger to Ethiopia of continuing American support for the tyrannical Barre government. Washington also began to examine the Eritrean situation more carefully and in 1990, started to change its tune and acknowledge the country's right to self-determination. Now that Isaias Afwerki, a Christian, headed the EPLF, they no longer saw the rebel group as Muslim fundamentalists, nor even as Marxist anymore.

By the end of 1991, the once powerful Soviet Union had broken up, and both Ethiopia's Mengistu and Somalia's Barre had fled their countries. The Cold War was at an end, and the United States, seemingly indifferent to the disaster it had created in Somalia, turned its attention to Iraq while Somalia imploded. "In 1991," Mowliid recounts to me, "chaos reigned everywhere, and everyone was in hiding in Mogadishu. The city was big and diverse so it was easy to conceal yourself. But the violence . . ." he throws his hands into the air, "the violence was impossible! In the absence of a government, all of the clans sought power, and in Mogadishu, the Hawiye, who were the largest tribe, were fighting one another for control. As you know, I am Biyomaal, so we were Hawiye targets, and we lived in constant fear of our lives."

Stories like Mowliid's, plus others about starvation in the city, brought the United States back to assist in the distribution of relief supplies in November 1992. But this supposedly humanitarian gesture turned into the debacle Americans now know as "Black Hawk Down." For by this time, Somalis associated the Americans with the Barre regime and saw them as a foreign presence, and when U.S. troops began disarming some of the warlords in an escalation of purpose known as "mission creep" and bringing about armed fighting in Mogadishu neighborhoods, the Somalis turned on them, killing eighteen marines. In March 1994 President Bill Clinton withdrew U.S. troops.

Seven years later, with the horror of the September 11, 2001, attacks that killed 2,752 Americans, U.S. foreign policy in the area assumed a different controlling narrative. The new war ideology, the war on terrorism, like that of the Cold War, divided the world into pro- and anti- stances that quickly segued into a battle of good against evil. Underneath it all lay U.S. oil hunger, which rewards regimes that facilitate the extraction and transportation of oil.

In the vacuum left by the Barre government, numerous warlords staked out their territories, and, in the fighting that ensued, Somali civilians fled for their lives. Since the United States was prepared to support any warlord who could deliver terrorists to its door, it wittingly or unwittingly financed the further destruction of the state. Fourteen failed attempts by the Somalis to establish a government had made the United States wary, but when the Transitional Federal Government led by Abdullahi Yusuf Ahmed finally emerged in 2004, the Americans did support it, even though numerous warlords could be found in its ranks and it had little support among Somalis, who favored a Somali Islamist umbrella group, the Islamic Courts Union. The ICU actually brought an end to the violence by negotiating with the warlords. The Americans, however, convinced that the ICU harbored al-Qaeda elements, persuaded the Somalis' longtime enemies, the Ethiopians, to invade in July 2006 in support of the TFG. The ICU, now forced from the country, left in its wake further violence as the Hawiye clan in Mogadishu, the ICU's main supporters, attempted to regain the momentary peace it had glimpsed. The U.S. Navy blockaded the Somali coast and launched a series of strikes in the south against al-Qaeda, killing numerous Somali citizens in the process. The region continued to reel, the chaos providing even more opportunity for terrorism to flourish. In the two years that followed the invasion, the TFG lost territory to the ICU, and the Ethiopians eventually left in January 2009. In an attempt to control the situation, the United States negotiated a power-sharing deal with TFG, Prime Minister Nur Hassan in Djibouti, and the Alliance for the Re-liberation of Somalia, a moderate splinter group of the ICU. The ARS leader, Sheikh Sharif Ahmed, was then elected as TFG president. The fighting, however, continues unabated as the more militant al-Shabaab pursues its Islamist cause through terrorism, and another Islamist group, Ahlu Sunnah Waljama'ah, supported by Ethiopia and allied with the TFG, struggles against al-Shabaab.

IDENTITY IMPOSED

Given these two narratives, when East Africans arrive in this country, powerful paradigms are already in place, and newcomers must compete for the right to their own versions of identity. If their personal stories differ from the U.S.-imposed narrative, they face an uphill battle, for the U.S. master code carries the weight of repetition, familiarity, and power.

If, however, their stories coincide with preconceived images, finding acceptance from their American neighbors follows a much simpler path. Thus, the Ethiopians have had it easier than most, in that the U.S. State Department for its own purposes projects positive images of Ethiopia, which are picked up by the media and catch the attention of different segments of an admiring public in the Pacific Northwest. Americans thus offer Ethiopian immigrants and refugees a degree of acceptance not granted to many other African peoples. Ever since Ethiopia became associated in the Western imagination with the mythological Christian kingdom of Prester John, supposedly a descendant of one of the Magi who followed the guiding star to Bethlehem to see the baby Jesus, people here have been fascinated by the country. And when singer Bob Geldof, the Live Aid concert organizer, raised funds for starving Ethiopians during the famine of 1985 by setting up a multi-venue rock concert hooked up by satellite, the music put Ethiopia on the map for young Americans of all races. As the country hit the airwaves on live television amid the sounds of "We Are the World," the younger generation caught its first glimpses of a tall and dignified people they would come to know as special.

Three stories about Ethiopia have paved the way for this attitude. These same narratives also cause dissension among members of both other communities from the Horn and within the Ethiopian community, too: the Amhara Solomonic lineage through the Queen of Sheba; Ethiopia's status as the home of mankind through the discovery of the hominid Lucy; and Ethiopia's resistance to colonization.

"Look," Haddis says diplomatically, when I ask him whether Ethiopians really believe themselves descended from the Queen of Sheba and King Solomon of Israel, "I see no reason why any objections to the story would emanate from within because the story has been told many times and is favorable to us." Although the visit is mentioned only briefly in Chronicles 11:9, the account in Ethiopia's national epic, the fifteenth-century *Kebre Negast*, or *The Glory of Kings*, claims that Solomon seduced the beautiful and wealthy Sheba, who subsequently gave birth to a son, Menelik, who became the first king of Ethiopia. Thus began the royal dynasty that ruled the peoples of that area. Ever since, Ethiopian emperors have turned to the *Kebre Negast* for endorsement of their positions. Thus, for example, when Ras Tafari, an Amhara, came to power in 1930, he claimed kinship with Menelik as the 235th ruler in a line of direct descent from the queen. He renamed himself Haile Selassie, King of Kings, Conquering Lion of Judah, and claimed in Ethiopia's 1955 revised constitution that the royal line "descends without interruption from the dynasty of Menelik I, son of the queen of Ethiopia, [who is] the queen of Sheba, and king Solomon of Jerusalem."[3]

"Frankly," says another Ethiopian, Dawit Nerayo, recalling from his Addis schooldays how Amhara kings were heroicized, "I don't remember any event in school depicting other ethnicities in heroic form, not Tigrayans, Oromo, nor the Afar or Issa."

"Besides," Jamal adds, echoing the skeptical attitude expressed by many Somalis to whom I spoke of the Sheba connection, "who knows who slept with whom?"

Still, Amhara Ethiopians believe in the Solomon legend, despite the lack of firm evidence, and the *Kebre Negast*, as a written document much treasured by the nation, confirms Amhara belief in their special lineage and status. With the connection now enshrined in the Ethiopian constitution as well, it has created a national sense of superiority in the region, one that other groups resent. Eritreans, for example, perceive the appropriation of the Sheba myth as simply an Amhara political strategy that supports the Ethiopian state in its imperial designs. The myth, they say, enables the state to claim an anointing of the Amharas as the chosen people and to denigrate other groups, creating resentment that carries over into relationships here in the Pacific Northwest.

Abraha was a third-grade Eritrean student in the 1960s when the Ethiopian government, having annexed Eritrea, changed his school curriculum into an Amhara one that included the *Kebre Negast*, with its Amhara claims about royalty.

> I had forgotten how painful those days had been. I guess I must have suppressed the memory, not wanted to go back there. I'd made it taboo to read Ethiopian histories that claimed royal status for the Amhara and made my culture inferior. You'd think I should be able to live with it by now, but it all came back, the way those stories made me feel as a child. By the end of my schooling, I was fluent in Amharic, but to this day, I would *never* write or speak in Amharic.

Abraha echoes the views of other Eritreans who take exception to Amhara hegemonic claims and in particular to the role supposedly assigned to Ethiopians as God's chosen people. According to the *Kebre Negast*, Ethiopians were selected from among all others to bring light to the world. The story justifying their claim recounts King Solomon's dream on the night of his seduction of Sheba, about a brilliant sun that departs from Israel and installs itself over Ethiopia to shine there forever after. Disturbed by the dream, Solomon accepts the idea that perhaps Ethiopia rather than Israel is now God's chosen land. Some years later, when Menelik (literally, "Son of the King") has grown to be a handsome young man of twenty-two, he leaves Axum for Jerusalem, where he is to meet with his father and hire men who could advise Ethiopia and help build and beautify the country. As things turn out, however, Menelik and a companion instead make off with the Ark of the Covenant, carry it back to Ethiopia, and install it in Axum.

Michael Damtew, our Eritrean history buff, explains to me that wherever Menelik's group rested on its way to Axum and lay down the Tablet, they placed a couple of rocks on the ground. Many generations later, on those exact spots, churches were built.

Today, in Ethiopia, God's gift of the Ark of the Covenant is still celebrated every November. The Ark is believed to be housed in the city of Axum, in the Chapel of the Tablet, a kind of outbuilding within a compound that includes the circular church of Saint Mary of Zion and the monastery church of the House of Zion. A lone monk guards the Holy of Holies in which the tablet is enshrined, and nobody, except a few select priests and monks, is allowed to enter and pray. The stone is said to be a single tablet, polished and inscribed with the Ten Commandments in Hebrew.

With ownership of the Ark of the Covenant, the Ethiopians believe that they are now the chosen people, that they were selected to be moral models, as it were. That is why they are mentioned so often in the Bible, they say. Eritreans maintain an awkward position in relation to these Ethiopian claims. In the first place, by choosing to establish themselves as a separate nation, which came into being in 1991, Tigrinya Eritreans have had to relinquish the history they shared with the Ethiopian Tigrayans in the trans-Mereb. For example, the Axumite Empire arose in those same highlands where both had their homes and where the Ark of the Covenant is said to lie. Both Tigrayans and Tigrinyas can claim this rich cultural past, but the latter, in choosing an identity that merged with other ethnic groups inside the boundaries drawn by the Italian colonial powers rather than with their brothers outside those boundaries, cut their ties to their shared past. Axum now lies below the border in the southern-Mereb Tigray area of Ethiopia, where it remains the religious and political center of the Tigrayans. Its cultural achievements have been appropriated totally by the Ethiopians, whose ruling power was established in 1991 by the Tigray People's Liberation Front, which still uses Axum as its insignia. The Eritreans, in disavowing their Tigray-Tigrinya identity, Alemseged Abbay argues, lost their "anchor in the past" and actively practiced "ethno-historic amnesia." Alemseged distinguishes between the EPLF elite and ordinary Eritreans, suggesting that, among the former, having social descent from Tigray is unmentionable and that President Afwerki keeps his Tigray parentage secret.[4]

The Eritrean leadership may have circumscribed Eritrea's history to actual territory that now lies within the new Eritrea, but keeping inherited memories within boundaries is not always easy. Thus, for example, while one may hear some Eritreans denigrating the Menelik connection as just so much mythical nonsense, to other Tigrinya Eritreans, the subject has been so deeply internalized that it has archetypal resonance. At the very least, such Eritreans would not deny that Sheba gave birth to Menelik, since they claim that Menelik was actually born in Eritrea, not Ethiopia. As Sheba was making her way back to Abyssinia after her visit to Solomon, it is said, she gave birth at a spring at Maibella in present-day Eritrea. Michael recounts the story as his wife, Sonya, and I sip coffee in a small café on the south side of Portland. Hip-hop music from ceiling speakers lends a strange surreal feel to the conversation as he relates this 950 B.C.E. narrative:

> When the mother, the Queen of Sheba, was in labor, the people who were around there, knowing that when a mother is in labor she needs water, they said "mi bella," "say 'water,'" "call for water." "Mi bella! mi bella!" They were saying it back and forth. There's a river there, known as Maibella, as you know. Today, it flows through the center of the city

of Asmara, taking the city's refuse all the way to the Sudanese border. But legend says that "running water" is what they said. So. He was born there, Menelik, at Maibella.

Given Menelik's birthplace, Eritreans do not reject the myth straight out, for to do so would be tantamount to denying their own special link to the biblical king. Since the royal lineage began in Eritrea, justification would therefore exist for claiming part of the Solomonic glory for Eritreans. The claims on Sheba, however, are multiple. Seattle's Abraha Alemseged notes, with a wry smile and just a trace of schadenfreude in his voice, "The Yemenis get so mad when the Amharas claim Sheba as their own." He goes on to explain, "To the Yemeni, she is Azieb; to the Arabs, Balqis or Bilqis; and to the Ethiopians, Makeda, Magda, Maqda, or Makera." Scholars themselves are undecided about her ethnicity and even her very existence.

It is not surprising that Ethiopians are proud of their biblical history. Nor is it surprising that American politics, with its Judeo-Christian bent, found common cause with the Amhara during most of the last century. American Christians felt a common bond in the religion they shared with the Ethiopians despite differences in Coptic belief. What is more, the power of Ethiopia's Orthodox Church provided the United States with a bulwark against Muslim encroachment from the Arabic world. Equally pertinent at the time, however, were the Eurocentric views of many scholars, writers, and journalists who perceived the Ethiopians as more "white" and "civilized" than the rest of Africa because of their Davidic lineage. Hamites belong to "the same great branch of mankind as the Whites," Joseph Harris quotes English anthropologist C. G. Seligman declaring and, in so doing, allowing European scholars and writers to characterize Ethiopia as the "cultural link between themselves and the non-Hamitic Africans who were regarded as the ancestors of African descendants in the Diaspora." Menelik himself, Harris writes, claimed to be Caucasian, though he was in fact "dark and Negroid."[5]

In the eyes of Americans, while the origin of the Ethiopian past in biblical history adds an aura of glamour and spiritual gravitas to Ethiopian cultural identity, the possibility that it is also the founding place of humankind imparts an importance beyond the claims of other countries. From the soil of this portion of Africa may derive all human life, scholars claim, for the oldest fossil fragments of a species of hominid were unearthed by Tim White and his colleagues from the University of California, Berkeley, at As Duma in Ethiopia's Afar region in 1993. Dated between 4.3 and 4.5 million years ago, *Ardipithecus ramidus* is thought to be bipedal and appeared on the scene sometime after hominids split from their common ancestor. Prior to these findings, in November 1974, Ethiopia drew worldwide attention with the discovery at Hadar by Donald Johanson and Tom Gray of fossil bone fragments that, when assembled, completed 40 percent of a 3.18-million-year-old hominid skeleton that became known as Lucy, after the Beatles' song "Lucy in the Sky with Diamonds," or Denqenash (You Are Marvelous), as the Ethiopians call her. The Oromo Ethiopians, however, claim Lucy as their own because she was discovered in their territory, Oromia, and, since she is considered the mother of us all, they resent the Christian Semites' appropriation of her for the country as a whole.

As the source country of all humankind, Ethiopia exerts tremendous psychological effect on Americans and on the gaze they direct toward the Ethiopian community, but Jamal points out that although hominid remains were found in Ethiopia, we aren't certain of their ethnicity. They could just as well be of Somali origin, he says, as in prehistoric times, Somalis lived all over the Horn region, including parts of Ethiopia. The Somalis also have prehistoric finds, such as the Las Geel cave paintings, as do the Eritreans, including the rock paintings found at fifty-one sites across the country, but the Ethiopians have a longer history. Even in the Greek classics, Jamal admits, one reads about the "blameless Ethiopians." He doesn't know why "blameless," he laughs, explaining that they used epithets then. It was a formalized way of remembering while they were reciting. "But then again," he asks, "what did 'Ethiopian' mean at that time? Does it mean what we are talking about today, or does it mean something different?"

One would think that the Ethiopians have it made. Yet they have a further narrative to add to their market capital, one that local Ethiopians stress most frequently and of which they seem most proud. This third history, which has been embraced by Americans, in particular by black Americans, represents Ethiopia as the only nation in Africa to have successfully resisted colonization by Western powers. During the Scramble for Africa in the second half of the nineteenth century, the British encouraged the Italians to stake a claim on the Red Sea coast as a way of preventing the French, Britain's longtime rivals who had already colonized Djibouti, from encroaching further via the Suez Canal to the Indian Ocean, where the British conducted much of their trade. Italian forces moved in and took over Massawa on the Red Sea in 1885 but soon expanded farther inland, right into the highlands. Italy proclaimed the area a colony in 1890, called it Eritrea, and separated the Tigrinya-speaking people from their southern Tigray brothers in the trans-Mereb. When Italian forces then attempted to move farther inland, they were stopped and their expansion checked by the 100,000 troops of the Amhara king Menelik II at the Battle of Adwa in 1896. The victory at Adwa brought Ethiopia to the attention of the world, forcing Western powers to consider the possibility that colonialism could be turned back in Africa. Moreover, the success of Adwa represents the one undeniable victory of blacks over whites on the continent.

The very symbolism of that success inspired Africans everywhere, but particularly those in areas under white domination and racism, such as in southern Africa and the United States. Since the American Revolutionary War, slaves in North America had noted the numerous biblical references to Ethiopia, supposedly the only country in Africa to be mentioned, and had seen in this connection the possibility of black redemption and the coming of a black messiah who would save them from slavery and return them to their homelands.[6] Thus there arose among them a religious movement known as Ethiopianism.

Abdihakim Hassan takes issue. "Ethiopia is not the only African country mentioned in the Christian Bible," he says. Some Somalis point to a biblical reference to the ancient Land of Punt, or Land of God (Ta Netjeru), the paradise to which the Egyptians traced their origins and which Somalis claim as their own. The Old Testament refers to Punt as Püt, and in Ezekiel 27:10, the men of Püt are mentioned as members of the army of Tyre. More interestingly, however, in Jeremiah 46:9, they are listed separately from those of Ethiopia, an important distinction since some scholarship claims that Puntland refers to an area of Ethiopia. Similarly, in the prophecies of Ezekiel 30:5 and in Nahum 3:9, Ethiopia and Püt appear as separate entities, suggesting that Ethiopia is not the Püt of the Bible. Even so, scholars are uncertain of the exact location of Punt.

"When I was going to school in Mogadishu, we were taught that the Land of Punt was Somalia," Abdihakim informs me. He is a Dhulbahante Somali and community leader who came to the States from a refugee camp in Kenya in 1993. When I interviewed him in 2006, he was executive director of the Northwest Somali Community Center, which he was instrumental in setting up in Seattle's Central District. "But not the whole of Somalia," he qualifies.

"Was it just the point?" I ask.

"No, just the eastern part of Somalia. It is the area around the city of Bosaso that used to be called Bandar Qasim. It's about two hundred miles around and has now become a very politically charged area that still produces incense." Today, the Somali region centered around Garowe is called Puntland, and its people consider themselves the descendants of the men of Püt.

Jamal, a Somalilander, doesn't buy it and maximizes the area covered by Puntland. "Puntland is one of those terms you can make mean whatever you want it to mean," he says.

"Like a floating signifier?" I ask.

"Exactly! It refers to the whole East African region, all the way down to Mozambique."

Whether the biblical Puntland is in Somalia or not, the success at Adwa reinforced black faith in Ethiopia as God's guiding light, and numerous independent churches sprang up symbolizing this faith, for example, the Ethiopian Zion Church, the Ethiopian Methodist Church, and the Abyssinian Coptic Church. Pan-Africanism spread throughout the world. Black people raised funds for Ethiopia and, with the 1930 coronation in Addis Ababa of His Imperial Majesty, Emperor Haile Selassie I, King of Kings, Lord of Lords, Conquering Lion of the Tribe of Judah, Elect of God, Light of the World, King of Zion, many were convinced that the covenant between God and King David, as recorded in the Old Testament (Samuel 7), had been fulfilled in the person of Selassie (formerly Tafari Makonnen), who would restore the Solomonic dynasty. In Kingston, Jamaica, Selassie was the messiah, the black Christ returned, and his worshippers formed their own spiritual culture, Rastafarianism, after his pre-emperor title, Ras Tafari. Rastas, as his followers call themselves, revered the Conquering Lion of Judah for his resistance to the Italian fascist invasion of Ethiopia during World War II, and he, in return for their support, granted land in Shashamene, as a home to any people of African descent who wished to return and settle in the "motherland."

Portland's Tesfaye Kumera, an Oromo Ethiopian, shakes his gray head at the mention of Shashamene. He leans forward on his elbows and speaks directly into my microphone:

> Yes, Ras Tafari *did* give them land. He gave them *our* land [*his voice rises*], Oromo land in *our* area. As far as we know, Haile Selassie is no god. If the Rastafarian religion started this way, the workings of God must be very strange [*shakes his head in amusement*] . . . very, very strange. When Mengistu was escorting Selassie to the car when he was being deposed, they say that Selassie—the Rastafarians' god—looked at him and said, 'You slave boy!' Now, no decent person would say that, never mind a god. At that, they say that Mengistu then pushed the emperor into the Volkswagen, just shoved him in, kicking him on the head. That's what people say. You see, Mengistu was born of a slave woman, a servant, and his father was a gatekeeper. Also . . . people don't say these things out loud, so we don't know for sure, but . . . Haile Selassie was suffocated while he was sleeping. He was a very frail man. Books say it was prostate disease that killed him, but that was not true. [*Tesfaye's more soft-spoken brother, Shigut, cautions him that he doesn't know for sure, but Tesfaye won't be sidelined.*] Let me finish. Mengistu killed him, and they buried him under his workbench, a table like this [*pointing to the one at which we sit*]. They buried him ten feet down and poured concrete on him. And when they exhumed the body, they saw only the rope, no clothing whatsoever. They didn't even give him *that* much, they didn't even cover him up, just lowered him by rope ten feet down and poured concrete on him. That's the way he *really* died [*nods*], not the way it is in the history books.

Today, in the United States, Rastafarianism still thrives, and pockets of New York, for example, are characterized by dreadlocks, marijuana, the reggae music of Bob and Ziggy Marley, and the colors of Ethiopia.

Pan-Africanist leaders, believing that redemption lay with Ethiopia, encouraged diaspora blacks to return to Africa. Among such leaders was the politician and black nationalist Jamaica-born Marcus Garvey, who led a movement "home" under the slogan "Africa for Africans." So closely did American blacks identify with Ethiopia that when Italy once again invaded that country in 1936, its actions were seen not merely as a David-and-Goliath attack on a small nation, as white Americans perceived it, but in racial terms as a white attack against black. Ordinary black Americans donated money to Ethiopia, and everywhere in the United States, pictures of Haile Selassie decorated African American homes. When finally, in 1941, Italy was forced out of the country, African Americans rushed in to help rebuild it.

Ethiopians take great pride in their uncolonized status, as indeed they should. When Italians seeking revenge for their defeat at Adwa successfully attacked Ethiopia on October 3, 1935, Britain and France did nothing to help. Selassie was forced to flee into exile in London, and Ethiopia together with the Italian colonies of Eritrea and Somaliland became part of Italian East Africa (Africa Orientale Italiana).[7] Only when Mussolini entered World War II on the side of Germany in 1940 and Britain responded by attacking Italian forces in Eritrea were the Italians pushed out, Addis Ababa liberated, and Haile Selassie returned to his throne. For the Ethiopians, the victory was all theirs. "Thanks to her brave sons and daughters," Haddis tells me, "Ethiopia was never colonized. It is a fact that is a source of pride not only for Ethiopians but for all people of African descent."

Seattle and Portland Ethiopians share Haddis's pride, and Adwa stands in their minds as a symbol of their united strength as a people. Aware of what it means to black Americans, too, local Ethiopians jumped at the chance to show the documentary film about Adwa by Ethiopian filmmaker Haile Gerima in 2001. *Adwa, an African Victory* thus became part of the community's cultural marketing efforts and was shown in Seattle and Portland on Adwa Day, March 2. Drawn from oral sources and narrated by the filmmaker himself, *Adwa* tells the story of the 1896 Ethiopian battle against the Italians, whom the film's chorus calls "the hyenas" and "the offspring of scattered lice eggs." The film presents the victory as a triumph of good over evil, the evil of colonialism. For a short period, it instilled cultural pride and united Ethiopians in both cities. What is more, it proved a winning vehicle for gaining support and respect in the Pacific Northwest.

Added to these three selling narratives was Haile Selassie's projection of himself as King of Kings, Lion of Judah. While he certainly had his detractors, Selassie nevertheless remains a historical figure of major importance in the American mind. For more than fifty years, he played a dominant role in the affairs of Ethiopia. Wearing his biblical nobility with aplomb and conveying his military status with a dramatic uniform (sash, medals, gold braid, black cloak, white gloves, curved sword, helmet headdress), Selassie created a personality cult through which he ruled as a benevolent autocrat. His picture hung in all official buildings and even in private homes, and numerous state institutions were named after him. He would regularly visit the schools of Addis Ababa, handing out cakes and oranges to the local children. So strongly did his personality dominate that the whole country, not only the Amhara, were identified with him. He impressed officials and dignitaries from the West—*Time* magazine named him Man of the Year in 1935—and they looked to his rule as a stabilizing influence amid the chaos of Africa. In international circles, he became a venerated father figure who, in 1963, presided over the creation in Addis of the Organization of African Unity (OAU).

Ethiopian immigrants and refugees arriving in the Pacific Northwest thus enter an American climate of acceptance and cultural respect not afforded many other peoples. Their stories precede them, and they are made welcome. Members of African American communities here embrace their brothers and sisters, and while black churches celebrate Ethiopia's biblical connection to Zion, white Christian communities also perceive their Christian brethren as having been faithful bearers of light in a world beset by Islam.

Eritreans, who are less known by their American neighbors, have their own challenges. "When I first arrived in the U.S. in 1972," Abraha tells me as we walk around Yesler Terrace, where we are visiting Eritrean friends who have invited us to share the coffee ceremony with them, "I would say, 'I'm from Eritrea.' People would ask, 'Where's that?' 'Next to Ethiopia,' I'd answer. Then they'd say, 'Oh, Haile Selassie!'" Abraha's face has about it a shadow of intensity that makes him look angry, and when he states dismissively, "That's all they knew! All!" his jaw locks up, as if he holds back a stream of fiery words. But he's used to controlling himself, I know, and now he merely comments that the myth Haile Selassie gave Americans was "truly immense. It has died everywhere," he concludes, "except in U.S. policy making."

Since then, the situation for Eritreans has improved somewhat, but they remain unknown entities to most Americans. Having discarded their early shared history with the Tigrayans, they have stood silently by, they say, while Ethiopia claimed *their* stories as its own. Eritreans officially acknowledge only their immediate history, dating from their Italian colonization in the 1890s, through their thirty-year war against Ethiopia, and their ultimate victory in 1991. Unfortunately, this recent history is one that few Americans know. The United States' covert pursuit of its strategic interests in the Horn of Africa after World War II at the expense of Eritrea never made the front pages of the *Seattle Times* or the *Oregonian*, and few radio or TV commentators ever pursued stories that would have enlightened their listeners about the Eritreans' history and culture. Eritreans arriving in the Pacific Northwest before independence in 1993, therefore, were simply lumped in with Ethiopians, only recently emerging as a separate people who insist on their own constructed identity. As such, their identity in the eyes of Americans is simply a blank slate, neither positive nor negative.

This view had certain advantages for the new arrivals because it offered them the opportunity to write their own stories, untainted by the preconceived notions of their host compatriots. They had already chosen what Alemseged Abbay calls an "instrumentalist option," namely, to separate their history from that of their Tigray brothers south of the Mereb and to invent for themselves a brand new identity. Yet, given that most Eritreans I interviewed perceive Ethiopia as their ex-colonizer, their desire to separate culturally as well as physically is understandable. Liberating oneself from the past, as Chinweizu writes in *Decolonizing the African Mind*, involves a cultural housecleaning, ridding oneself of the colonizers' effects, and a psychological excision of memory that frees one from traditions associated with them.[8] Still, in my own interviews, I found that while the Tigrinya seldom mentioned this common past, it was nevertheless present, a mutually understood history. Occasionally, in the heat of conversations about Eritreans being underappreciated by the local population, someone would burst out with reminders of heroic deeds and historical events from precolonial times, thus providing heartfelt grist for the mill of Tigrinya pride.

The publication in 2005 of Michela Wrong's *"I Didn't Do It For You":How the World Betrayed a Small African Nation* improved the situation slightly in that it introduced Eritrea to the reading public in the Pacific Northwest. In so doing, the book pushed the blank slate of that people's identity in a direction in which local Eritreans have long been trying to steer their Pacific Northwest neighbors. The world betrayed Eritrea numerous times, and Wrong's book describes in shaming detail the behind-the-scenes maneuvers involved. Before the book's publication, Abraha had described to me an event known to him through oral stories. Wrong would later report Eritreans' description of the same event in her book. Here, in much the same words, is Abraha's version:

> As the British soldiers trudged from Keren to Asmara, they were met on the road by an elderly Eritrean woman who was ululating in the traditional way and holding her hands up in thanks to them for liberating her and her people from their Italian oppressors. As the soldiers marched by, the captain turned towards the old woman and said, "I didn't do it for you, nigger!"

The British may have been fighting a world war in part against racial genocide, but their attitude toward Africans remained condescending and downright racist. They were convinced the Eritreans would not be able to maintain the productive industries the Italians had built, so they dismantled the factories and transferred them, together with railway tracks, carriages and equipment, cranes and vessels, to their own colonies in Africa, the Middle East, and Asia. This asset-stripping would have remained a secret, kept under wraps by the British government, Wrong suggests, were it not for the British activist and suffragette Sylvia Pankhurst, who, in her book *Eritrea on the Eve*, investigated the devastation in person and publicly denounced her country's plundering. Her son, Richard Pankhurst, confirmed through his own research in the 1990s the systematic looting of Eritrea by the British caretaker government.[9]

Eritrea's treatment at the hands of Italy, Britain, and the United States, has led to a loss of trust, which is why Eritreans in the Pacific Northwest prefer to rely on themselves to get things done. Recent developments on the terrorism front, however, have raised suspicions about this unknown, victimized people from the Horn. The identification of one of the terrorist suspects in the attempted London bombings of July 21, 2005, as an Eritrean of Muslim descent brought negative attention to Eritrea at that time. While the two other Muslim defendants were born in Somalia and Ethiopia, a terrorist from Somalia, sad to say, does not elicit surprise and one from Ethiopia is seen as an anomaly, since most Americans in Seattle and Portland assume Ethiopia is entirely Christian and therefore a bulwark against Islamic terrorism. But for Eritrea, about which so little is known, the attention is new and unwanted. Even though the suspect lived in Britain and had not been back to Eritrea, the connection pulled Eritrea into the limelight.

Muslim aspirations and guerrilla potential in the United States has long been a concern. In the heightened atmosphere of fear and suspicion after the 9/11 attacks, the CIA investigated the Eritrean Islamic Jihad for possible connections to al-Qaeda. No links were found, and the government of President Isaias Afwerki convinced Washington that it would in no way tolerate terrorists in its midst. In 2002 it offered access to its military bases for use in President George W. Bush's war on terrorism and ever since has been working closely with Washington. Nevertheless, it now finds itself on the radar screen of the more terrorism-phobic members of the Pacific Northwest population.

To make matters worse, during the December 2006 unrest in Somalia, Eritrean soldiers supported the Islamic Courts Union against the government of President Abdullahi Yusuf, which was supported by Ethiopia and the United States. In fact, they were believed to have been supporting Ethiopia's dissident Muslim Somalis in the Ogaden. The Eritrean president denied it, but because the United States believed the Islamic Courts Union to be infiltrated with anti-American terrorists, Eritrea found itself once again installed against its will in a U.S. narrative of terrorism. Local Eritreans are confused, and when I tell Abraha that I read that two thousand Eritrean soldiers had been deployed in Somalia, he reacts defensively. We sit in a restaurant near Green Lake, sipping tea, and between sips, he attempts to put me straight by reiterating Isaiah Afwerki's denial:

> The president is on record as saying, "We do not have any soldiers in Somalia." Somalis and Eritreans look alike, and Ethiopians have been creating false identity cards for these Somalis to pose as Eritreans. It's on record. Eritrea is *not* supporting the ICU. [*His face is set, adamant.*] This country [the United States] is just biased against Islam. It goes way back before al-Qaeda and Iraq. When Eritrea's struggle started, one of the myths created about Eritrea was that the Muslims and the Middle East were funding this small piece of land because they were interested in Red Sea access. So [*he challenges me*], just because it's an Islamic country, it should not be supported? For years, Sandra, fifty years, we lived with that myth. People don't know that Eritrea was 50 percent Christian and 48 percent Muslim and that we fought side-by-side to gain our independence. I remember when we first brought Eritrean fighters to this country, people were saying [*his voice leaps an octave*], "Aren't you Muslims?" [*His mouth tightens and he shakes his head.*]

Jon Lee Anderson, in "The Most Failed State," published in the *New Yorker* on December 14, 2009, writes of the current president of Somalia's Transitional Federal Government that this ex-chairman of the ICU fled to Eritrea after his release from Kenyan custody in February 2007. And from there, he and his allies fought a jihad against Ethiopia's occupying forces and Western "crusaders" in Somalia. However, outside of scholars, Peace Corps workers, and others involved with the Eritrean communities in Seattle and Portland, the terrorist narrative, like that of the underdog, resonates among very few Pacific Northwesterners. On the whole, the "blank slate" perspective continues to dominate, and a certain openness to learning more about Eritrea defines the attitudes of ordinary citizens, an attribute that gives the Eritrean community a definite edge in the market.

The same cannot be said of the Somalis. When it comes to preconceived ideas, not only are many Americans ignorant of Somali history and culture, but what they do know is often mediated through political and religious lenses that so drastically "other" the Somali that finding a connection may sometimes seem impossible. Of the three Horn of Africa communities, the Somalis in the Pacific Northwest perhaps start their new lives with the worst handicap.

The U.S. debacle in Mogadishu in 1993, when angry mobs of Somalis dragged the lifeless body of a slain U.S. Army Ranger through the streets amid jeers and anti-American shouts, still resonates in the minds of local Americans. It accounts for a perception here of Somalis as a bloodthirsty, vengeful people. Even though Seattle and Portland by and large support antiwar efforts of all kinds, they experienced deeply the humiliation suffered by the U.S. Army at the hands of warlords and their clans, especially since they understood the army's actions to have been benevolent initially, namely, to make the area safe for the distribution of famine relief by the United Nations. In attempting to remove Somali warlord Mohamed Farah Aideed from his stronghold in Mogadishu, however, the use of helicopters and massive force in the area alienated ordinary Somalis who subsequently saw Aideed as their protector. When the movie *Black Hawk Down* played in cinemas and Somali moviegoers greeted the downing of the U.S. helicopter with cheers and laughter, Seattleites were shocked. To them, it seemed that Somalis were biting the hand that fed them. While, from a psychological viewpoint, one could perhaps understand the "we showed you" aspect of the struggle between a superpower and a small African country, Somali reactions to its representation in *Black Hawk Down* nevertheless did nothing to endear the immigrants to the Pacific Northwest population.

The events of September 11, 2001, and the subsequent U.S. Operation Enduring Freedom, with its anti-Islamic fallout throughout the world, further fanned local antipathy to the Somalis. In the traumatic days following the attack, Somali cab drivers were harassed, fearful Somali parents kept their children at home, and all lived in terror of the irrational rage flaring at schools and on the streets. In spite of the vigilante attitudes of some Pacific Northwesterners, however, cooler heads prevailed on the whole, and when, on September 13, worshippers at Idriss Mosque in North Seattle were threatened by one such vigilante, Patrick Cunningham, toting a can of gasoline, local Americans stood up in support of Muslim civil rights and deplored the cruel harassment.

The nongovernmental organization Hate Free Zone, now called One America, With Justice for All, reported a series of anti-Somali events that occurred in Seattle in the aftermath of 9/11. On September 15 a sixteen-year-old Somali girl was attacked and stabbed at a gas station in West Seattle and, about four days later, six Somali women were fired from their jobs for wearing *hijabs*. Women were harassed on the street, and a Somali woman had rocks thrown at her when she went to pick up her children from school. Also in Seattle, on November 7, 2001, agents acting under the authority of the U.S. Treasury Department's Office of Foreign Assets Control, raided the Barakat Wire Transfer Company, which transmitted money from local Somalis to their families in Somalia. The government suspected that the company was being used to channel funds to foreign nationals who were alleged to be supporting terrorism and so authorized agents to seize the company's assets. At the time of the raid, the agents also raided two other businesses that shared the same building, the Maka Mini Market and the Amana Gift Shop, neither of which had anything to do with the bank. The Seattle branch of the American Civil Liberties Union (ACLU) took on the cases of the market and gift shop owners, Abdinasir Ali Nur and Abdinasir Khalif Farah, and won compensation for them two years later.[10] By the time the store owners were cleared of any wrongdoing and allowed to reopen their stores, months of revenue had been lost and, in the case of the grocery, perishable items had been thrown away.

I list these traumatic events in part to record them and bear witness but also to point out that the majority of Seattleites did not take them lying down. Letters of protest expressed the horror many people felt about the racist backlash; the local branch of the ACLU jumped into action; and, as early as September 16, a group of angry young people led by author and activist Pramila Jayapal set up Hate Free Zone, in Washington. On September 21, the group hosted the nation's first public hearing on the post-9/11 backlash against Muslim peoples including Somalis. On January 13, 2003, hundreds of Seattleites rallied again, this time in the International District, to denounce the Immigration and Naturalization Service's roundup of mostly Muslim students, tourists, and workers on short visas for fingerprinting and photographing.

In the months that followed the 9/11 attacks, the United States extended its Operation Enduring Freedom to the Horn. Since chaos reigned in government-less Somalia in 2001, the United States feared that al-Qaeda members would try to set up bases there and so sought to prevent terrorist cells from reemerging and becoming active. To that end, it outlawed al-Ittihad al-Islamiya as a terrorist group in 2001 and the following year established a Combined Joint Task Force base at Camp Le Monier in Djibouti, from which it could monitor activities in Somalia as well as elsewhere in the region. Al-Ittihad al-Islamiya is believed to have evolved from Wahabi roots and is a Salafist group that seeks a return to the Muslim orthodoxy of the past. (Wahabism is an ultra-conservative form of Sunni Islam founded by Muhammad Ibn Abd al-Wahhab in eighteenth-century Arabia.) Unlike other groups whose members are mostly nomads, Al-Ittihad al-Islamiya recruits urban and semi-educated youths in Somalia and the Ogaden and receives support and training from Sudan.[11]

Outside the Abu-Bakr Mosque in Seattle's Rainier Valley on February 9, 2006, members of Seattle's Somali community gather. There must be at least a couple hundred people, mostly men, rallying around their leader, Aziz Junejo, and talking to one another in guarded but angry voices. Some of them look nervous and ill at ease, but they are present to show solidarity. On November 14, 2005, the FBI's Puget Sound Joint Terrorism Task Force (PSJTTF) arrested their prayer leader Abrahim Sheik Mohamed at Sea-Tac Airport, supposedly on an immigration violation charge. Now the locals wonder who will be next? The PSJTTF accused the imam of once belonging to al-Ittihad al-Islamiya and of coming to the States as a covert member of the rebel Ogaden National Liberation Front (ONLF) to collect money to pay for its war. The ONLF wants to secede from Ethiopia, a move the United States does not favor. The mostly Darod-related community believes that its leader is being made a scapegoat in order to keep Seattle Muslims under control. They wonder if perhaps another clan is trying to make trouble for him. They have known the sheikh for five years and have never heard him preach jihad. The *Seattle Post-Intelligencer* of February 11, 2006, however, notes that the imam is said to be the spiritual leader of a group whose rallying cry is "Black Hawk Down." They meet at the mosque or at Crescent Cut Barbershop on Rainier, where young people supposedly are trained in weaponry and anti-American rhetoric.

The day after the rally, the FBI visits some of those who were there, perhaps justifying their concerns. Fear abounds in the community, and few

Somalis at the time will talk to me about the case, except anonymously. Fourteen months later, however, in my interview with Koshin Mohamed, the topic comes up again, and a different view of the prayer leader emerges. Koshin was appointed in January 2007 as Somalia's ambassador-designate to the United States by President Abdullahi Yusuf of the Transitional Federal Government. Some local Somalis, particularly those of other clans, look askance at Koshin's title and express skepticism about his position. "How can there be an ambassador when there's no country?" they ask and suggest that he simply gave himself the title. Koshin, when still a student at the University of Washington, was an advisee of mine. I interviewed him a few days after his Discovery Institute–sponsored press conference at which he announced his position and was immediately reminded of the impossibly lofty aspirations I had noted in him as a student. Now he sports a smart suit and tie but still retains the same irrepressible, bubbly personality I knew from before. Over a rushed lunch in the University District, he tells me bluntly that the sheikh is no struggling immigrant but a combatant on the Saudi Arabian payroll. He'd been sent to brainwash people in Seattle— particularly black American converts—to wage jihad here:

> The Somalis who went out onto the streets marching and protesting, they didn't know the sheik. To them, everything the U.S. government says is a lie, because they don't believe in it, because that's the culture. Again, no one listened exactly to what the sheikh said, so anything the government said against him, they dismissed. But he showed up in Mogadishu with his supporters, claiming his title as leader of the Ogaden liberation force. And the Somalis here were like [*he assumes a soft credulous voice*], "Oh, the sheikh, he's actually the leader of the Ogaden liberation force? Isn't he kidding?" [*Returning to his own voice, he says emphatically*] No, no, no, no!

Despite the willingness of local Americans to believe the best about Somalis here, a certain degree of underlying uncertainty remains. When the ICU gained its foothold in the country in 2006, this uncertainty turned to suspicion. On July 1, 2006, Osama Bin Laden posted a Web message encouraging Somalis to build an Islamic state in their country and threatening to fight any Western nation that interfered with its creation. U.S. Assistant Secretary of State Jendayi Frazer further fanned the flames of uncertainty on December 14 by claiming that al-Qaeda cell operatives controlled the ICU. Six days later, the ICU attacked the government seat in Baidoa and soon succeeded in spreading its forces across the country. Despite some of its more conservative practices, a ban on music and Western movies, for example, most Somalis welcomed the relative order the ICU brought in its wake.

"Some Somalis here support the Courts, you know," Abdihakim tells me as we sit opposite each other at his desk at the Northwest Somali Community Center. The center is housed in an office building close to the corner of East Union and Twenty-third in the Central District. On the corner, drug dealers hang around the Philadelphia Cheese Steak and complete their transactions with solitary people who wait outside the post office across the way. Sometimes, the dealers drive through the parking garage, slowing down just long enough to put a hand out the window in a fast-paced exchange. Police cars cruise the neighborhood, keeping a wary eye out for action, but scouts with cell phones stand on street corners ready to warn of the cars' approach. I'm not surprised therefore that when I walk up the stairs to the center, a burly man stops me and asks about my business.

"Somalis are sick and tired of the warlords," Abdihakim explains to me now, "and some of those that America supports *are* warlords." Since most local Somalis still have family back home, ending the violence and uncertainty has become a priority. He continues:

> We've been asking U.S. senators for their help, and I personally contacted Senator Maria Cantwell's office. A lot of U.S. elders, we asked them to do something about Somalia, even a year or two ago. That's when the proposition was born to support them so we could see good things happen in Somalia. [*His mouth tightens.*] But no response at all! They say, like "OK, we'll see."

As early as March 2006, Jamal Gabobe had given me his take on the situation in Somalia, explaining that the TFG was just a legal cover for the Americans, whose main goal was to destroy the ICU. Although Jamal's a full-time graduate student, pursuing his interest in the Somali poet Elmi Bodheri, he also actively involves himself in Somaliland politics in the Pacific Northwest. He explained then that "the U.S. knew all along the warlords were not to be trusted and that the transitional government was not viable." That's why, when the Americans realized the warlords were bringing them only minor terrorist figures, they decided to use the Ethiopians for their purpose instead. He summed it all up by saying that "the U.S. provided the money and logistics, Ethiopia produced the brawn, and the TFG gave a fig leaf."

"So, what happens next?" I ask.

"The two most likely scenarios are the use of force, which in this context would mean the ethnic cleansing of the Hawiye clans in the south, who see the TFG as a Majerteen-Darod government, or else the withdrawal of the Ethiopians and the failure of their intervention."

In December 2006 the Ethiopians took Mogadishu, enabling President Abdullahi's government forces to disarm the people, particularly the Habr Gidir and Abgal supporters of the ICU, as they attempted to restore order to the country. When the Ethiopians moved on Kismayo, they sent ICU leaders fleeing toward the Kenyan border. Despite U.S. strikes on these supposed al-Qaeda operatives, the Islamists were not defeated. Their fighters bounced back with renewed determination, and over the next two years, their insurgency against the TFG and the Ethiopian army won back both territory and supporters. When moderate Islamists of the Alliance for the Re-liberation of Somalia negotiated a cease-fire with the TFG in 2008, the United Nations brokered a deal to include them in an expanded parliament. This new development persuaded the Ethiopians that their job was done, and so, having accomplished their mission, they withdrew their troops in January 2009. From the ICU perspective, however, the Ethiopian departure merely signaled the failure of the Christian enemy.

As events evolved in Somalia and locals did not speak out against the ICU, Islamophobia took hold among Americans in the Pacific Northwest. While not overt, it still lies beneath the surface and leads to the suspicious eyeing of *hijab*-covered women and reluctance to hire Somali men in local businesses. Most Somalis open small groceries, interpret at local hospitals, or work in programs that serve the Somali community. Abdihakim is typical of the men who create their own nonprofits in order to provide social services. An energetic and personable young man, he is the executive director of the community center. It consists of just a couple of rooms, but from there, he and his partners attempt to provide the Somali community with valuable social services related to housing, immigration, and education. As with all social services, however, money is short, and nobody is coming to the Somalis' aid. As he tells me:

> The city offers grants, but not a single Somali that I know of has received one. We're a low-income society at the moment, and most Somalis live below the poverty line. They need a lot of help from service providers. Like in housing, from Seattle Housing Authority. SHA isn't even trying to know who they are servicing, you know what I mean? I don't see any research or any study conducted by anyone about this new community, this new group, who they are, what they do, what are their customs.

Some organizations that serve Somalis have indeed attempted to research Somali culture and practices. Among them is EthnoMed, which provides online information to medical providers at Harborview Medical Center. The International Rescue Committee, too, has been working directly with Somali service centers like Abdihakim's. The IRC hired Katie Barnett, the ethnic communities program coordinator, to help create a coalition among seven Somali service groups—Somali Community Services of Seattle, Northwest Somali Community Center, Somali Community Services Coalition, East African Community Development Council, Refugee Support Service Coalition, Northwest Somaliland Society, and Refugee Social Development Resource Center. Nevertheless, many in the community, like Abdihakim, feel isolated and marginalized by the larger American community of Seattle and perceive Americans' knowledge of Somali culture as minimal.

Perhaps it was this sense of alienation that made some young Somali Americans respond when al-Qaeda deputy leader Ayman al-Zawahiri called upon Muslims worldwide to fight against Ethiopia and against the TFG in Somalia. Often, local Somali males, disconnected from their clans and not really fitting into the African American scene, feel that they do not belong anywhere. Thus, they become easy recruitment targets for those who manipulate their Somali nationalism by conflating it with religious ideology. Al-Shabaab, the more radical ICU youth movement that still battles the new TFG in Somalia, recruits young Somalis in all the diaspora cities, including Seattle. In 2009 Abdifatah Yusuf Isse, a twenty-five-year-old Somali refugee from Seattle, pleaded guilty to providing support to terrorists. Eighteen-year-old Omar Mohamud, another Somali Seattleite, is still being investigated by the FBI, which suspects him of involvement in a suicide attack on an African Union peacekeeping base in Somalia that killed twenty-one peacekeepers and civilians on September 17, 2009. Al-Shabaab claimed credit for the attack.

The uncertainty of the situation in the Horn reflects back on the transnational Somalis in the Pacific Northwest, making them worry about their own futures as the American gaze turns from Somalia to the streets of Seattle and Portland. Like Somalis elsewhere in North America, those in the Pacific Northwest are caught within an American narrative that is itself changing constantly as it attempts to follow the parameters of its own projected identity, that of a global power that makes the world safe from terrorism.

Alternating with the American perception of Somalis as potential terrorists is the common view that their clan affiliations rule the community and prevent members of different clans from working together for the common good. Ever since Ioan Lewis's 1961 book *A Pastoral Democracy* enlightened the West on Somali kinship, U.S. State Department reports, scholarly books, and newspaper accounts have focused on clan divisions to explain the crippling of the country and the displacement of so many of its people. When Siyad Barre came to power in Somalia in 1969, he aimed to lessen the hold of the clans and create a modern state identification for the peoples of Somalia with the help of intellectuals and technocrats. He wanted them to think of themselves as Somalis first, not as Hawiye, Darod, or Isaq, clan identities carrying historical overtones of hatred and revenge that threatened future peace and cooperation. Later, he called his policies Scientific Socialism, after Friedrich Engels's term, which added an empirical element to Karl Marx's social-political-economic theory. The name, however, had little bearing on what actually happened on the ground, and by the time Barre was overthrown in 1991, his regime had become the most clan-driven and repressive ever. Since that time, warlords representing different clans have terrorized members of other clans, creating what some call civil war and others an economic war.

Clan membership is determined by patrilineal descent and binds Somalis in a support system that protects the group against outsiders and is conducted through a number of generally agreed-upon codes. The system requires loyalty to the clan family, the subclan, the *diya*-paying group, and the extended family. The *diya*-paying group functions much like a system of economic cooperation for its members, who pay compensation for crimes committed by one of its members against another lineage, including blood money in the case of homicide. In the north, for example, though costs vary from nomadic clan to clan, one man generally is valued at one hundred camels, one woman at fifty.[12]

"Somalis don't have any enemies but themselves," Mohamed Omer says, claiming to echo the general opinion among the Seattle community, whose members are clan conscious and do not trust one another. Mohamed, an Isaq from Somaliland, came to Seattle as a twenty-one-year-old student in 1986. He hoped to return to Somalia at some point, but when Hargeisa was destroyed in 1988, the fighting forced his family to flee to the Harata Sheik refugee camp, one of the last in Ethiopia. Now a research technician in the Division of Metabolism, Endocrinology, and Nutrition at the University of Washington, he meets me in one of the Health Sciences Building cafés. Above the din of conversations among nurses, doctors, and students, he tells me that he feels sorry about what happened in the south. "They were such law-abiding citizens and believed in the law much more than Somalis from other parts," he explains, adding with a degree of pragmatism that "bad government [was] better than no government at all."

Sympathetic sentiments crop up often in my interviews with Somalis (as well as Ethiopians and Eritreans), hinting at other narratives that selective memory has pushed to the side in order to project a different story. Seattle's older Somalis, however, have less sympathy than Omer, and, caught up in ghostly rivalries and dreams of revenge, they cannot trust members of clans that have done them harm. Even the community and service centers tend to be clan dominated. Although only seven Somali service centers have offices, Ubax found, by checking out 501(c)(3) lists, that there are at least eighteen Somali service centers, each run by a different clan. "If we only had one organized community," she muses, "it would make so much difference; it would help so much."

After the International Rescue Committee's three-year project, which attempted to do just that, there is still no coalition. "It's been really challenging," Katie Barnett says, when I interview her on April 4, 2006, at the IRC office in Seattle, explaining:

> We have to figure out . . . well, what do they want to do? What is their vision? Do they have a vision? A couple of leaders feel very strongly that they want to see a united Somali community in this area. I think most of them want that, but they want it on *their* terms, if *they* can manage the contract.

As the ethnic communities program coordinator for the IRC, Barnett helps the executive directors of the Somali service centers develop their resources and build their capacities so they can better compete for funding. For that reason, she doesn't ask about the clan makeup of the agencies. She gives the same information to everyone.

> We are not favoring one agency over any other, although we've been accused of doing that many times [*smiles wryly*]. It can really make you crazy just trying to figure out, you know . . . Well, if someone is accusing you of doing a horrible thing like dividing the community, then you start to think, "Well, am I?" Obviously I'm thinking of it all the time. I'm trying to be neutral. Everyone gets the same opportunities.

Few Somalis I interviewed trust the neutrality of Americans or their understanding of clan loyalties and obligations. "Only Somalis can really understand the Somali clan system," Mowliid informs me when I become confused about which sub-subclan belongs to which subclan. Mowliid, too, is now the executive director of a Somali service center, which he started in 2002, the Northwest Somaliland Society. Needless to say, he serves Somalilanders, while Abdihakim, a Dhulbahante, serves Darod Somalis.

In spite of the insistence on clan affiliations, clan need not be the only source of identity. Religion, *tariqa* (religious order), neighborhood, village, education, gender, paternal or maternal lineage, and work patterns can supply identity. People have choices depending on the context. But as Maria Brons points out in *Society, Security, Sovereignty and the State in*

Somalia: From Statelessness to Statelessness? it suited the nomadic Somalis to emphasize clan identity because doing so allowed the major clans to dominate culturally, politically, and economically. Although these *Samale* were arguably only 60 percent of the population, they claimed to be the "real" Somalis, the ones who were ethnically homogeneous and who spoke the same language. To further the distinction between them and the rest of the people—the blacksmiths, shoemakers, tanners, fishermen, and farmers, but particularly those who look more African—they emphasized their mythological origins, claiming Arabic descent. The camel became a symbol of the state, and the pastoral identity of Somalia was woven into the poetry of oral history. The destruction of the state in the 1990s, however, and the increasing importance of the food-growing areas around the Juba and Shabelle rivers in the subsequent years of strife and famine shifted the emphasis of identity away from the nomadic and pastoral that had long dominated Somali life. Without a state, Brons argues, Somalis were thus free from this version of national history and identity and could choose another identity, beyond the state.

Here in the United States, however, constructing another Somali identity in the face of such powerful American versions of their identity and worth is a major challenge. Fearful of any word, act, or gesture that might resonate with any of these unflattering and dangerous American narratives about them, Somalis in Portland and Seattle sometimes police themselves, instituting a kind of internal panopticon that exercises a controlling influence on both individuals and the communities themselves. It is not only Big Brother, the Joint Terrorism Task Force, on the watch but their American neighbors, teachers, and bosses who seem also to be looking for signs that reaffirm these narratives.

Somalis, Eritreans, and Ethiopians all enter the United States bearing the weight of their national stereotypes, which they must negotiate in a way that best helps them pursue the American Dream, both for themselves as individuals and for their people as a whole. It is not an easy task. Although many ethnic groups have been in that sometimes schizophrenic place before them, there are no rules for mapping out safe passage, no consensus on crossing the big divide. They cannot erase the narratives that reflect badly on their people, nor can they bite the hand of their host country, which has given them safe harbor. What they can do, however, is displace harmful narratives with their own more positive ones, narratives of their own construction, and begin the slow process of renegotiating their own identities with the representatives of those other communities that make up the state.

THREE

WITH EYES
OPEN

We must stop saying this tribe is good or this one
is bad, because if we keep doing the same thing,
nothing will change and we will never be safe.

—SAHRA KHALID, PORTLAND, 2009

AT THE halal meat store in the shopping center off Barbur Boulevard in Portland, Somali women buy small portions of goat for their families' dinners. The meat is frozen, and they carry it in their shopping bags along with other groceries, lugging them to the bus stop on the street below. For these mothers, the outing is a break from their children, who at this time in the morning attend school or, if not yet of school age, remain in the care of other Somali mothers at home. Although the women have modestly covered their heads and arms, they are lively and animated, and as they talk, they point and gesticulate, laughing and teasing one another and seeming not much more than teenagers themselves. We have been talking about what *they* want Americans to know about them and, as important, how to get that information to Americans since the women live almost entirely within Somali communities and are busy just surviving.

One responds, "The newspapers and TV aren't interested in us here. We Somali immigrants don't have fancy names like some of the others, like the 'Lost Boys of the Sudan.'"

"Or like the 'Boy Soldiers of Sierra Leone,'" says another.

"You mean sound-bite names?" I ask.

"Yes, yes, sound bites," they agree, revealing more media awareness than many American-born citizens. It is true, they do not possess exotic titles to attract the American media and draw attention and funds to their communal causes. Neither do the Eritreans. Each group wants a catchy national narrative that it can present to its American hosts, but, as with all immigrant groups, contradictory stories from Horn neighbors keep that would-be unifying story constantly fluid.

At some level, though, even as the members of each community contradict one another, they know what aspects of their identity their stories must promote in order for them to claim the American Dream for themselves and their communities. While they may rail at the manipulation of memory by some and the cultural amnesia of others, they acknowledge their dependence on the goodwill of their American neighbors and the need therefore to present communal images that most satisfy American wants.

To the Somalis, the first and foremost goal, they say, is to allay American fears of Islamic jihad. Terrorism threatens both life and democracy in the United States and conjures up that much-aired bogeyman, a Muslim–Judeo-Christian war. As long as Somalis inspire fear in their neighbors, they believe, they can expect an uphill battle as far as acculturation and integration are concerned. Certainly every Somali I spoke to condemned terrorism. "Islam is about minimizing hate," Koshin explains to me. Like other Somalis I interviewed, he separates the mainstream religion from the extremist sects, which he denounces as having been influenced by the Wahabists of Saudi Arabia and their philosophy of hate. As we talk, he gets worked up about the debilitating shadow that extremists' actions unfairly cast on him and other innocent Muslims by association. "It is up to us to get our religion back from these guys and make sure they don't intercept us," he says. "It is not the responsibility of Christian and Jews, it is *our* responsibility. We must take control of our lives and say 'no!' to them. Islam is not a religion of hate, and I want Americans to know that." A Seattle Somali community press release of September 25, 2009, written by Abdurahman Jama and published on the Web site Bartamaha on October 9, denounces violence and terrorism and decries the media's accusatory portrayals of Somali Americans as homegrown terrorists in the United States. "It's unjust and un-American," it reads, "to denounce wholly a law-abiding community of American citizens for the barbaric acts of violence of individuals. There is no evidence of radicalization happening within Seattle, and the Somali community in Washington requests respect as good American citizens."[1]

Local Somalis also strongly disapprove of the kind of clan rivalry that divides them as a community. They want to show their commitment to overcoming clan differences so that they can work together for their community's benefit. Since Somali women are most often the innocent victims of clan violence, they particularly appreciate the importance of transcending clan. "We cannot speak as tribes anymore," Portland's Sahra Khalid tells me in a follow-up telephone conversation. "We must stop saying this tribe is good or this one is bad, because if we keep doing the same thing, nothing will change and we will never be safe. We have to be united as Somalis." To be united, of course, means both men *and* women working together across clan differences, which brings me to the third goal to which Somalis say they are committed, namely, greater gender equality. Asia claims that, in Somalia, "though Somali women are incredibly strong and powerful, they are generally marginalized in all aspects of life." Somalis here want to make it clear to Americans that as modern people they respect gender equality and aspire to treat Somali women fairly at home and in the workplace.

The project for Ethiopians looks much easier. It's a case of "If it's not broken, don't fix it," many locals say. They need merely to continue to promote that which America already believes, namely, that in a region ringed by anti-American Muslims, Ethiopians represent the only Christian U.S. ally capable of maintaining the security and trade on which the United States depends. Ethiopia has a Muslim population as big as its Christian one; nevertheless, Christian Ethiopians here feel that they must keep reminding the United States of their people's suitability to play this role in terms of the power they wield in the Horn and the control they maintain over their own dissident Muslims. Second, by emphasizing the stories Americans already know—that Ethiopians are the chosen people of God, descended from the biblical King Solomon, that they are the only country in Africa to successfully resist colonization, and that they are the cradle of all humankind—such stories will further cement the respectful view their American neighbors already hold of Ethiopians.

The Eritreans, for their part, face a greater challenge. "The U.S. never wanted Eritrea to be independent," Abraha reminds me as we sit in his office, hunched over our respective notes. "They still don't believe Eritrea should be independent. You'd think that since we're the only African country to have a diplomatic relationship with Israel, even though half our population is Muslim—that would mean something to the U.S." He cannot understand it. The fact is that Washington favors Ethiopian hegemony in the Horn, and while Eritreans may not be able to change government attitudes, they can reshape those of their neighbors in Seattle and Portland. Eritreans, they say, are moral people who, ignored by the rest of the world, were colonized by the Ethiopians. Their past wars, they insist, were heroic efforts at self-determination, struggles to gain the same freedom and independence to which all countries have a right. If they can be seen by their neighbors as people who hold the high ground, as self-reliant, honest, and moral people, which, they insist, they are, their path to the American Dream will be eased.

CULTURAL ASSETS

Whatever the challenges ahead, the newcomers do not come to the table empty-handed. All of them possess rich cultural resources that equip them well to make their mark on the larger Pacific Northwest community through story: their storytelling skills, their rich narrative inheritance stockpiled for use in appropriate situations, and finally the cultural values contained in those stories, which fortify them for the road ahead.

"We grew up on stories," Mehret says. She has a ribbon around her hair and wears a red T-shirt that matches her daughter Bilen's red jacket. Leaning on her elbows, she clasps her hands in front of her face and says with determination, "I want my children to grow up on them as well." In the Horn countries, history is passed on to the next generation via storytelling that takes place in the home or around a roaring fire. The father usually starts the narration, the mother picks up where he left off, and other storytellers follow. The whole process stretches late into the night and lulls the children to sleep within a comforting circle of warmth and security.

In Eritrea and Ethiopia, the coffee ceremony with its specific rituals provides storytellers with a central point of togetherness, which Mehret's brother Redi Mehanzel remembers well. He has been in the States since seventh grade and graduated from the University of Washington in economics. In his white T-shirt, he looks like the American he is, but Eritrean history fascinates him, and he tries to find out as much as he can. He speaks nostalgically now of that time, back home, when the coffee was being made and they would "just sit there and chat." As he reminisces, we sit around my dinner table with other members of his family and some friends, also young Eritreans. We are waiting for the water to boil so I can pour it over the French roast I have ground medium-fine and transferred to a large French press. "We would just sit and tell stories, especially about family values," he recalls, hugging his niece, Bilen, who enjoys all the attention. "It touches me when they tell stories about family history, and about the liberation group, and the struggle." The wistful tone in his voice makes me wonder how many of the people in his family history were lost to the liberation war. I press the plunger on the coffee grounds, and the smell wafts through the room, simulating but never even approaching the powerful scent that I myself recall from the coffee ceremonies of Asmara, where young women roast beans over a fire and, as they stir and shake them in the pan, fan the smoke across the waiting circle. "We used to go to Starbucks to try and re-create the feel of those evenings," he says. "We would tell stories to one another, and, although it was not the same, you could feel the sense of history and values that had been passed down through the generations."

Those values were not rules drummed into them by their parents, Redi's brother-in-law, Yegizaw, explains. "The dads don't sit like this"—he leans on his elbows, looking stern—"and say 'This is what you should do!' No. Instead, they tell you the stories and they say, 'This is how we used to do it.' And you learn through them how to live your life. Meaning, this is what they've done and what worked for them. They pass on their knowledge through storytelling, which is a tradition I think just as valuable as attending school."

Growing up in such storytelling environments inspires everyone to speak effectively. Even when some of the more recent newcomers lacked the appropriate grammar to present their stories and opinions with proper syntax, they still wielded their words with a skill that many native speakers would envy, myself included. Obviously, poetry and debate ran in their blood. I wondered sometimes whether I was catching everything they meant beyond the words, especially since Jamal explained to me the kind of wordplay that some Somalis bring into dialogue when they want to speak at different levels so that the appropriate message gets through to the right audience without other listeners catching on. In Somalia, such wordplay is called *gabay* and has several layers. In Eritrea and Ethiopia, the equivalent is known as *sämanna wärk* (wax and gold) because the real meaning or message—the gold—is hidden from all except those in the know and to whom it is directed. Different levels of complexity exist, seven in the case of Somali *gabay*, but most people never get beyond the first two. Sayyid Mahammad Abdille Hasan, the warrior-poet who became the scourge of the British forces in Somalia in the early 1900s, is the master of *gabay* and the only one ever to have reached level six. "But he has competition," Abdihakim tells me eagerly. "The one who really excelled at *gabay* is the poet Cali Dhuux."

While only the educated are likely to have studied the more academic traditional forms in depth, many Somalis have picked up the concept. In fact, I thought I had, too, when I noticed Koshin using the word "Somalians" as opposed to "Somalis" the last time we talked. My hunch was that he consciously used that old Western signifier to ensure that I understood he spoke only of Somalis from Somalia and not from Somaliland, Djibouti, Kenya, or the Ogaden. It turned out, however, that he was merely falling back on Western terminology for convenience since Westerners use "Somalian" even though most Somalis consider that use ignorant. So much for my powers of *gabay* detection!

Verbal skills thus put Horn Africans ahead and allow them to jump hurdles that few first generations can manage. Those who arrive already fluent in English generally represent the more educated of their groups, and, as such, they are the ones who assume the role of spokespeople for their communities. The elders and ex-fighters who traditionally would fill these roles may have the wisdom but not always the education needed to work with U.S. politicians and bureaucratic institutions, such as funding agencies, and to produce the paperwork so necessary for improving their community's lot.

Beyond their storytelling skills, the Horn Africans also carry with them tales drawn from both their recent past and the historic past right to the very dawn of life. These national, ethnic, or clan stories, internalized at home, in the field, or at school, impart a sense of historical significance. The stories bestow on the exiles the pride and dignity with which they now face the world. Among the most meaningful of these narratives are the foundational stories that, in the telling, like muscles frequently flexed, add cultural heft to their images and instill confidence. The Ethiopians, as mentioned, cherish the *Kebre Negast*, which recounts their origins. They also keep a special place in their hearts for the novel *Tobyā*, which signifies on that foundation story. But although Eritreans share the historical Sheba narrative with Ethiopia and accounts of happenings at Adulis and Axum fill the National Archives of Eritrea, it is the story of the liberation war that most Eritreans consider their foundational narrative. This is the story they recount with the most pride, pointing to this formative experience as the one that shaped their sense of themselves as a people and gave them the fighting spirit to take on the challenges of the diaspora. Before that, they say, their history related to specific ethnic groups within the broader area, but once resistance to Ethiopia's colonial oppression became organized, ethnicity and religion took a backseat to the newly minted nationalism.

In Portland, Aklilu Foto, a singer and former fighter with the Eritrean People's Liberation Front, sings lyrics about that history. His admirers know him popularly as Tefono, which in Tigrinya means "A Person Who Talks Too Much." "I don't really talk too much," he chuckles, "but when I was in the field in 1976, you know, every freedom fighter had a nickname. Really, I was a quiet person, but after three years in the EPLF, I started to talk. So, someone named Yemane . . . he was a freedom fighter . . ."

"He died?" I ask.

"No," he corrects me, "he was a martyr. He sacrificed his life for our freedom." I accept the rebuke, and he continues, "He told me I talked too much at that time, and so from then until 1991, I was known in the EPLF as Tefono."

"That was a long time," I say. "What did you talk about?"

He explains that he doesn't distinguish between talking and singing.

I was always singing about battles and fighting. You see, you want to wake up the *tegadelti*'s morale and make them hungry for their freedom. So you sing about the old history and about Eritrean history, because, maybe, he or she doesn't know about it, and we can explain it all by song and by music. We can express the history by *krar* [a traditional six- to ten-string instrument something like a lute] and by different types of instruments.

He continues:

We also sang about heroes. One of my songs about a hero is called "Gualmeki." I dedicated it to my first love. Her name is Meriem, and I saw her for the first time in 1978 [*looks away*]. At that time, my first love, Meriem Meki, she died in *maemide*, they call it, "killed in action." She was a *tegadalit*, and they killed her. So this song is dedicated to Meriem. It's a very emotional song.

He sings it beautifully, and afterward there is silence in his taxicab. We are parked in an empty lot in downtown Portland, the recorder on the seat between us. We watch the tape spin round and round as cars and trucks drive past us. Then another taxi driver honks his horn, breaking the spell and returning Tefono to the present. I ask him whether he wouldn't mind singing one of his other creations, and he breaks into a smile. He sings it in Tigrinya and then explains for me:

Moon said, "This song is for Eritrea." The stars are the Eritrean people, so I express by that song how the Eritrean people united for their freedom, for their betterment at this time. So I say [*sings a couple of lines in Tigrinya*], working in Eritrea, the stars, they united together, and they brightened the Eritrean land. If the stars are united, Eritrea will be bright.

I tell him it's beautiful and he accepts the praise nonchalantly, as if he's used to groupies.

The stories that coalesce around the central narrative of the liberation war supply the Eritreans with the wealth of material that they want Americans to know. No family is untouched by the war, and each member has a personal investment in the foundational narrative that recounts

Eritrea's David-and-Goliath struggle against the imperial might of Ethiopia. From the point of view of cultural resources with which to make their case, therefore, everyone has a plentiful supply. Poet-warriors among the *tegadelti* contributed many of these stories, and in their recounting of heroic deeds, they bind their countrymen and countrywomen ever further in patriotic camaraderie.

Although every Eritrean contributed to the war effort, three Eritreans are considered to be the founding fathers of the country: Woldeab Woldemariam, a writer and intellectual fondly known to his people as Welwel; Ibrahim Sultan Ali, founder of the Eritrean Muslim League and a spokesperson for unity; and Hamid Idris Awate, said to have fired the first shot against the Ethiopian colonizers in 1961.

Somalis, too, pride themselves on their foundational narratives and frequently refer to their known origins. In fact, each of the major clans traces its roots to Arab holy men, sheikhs, and relatives of the Prophet Muhammad, thus establishing through genealogy the spiritual authenticity that gives its members status and standing in Somali culture. Most of the major-clan Somalis interviewed in Portland and Seattle have internalized this Semitic connection, which distinguishes them from other Africans. Their stories are thus as much part of their identity as are the tales of their immediate kin.

Jamal summarizes the Isaq legend for me. "The Isaqs are descendants of Sheik Isaq, who came of the Beni Hashim, which is the noble house of the Prophet." He is brief, to the point and matter-of-fact. "Sheik Isaq came to Somalia, and there he married a woman of the Dir clan."

The brother of Sheikh Isaq, Ali Samarroon, is believed to be the founder of the Gadabursi, who are traditionally of Dir descent, with the Dir in their turn tracing their connections to Aqiil Abuu Taalib, whose shrine can be found in Djibouti. The Darod legend presupposes an original eponymous Darod, the son of an Arabic saint, who crossed the sea to Somaliland and settled at the port of Bosaso, where the Dir Somali on the northeastern Somali coast welcomed him. He eventually married a woman of this clan, the marriage producing so many descendants, the Darod say, that eventually their numbers overtook those of their Dir hosts.

While none of the members of the main *Samale* clans questions his Semitic connection to the Prophet, some scholars, such as Mohamed

Haji Mukhtar and Abdi M. Kusow, dispute it and point to various other groups from whom they could have derived. The accuracy of the foundational narratives, however, has less relevance in the context of this book than the extent to which Horn Africans embrace these narratives. When I was growing up in South Africa during colonial days, some Afrikaners considered themselves God's chosen people, as did some Jews, and even today some Americans consider their rolling hills and craggy mountaintops to have been bequeathed to them as God's own country. More interesting is the understanding of self conveyed by such foundational narratives, the sense of lineage and history that situates them in time and space and elicits their pride and dignity. It is that which Eritreans, Ethiopians, and Somalis bring to their new home.

While the newcomers arrive in the Pacific Northwest swaddled in their foundational narratives, once here they add on the contemporary memoirs and autobiographies written by Horn authors who are themselves in exile. These works offer role models as well as cultural identification and historical instruction. In the difficult situations found in Eritrea, Ethiopia, and Somalia, young people often had little detailed knowledge of their own histories, and many of the autobiographical texts written by scholars perform secondary functions as cultural histories. They explain the reasons behind the ceremonies and the beliefs behind the actions, thus educating readers and reinforcing their cultural memories.

At the University of Washington some years back, Ethiopian Nega Mezlekia read from his *Notes from the Hyena's Belly*. The book traces his autobiographical character's journey of struggle in the Ogaden through the years of Emperor Haile Selassie's fall and the rise to power of Ethiopia's Communist junta. Ethiopian men from the local community packed the room and hung on Nega's every word, forming a circle around him after he had finished his reading to ply him with questions in Amharic. One seldom sees Ethiopian women other than students at events like these. This night, the men in their business suits and ties reconnected with old acquaintances, kissing cheeks and shaking hands while catching up on news from home. Even as they relived their own experiences through Nega's memories of childhood and later times as a student during the Red Terror of the Mengistu regime, they expressed thanks for their adopted home in the United States.

When, some years later, I interview Dawit Nerayo, who, like Mezlekia's student hero, also fled Ethiopia to avoid being picked up by Mengistu's army-recruiting thugs, he tries to make clear that the Derg were not trying to pick up able-bodied men. It was just twelve- to fifteen-year-old kids being thrown into a truck and taken to fight. "What people don't realize," he explains, "is that when you talk of a twelve- or thirteen-year-old in Ethiopia, and you compare it to someone from the U.S., a kid that age doesn't have the same body size and strength. Can you imagine a nine- or ten-year-old child being drafted to war here in the U.S.?" he asks, then adds, "It's unthinkable."

"You were really still a child, then," I say. "So how did you escape them?"

"Well, they were going house to house—this was the public security and community police—and they were looking for any male who could hold a gun and help keep the freedom fighters at bay. The fighting wasn't necessarily designed to win the war—the well-trained militia hadn't accomplished this—so the Derg were just buying time for Mengistu to make a clean getaway." He continues:

> They came to our house a couple of times looking for me, and the first time, I hid in the dog's house. They didn't think to look there. The second time, I climbed up a peach tree about twenty-five feet up and from there jumped on the roof of our house and lay flat. It was so cold and uncomfortable . . . but I spent the night there. I was about fifteen and couldn't avoid being drafted. If you knew someone with authority in the Derg or had a military person in the family, you might get out of the draft. Otherwise, as an ordinary person, the odds were against you.

Many local Ethiopans and Eritreans have stories similar to Dawit's. At the same time, each story is unique and adds another strand to the story-tapestry. Autobiographical success stories also offer beacons of hope to local immigrants and refugees. Mawi Asgedom's *Of Beetles and Angels: A Boy's Remarkable Journey from a Refugee Camp to Harvard*, for example, inspires young Ethiopians who dream of making it in America. "The most impressive thing about his book," observes Mawi's friend Haddis, "is the fine line he walks between Ethiopians and Eritreans. His family happens to be part Ethiopian and part Eritrean, yet in telling his story, he maintains a good balance because he brings out the best of both sides without favoring one or the other." Haddis turns to me then and adds with a degree of wistful insistence, "I hope Mawi's background and balanced approach will be the norm here rather than the exception."

For Somali women, the autobiographies of the super models Aman and Waris Dirie appear to be the most inspiring, and they frequently inquire whether I am familiar with *Aman: The Story of a Somali Girl* and *Desert Flower: The Extraordinary Journey of a Desert Nomad*. Nearly every Somali woman I interviewed had read the books, and many identified with the stories, seeing in the books' public acclaim acknowledgment of their own traumas. In Portland, Amina Sheikhuna, a Darod, confided that her escape from Somalia was just like Waris Dirie's and asked that I record her story, which she immediately began telling me in a monotone, showing no emotion or facial expression, stopping only to answer my questions. I would encounter this dispassionate telling with some of the most traumatic stories and frequently found myself unable to maintain similar decorum. At the same time, I felt that too emotional a response on my part might threaten the fragile barrier the storyteller had erected between herself and the person in the story. Amina sat now on the carpeted floor of a Somali friend's house and in broken English, using the present tense as if watching a reel playing in her head, she spoke into the microphone, telling me of her blind father in Mogadishu who in his eighties impregnated her mother. When the family received news he had been killed, she said, they realized they were on their own.

> Then one day, we have civil war. Boom-boom-boom! And we go to this area in Somalia called Kismayo. When we stay over there, the people of Mogadishu, they come in where we are and it's scary. Every night, every girl they rape, every house they break in. They rob everyone, everywhere. It was scary. Then some kind people gave us safe haven, and some big men offered us protection in return for food and a place to sleep. So that day, we got lucky. The big guys say, "We fight for money, we don't need women and children." OK? But we already had too many Somali people living there. So after ten days, one of the guys says to me, "I need to marry you and go back to Mogadishu." I say, "Well . . ." [*Her voice reveals no*

expression.] I was so scared to go back over there, because people were fighting. I mean, if I go back and get married to this guy, maybe next time he's going to kill me. So there you are. He says, "Come with me." He was going far away, and he told me, "Tomorrow I'll be back. You'll come with me." And he left. And I left, too, me and my mom and my sister. We run away from Mogadishu and away from him. I didn't want to marry him. He was thirty, I was thirteen. So. [*She laughs a little at having gotten the best of him, showing emotion for the first time since beginning her story.*] When we got back to Mogadishu, it was so scary [*in a monotone*]. The people there want to kill us. My mom used to lock the door. Everything's closed. It's scary [*no expression*]. You never see the guns outside. If you sleep nighttime, daytime is spent inside the house. I never sleep at my house; I sleep at the neighbors, me and my sister. So. We are virgins, so we are scared. Virgins in Somalia, they're sewn all the way. They cannot use the penis to open it, they use a knife. So I mean, your husband . . . [*doesn't finish the sentence*]. I told my mom, "I can't make it in Mogadishu, not anymore."

She narrates her various other escapes—running with bleeding legs through a lion-infested jungle, fleeing from a job cleaning house for a Somali woman who took advantage of her, and negotiating her way out of an unconsummated marriage. She is right; her escape is similar to that of Waris Dirie and is equally heroic. By comparison with this past, her present in the Tigard neighborhood where she lives surrounded by other Somali women appears utopian to her. Still, it is not glamorous, like that of Waris or Aman. Such American narratives are unobtainable for most refugees. Nevertheless, the women who live them provide positive cultural heroes that Somalis here perceive as fitting into the cultural value system of the United States.

The stories of Nuruddin Farah, winner of the 1998 Neustadt International Prize for Literature, also inspire. His novels deal with the same issues many Somalis here face—clan and national identity, discrimination against females, and the burden of accepting charity— and every Somali I interviewed knew of him even if they hadn't read his books. For many of the mixed-identity refugees and immigrants in the Pacific Northwest who ask "Who am I?" Nuruddin's own life provides guidance. Although born in Italian Somaliland in 1945, Nuruddin grew up in Kallafo, in Ethiopia's Ogaden, then an ethnically and linguistically mixed area where nobody bothered about difference.

"I love his writing," Ubax enthuses when I ask her about his many books. We sit in the small noisy library of South Center Mall in Tukwila, Washington, where the library displays a number of well-thumbed magazine-size Somali newspapers. At the counter display, a thin, elderly Somali man in a suit that perhaps once fitted his frail body leafs through one of them, looking longingly at the pictures. His is an earlier, unschooled generation, unlike Ubax's, and he looks askance at this dynamic young woman who speaks with so much confidence. She tells me now that some of that generation feel differently about Nuruddin's books and find the fantasy parts in them extreme.

> Like in *Secrets*. Some people say it was made up, that the things he writes about are based on stories or legends. But some of them are accurate, too. But people don't want to know, they don't want to talk about it. Most likely it has something to do with Somali culture, of not airing dirty laundry. As Muslims, they don't want people believing that things like that exist in our country, so they detach themselves from all the troubles that he talks about in his books. Most artists see these sorts of things as taboo and they go, like, "Oh, we can't talk about that," especially in a book that's going around. He's the only one who covers those stories, so I find it very interesting. I really enjoy his writing. I mean, I even found out a lot of things that I didn't know. When the civil war happened in Somalia, I was just eleven years old, and I didn't know much about what was happening. So for us, too, it's a way to connect to our country through him.

Identifying with characters of similar experience bears testimony to one's own worth and encourages further imitation, but reading books by and about the other enables one to experience what it feels like to be in somebody else's skin. Seeing what it's like to think and feel as a different kind of person, facing a situation unique to that person, and perhaps doing so in a different country, can turn out to be the reader's first step along the path to empathy and understanding of the other. So, finding among those I interviewed some Horn Africans who had read books by or about the other encouraged me greatly. Even when they perceived the accounts as biased or disagreed with the books for other reasons—"they're so full of political rhetoric that their arguments become numbing," David Makonnen says of some Eritrean texts he's read—the very act of reading them indicates a desire to know and convinces me that among the competing stories in this book lie the seeds of other more hopeful narratives that will bring these communities together for the common good.

Many of the stories—the myths, legends, fables, and anecdotes—also contain cultural values that have stood the test of time in Ethiopia, Eritrea, and Somalia. These values, like self-sufficiency and strength of character, along with the stories themselves and skill at telling them, constitute the cultural capital of the Horn groups. But not all narratives translate across cultures, and knowing which values are useful here takes time. Thus, Ethiopians, Somalis, and Eritreans may approach the challenge of competition with cultural values that have little resonance in the United States. Some of the tales handed down through the generations to instill values that might shape children of the Horn into upstanding young people who can live honest and productive lives, and which often have the imprimatur of Christianity or Islam behind them, sometimes fizzle or backfire outside their culturally specific context. Take loyalty, honesty, humility, and politeness, for example. Abraha says:

> In Eritrea, being humble is a good quality. People there don't talk about how wonderful they are or what great things they have done. But here, you have to love yourself. You have to market yourself. At one point I used to hate that. Loyalty, too. I was extremely loyal in my work, but it doesn't pay in this society. It's a self-serving and almost cannibalizing state of existence here. I'm being mouthy now [*smiles apologetically for criticizing the United States*], but loyalty is one of the values I brought from Eritrea, and I'm really tied to it. In Eritrea, it translates to strength of character, in consistency and in substance. It's a hallmark of one's character, especially as you mature. And then there is also honesty . . . really, that is a natural characteristic in Eritrea. If you lost your wallet, someone would walk two miles, looking at the address, and say, "I found your wallet." They wouldn't take a dime out of your pocket. That kind of honesty, it really defines your character . . . how you see the world and how you serve the world. Whereas here, one goes for

the jugular to be what you can be, defining yourself in terms of money only. Who cares how honest you are, or how polite you are?

Dawit talks about loyalty, too. Above the bookstore chatter, the clink of coffee cups, and the low strains of elevator music, he tells me about loyalty in friendship:

> I remember this one time, when we were, kids, there was this guy who always used to take my friend's and my money. Once, I was bringing milk home, and I saw that my friend had just decided to take on this guy and was being beaten up. I just put my milk down and I jumped in and helped my friend out. What is a friend, after all? I will talk to my friend and ask, "What was that all about?" but only afterward. That kind of loyalty is blind. You do it without . . . you go out on a limb. I had difficulty making friends in the United States, because that level of loyalty is hard to come by. You can phone me in the middle of the night and say, "My car is broken down on Freeway X," and I will get up and fetch you. I believe the philosophy that your friends are the ones that stand by you during your most troubling and trying times. Everybody will be there when you are having a good time. That's why you should cherish those that help you get up and stand on your feet when you are down.

Americans once aspired to live by those values, too. Today, however, reality demonstrates over and over again that in order to succeed in the United States, one needs to be competitive and assertive. Reality here shows, too, that age is not necessarily wisdom, nor is it privileged as such, for it is young people, we are told, who produce the big ideas, the great novels, the scientific discoveries, the next Google. While being competitive does not necessarily exclude politeness, loyalty, or respect, it very often does. In the United States, such values are subsumed in the greater narrative of success. It is just the way things are.

The American mind-set of individualism, which rewards individual initiative rather than the commitment to community valued by the Horn exiles, is probably one of the most difficult adaptations the newcomers must make. The Pacific Northwest could benefit from a little communal commitment, but in a city like Seattle, where the stereotypical loner, geek, software billionaire parades his reward in boats and private planes, the message would seem obvious.

"I was educated in both Ethiopia and America, so I know both worlds, and it's a real conflict at times," confides Sofi Mulugeta, a charming and poised young Ethiopian woman. Sofi has an M.B.A. from Seattle University and works as a senior credit analyst with Bay Bank in Bellevue, Washington. "Sometimes, it's hard to reconcile the two," she says. "When I'm in Ethiopia, I get tired of having always to conform, but when I'm here, I get tired of the me-me-me."

Reconciling the different cultural mind-sets is a continuing challenge for both Ethiopians and Eritreans, who find themselves pragmatically choosing one way or the other—my desires and needs versus those of my family and community. Given the traumatic stress that lingers everywhere, and the long hours some spend working two or three jobs, going to school, and raising children, it amazes me that they still can give of themselves. Some, like the Seattle Somali immigrants who volunteered to help those displaced by Hurricane Katrina in New Orleans in 2005 and the Eritreans and Ethiopians who continue to donate to Goodwill though they are needy themselves, go even further, offering their time and money to the larger American community.

While the American emphasis on individuality causes confusion, the notion of respect has many Horn Africans mystified. The American classroom, for example, seems a strange place to many of the newcomers, who watch in awe as teacher-student behavior subverts their bred-in-the-bone respect for authority and age as well as for the written text. When Dawit first began medical school, other students hinted that he was brownnosing because he would openly praise a professor if he deemed it appropriate. He was also reluctant to get into an argument or criticize his professors because his background didn't prepare him for that. In Ethiopia, you just don't do that, Dawit tells me. "You yield, and instead afford a significant degree of respect." To Dawit, therefore, their hints were hurtful, because he had no intention of seeking favor. He simply appreciated the opportunities afforded him and wanted to recognize his professors based on the values he brought with him from Ethiopia.

Somalis also find Americans misreading their gestures of respect. Averting one's eyes from the person to whom one speaks is just such an example. Omar Eno, who looks me straight in the eye as we sit in a conference room at Portland State University, explains why young Somali Bantu find it such a difficult thing to do. Omar is a large man with a powerful voice and big smile whose presence fills the room. He tells me:

> The Somali Bantu people do not normally make eye contact. If you are older, the young will always look down as a gesture of respect. Thus they don't make eye contact directly. Women, too, who are young do the same to older women and also to older men. In this country, you are viewed as someone who is lying if you don't meet the person's gaze. But in our culture, you would complain if a kid *did* meet your look—you would say, "This kid is bad!"

I'm older than him, so by his cultural standards, he should lower his eyes, but as I'm a woman, he is not expected to. Besides, he has been too long in the States to observe such practices and looks everybody in the eye straightforwardly, irrespective of age or gender. He is an ebullient and confident person who focused on the history and culture of the Somali Bantu for his M.A. and Ph.D. degrees. He knows his people well, and he explains to me other cultural anomalies that exist among them. "When you're good friends, for example, you hold hands, or I put my hand on your shoulder. That means we are good friends. But that has a very different connotation here." He looks to see if I understand and then offers another example of misunderstanding:

> The Somali Bantu kids, their teachers say, hit other children at school. But in Somalia, if you are my good friend, I hit you. Not hit you hard, but I hit you because you are my friend. Here, it is different, and they complain that the kids are hitting other kids [*chuckles loudly*]. Meantime, the kid just thinks he is a good friend of this guy. So the kid is taken out and punished for what he's doing, and he's surprised. He tries to explain, "But he's my friend." "Then why do you hit him?" "Because he's my friend." It's a cultural thing.

Young people, however, soon adapt to the ways of their host country in terms of both behavior and language. Part of an immigrant's survival skills revolve around knowing how to read the lay of the land and act appropriately. In high school, docile-looking young Somali women become as vocal, assertive, and competitive as home-grown Americans. But while they have at their fingertips the means by which to promote their Horn narratives, their interests may often lie more in promoting their new *American* cultural credentials, their music, their dress, and their speech.

TESTING THE WATERS

Still, it doesn't take Horn Africans long to adapt to the new American waters around them and, after a period of observation, to wade through the shoals, girded around with their stories, values, and skills. They plunge into the cultural deep of American competition; they are intrepid. As soon as they have secured a degree of stability in jobs and living spaces, they are out there proudly telling America about themselves.

The auditorium at the Seattle Art Museum is ablaze with head shawls of white, yellow, pink, blue, and even some purple. An Eritrean-themed night at the museum brings out virtually the entire community. Whatever their ethnicity or religion, they have come out in full gear, not only to celebrate proudly with their compatriots, but, as important, to display their cultures and tell their stories to the world. Behind them follow American friends they have invited here to see what they are all about. These visitors eye the flutter of traditional robes and listen in awe to the rhythms of different languages. They hang onto their friends like life-preservers in a sea of undecipherable sounds and sights. "What does this mean?" "What did he say?" "Why do they do that?" On a display table lie examples of Eritrean basketwork, while on another, an open prayer book shows handwritten verse inked on vellum. Although the Eritrean women move quietly in their long robes, as their cultures dictate, their children skip and giggle with excitement as if they can sense the importance of this night. On the stage, young people dance or recite, and Portland's Tefono sings of Eritrea with his *krar*.

Such scenes repeat themselves at different venues as Somalis, Ethiopians, and Eritreans become more public in their actions and look for opportunities to educate their neighbors about their histories and cultures. On the business side, Horn exiles join work and trade associations, where they interact with their associates and, over coffee, pass on episodes from their countries' histories and anecdotes about their cultures. Some even find time amid the numerous demands on their lives to join organizations that do charitable works. Members of the Rotary Club of the University District in Seattle, for example, are well aware of Ethiopia's needs in part because of Ezra Teshome's involvement. Ezra joined the organization in 1984 and ever since has been working with his fellow Rotarians on projects there. In 2005 *Time* magazine named Ezra a global health hero for his work on eradicating polio in Ethiopia.

Although some members of all three communities continue to look inward, working only within their own ethnic or national associations—like the Ethiopian support groups called Ekub or the single-clan enterprises of some Somalis—most others move into the mainstream and establish new links to the broader community. Thus, as events unfold in their home countries, they publish poetry or essays on the Internet, offer talks in their children's schools, or speak out in public forums to explain the history behind recent developments or the ethnic or clan differences that have brought matters to this point. Poet Hidaat Ephrem, for example, has been for many years a one-woman resource on Eritrea for students at the University of Washington. She gives of her time and energy unstintingly to help other Americans understand the complexities of the situation in the Horn. Sometimes, she wears traditional Tigrinya dress or offers *injera* to the students. Always, she shows eagerness to answer even the most difficult of questions.

Like all immigrant communities before them, Horn Africans have opened restaurants too, and encourage other Seattleites and Portlanders to explore these new tastes. At the Hidmo Eritrean restaurant, where the owners embrace diversity, local art and musical performances also educate Americans, as do the maps, pictures, and portraits, which represent the peoples' pride. As these Americans mix in restaurants and also in schools and playgrounds, they pick up snatches of Amharic or Tigrinya, which they try out on their friends. Horn students at local universities invite nationally recognized speakers to address their peers, and Horn musicians reach out to American youths by playing Ethiopian and Eritrean songs at their social functions.

Seattle and Portland provide numerous opportunities for promoting cultural wares, the potential niches for self-representation limited only by the imagination. At the Northwest Folklife Festival at Seattle Center, for example, where all three communities participate, visitors every year consume various features of East African cultures along with their food. In 2004 Ethiopia celebrated one hundred years of Ethiopian-U.S. relations, a choice theme that registered with American festivalgoers as more than just food and art. The celebration included a panel discussion sponsored by the Ethiopian Youth Association–Ethio Study group at Third Place Books. The communities also publicize their national films at local showings, and while Yegizaw Michael paints dramatic colorful images that reference his country's heroic history, others involve themselves with members of their religious congregations and teach them about Horn values.

Eritreans, Ethiopians, and Somalis all love to talk, and local taxi drivers respond enthusiastically to questions about their homelands. In the final analysis, this person-to-person encounter, albeit slow going, probably constitutes the most effective transfer of cultural knowledge to and development of empathy in Americans. As the members of these communities talk to their neighbors one by one, they teach about their pasts and create friends of Ethiopia, friends of Eritrea, and friends of Somalia who in turn share with others what they have learned about these newcomers. "If we can make a difference in two, three, or four people," Yosieph argues, "then we are making a difference."

"When it comes to promoting their cause," Haddis tells me in relation to Eritrean image management, "I really admire them. They have done a better job of giving back to their community than Ethiopians have." Haddis is generous in his praise, and my ears prick up at his ability to be open-minded about the other group while seeing his own in perspective. It is what I want to hear although I try not to reveal my delight at this evidence of impartiality. "They are good at organizing for things that matter," he explains, "whereas most East Africans I know operate individually or in small groups." He continues:

> The reality is, and I include myself in this, that people who have done well have isolated themselves from the community and have not really given back as much as they should. At first, it's not knowing where to begin and

out of fear of being labeled politically. But I think after a period of time, we use that as an excuse not to get involved. You know [*apologetically*], we're *all* busy, everybody's busy, and I understand that. I advocated early on that we should participate in the political system here. Because I'm in it, I see the value, the power, and how one can really make a difference in terms of who takes office. Look at the last gubernatorial election in our state—it was decided by 129 votes. Even my boss's first victory was only by 2,700 votes. If we are active, we can actually influence who gets into office. The Ethiopian community has been shy about getting involved in anything outside its own community. I don't know about the Somalis, but I think the Eritrean community involvement is much better. Just look at the community center they've just built. Have you seen it? That community center was built with the help of political connections they made with various organs in our state. It's remarkable. And they came into Washington way after the Ethiopians did.

In 2007 Haddis left the mayor's office to join the Bill & Melinda Gates Foundation's Global Development Program, which aims to help reduce the inequities associated with extreme poverty.

Sonya Damtew, program manager at the Immigrant and Refugee Community Organization in Portland, enthuses about Portland's Eritreans, too. Over the last ten years particularly, she has seen them move forward despite the odds against them. "One of them is a doctor now," she tells me proudly, "two are law students, and some are in engineering and nursing." Others went into real estate, while still more involve themselves in building the community. They are all succeeding, but it has not been easy. She explains:

When the Eritrean refugees arrived in the '80s, they were mostly unskilled and uneducated. No community infrastructure existed here to assist them, nor were there role models to provide them with blueprints about how to deal with government and institutions. With the Thai, Vietnamese, and Cambodians, for example, there already existed an Asian infrastructure that could access government funds to help establish businesses and homes for the members of those communities. So despite their wartime grievances, the different Asian groups could come together and help one another. For the Eritreans, Ethiopians, and Somalis, however, no such East African group existed to show them the ropes and encourage them to work together for their common benefit.

"And then, when the border war broke out, of course, the two groups moved even further apart." Sadness tinges Sonya's words. "There was little I could do," she says, "little anyone could do." I can sense her frustration as she tries to explain. A lively, intelligent woman, she is full of ideas for improving the lot of Eritreans in Portland, but sometimes, she says, she feels stymied when each group gets caught up in its own grievances and can't see beyond its personal beliefs and habits.

Sonya's husband, Michael, does not disagree and praises his wife's efforts with Eritrean refugees. "You can get them to the door," he explains, "but sometimes they just don't know how to turn the knob." For himself, he simply appreciates the example of other immigrant groups and expresses gratitude to those earlier refugees and exiles who, through their hard work and contributions to the growth of the United States, made good impressions on the country.

Although nobody likes to speak openly about the competition among the three communities in the Pacific Northwest, their members are well aware of the stakes and why they need to tell their stories. Control of the word means having the power to define reality. As we have seen, the Amhara, by promoting a linkage to biblical antiquity, succeeded in improving their status in the area and unifying Ethiopians as a whole. At the same time, the power of their story enabled them to situate other ethnic groups in the pecking order of their choice by using words to create the impression of the others' purported inferiority. Thus, by calling the Oromo "People of the Water" (Galla), the Amhara succeeded in denying the Oromo the reality of their own words, even though their numbers exceeded those of the Amhara and they owned most of the land. Likewise, the Amhara's signifying of the Ethiopian Jews as "People of the Trees" (Falasha) overwhelmed that people's own history as they knew it, leading to their ill treatment not only by Amharas but by other Ethiopians as well. Derogatory words imposed by those who have the controlling story strip people of both dignity and power. Thus, although Somali Bantu are skilled agriculturists and artisans of various types, the *Samale* clans' designation of them as *boon* or *adoon* (slave) or *jareer* (kinky hair) erodes their real standing and makes them second-class citizens.

In Eritrea, too, manipulation of the language helps cement the reality of the new country. Different spellings or pronunciations, such as Badme/ Badume, Eritrea/Erītrea, Tigrayan/Tigrean, create through connotations conceptual entities that become established within the mind-set of the Eritrean people and contribute to both identity and nationalism.

In the new host country, the United States, each community has the opportunity to translate words into power for the betterment of its position. By taking charge of their stories or changing the semantic weight of words to their advantage, the communities in the Pacific Northwest stand to benefit in both social and economic terms. That is why those I interviewed want to put the record straight.

FOUR

HAVING THE
LAST WORD

We didn't come to America to focus on our past
and create even bigger problems for ourselves.

—MEHRET MEHANZEL, SEATTLE, 2004

"IN MY opinion, honestly, I think we are all the same people," Dawit
Nerayo confides as we discuss the differences that cause conflict among
the peoples of the Horn and lead to tensions among their communities
in the Pacific Northwest.

You see, if you take the whole area from Egypt across to Sudan before
the Europeans divided it up, it was all one place. Just look at the people!
A lot of Sudan's people look very much like Ethiopians. And if you go
by looks alone, there is also practically no difference among Eritreans,
Tigrayans, and Harar people. Obviously, if you go very southwest in
Ethiopia, you run into much darker skins, and if you go southeast, into
very light skins. But . . . whatever they call themselves, in the end, they
all look the same.

Dawit is Ethiopian, but his father is Eritrean. I look at his face and
wonder if anything about his looks identify him as such. Sitting there in
his shirtsleeves, he could be any other young American, although a certain

graciousness plus a lack of cynicism mark him as different. "Obviously not many people share my opinion about looking the same," he smiles. "Just look at Eritrea, which wants to be a separate people." Whether they look the same or not, the members of the three communities nurture their own sense of who they are. Identity means everything, and nationhood sometimes provides the linchpin on which one hangs one's status in the United States.

Identity and nationhood, however, can be tricky subjects in a part of the world that has seen colonizers come and go. In fact, all three peoples at one time or another have been at the receiving end of challenges about their status as nations. Somalia experienced nationhood only for a relatively short period of time during the rule of Siyad Barre (1969–91), while Eritrea became an independent country only in 1993 and still feels insecure in its status. Also, talk of ethnicities too often segues into talk of nations, as it sometimes does with Ethiopians, and while specific ethnic groups may have lived in those lands for centuries, cooperation between unified nations of these ethnicities and other functioning entities signifies something different. Nationhood is thus a slippery subject and, with identity, complicates the issues that rankle the three groups. A legacy of ill feeling related to boundary perspectives, relocation, and resettlement intertwines with them, and most interviewees had something to say about these matters even if they refused to be quoted.

Ethiopians, Eritreans, and Somalis are not the first refugee or immigrant groups to struggle with historical resentment when settled among erstwhile enemies in their host country. In the various ethnic ghettos of the United States, immigrant Jews have lived back-to-back with Polish Catholics, Serbs with Croats, Chinese with Japanese, Indians with Pakistanis, Greeks with Turks, and Turks with Armenians. The greater challenge for Africans from the Horn, however, lies in the global reach of the Internet, which enables anyone with access to a server to take control of the word and manipulate it to his or her group's advantage. At the same time, online talk works to the advantage of all groups. Ethiopians, Eritreans, and Somalis *all* can tell their stories, selectively framing them for meaning while omitting anything that interferes. They also *all* can bad-mouth their enemies. Many of the people I interviewed have been offended and intimidated by the vitriol of much that appears on Horn sites. Nevertheless, they try to hold their own on that unstable pathway between freedom of speech and ethnic criticism.

"At least here, I can respond equally," Ezra points out. "If you go back to Ethiopia, it is only government that can speak; it's a one-way communication. If I tried to say something against that, I'd end up in jail!" Leaning too far in the direction of freedom of speech, however, may lead to accusations of political incorrectness, which, in Seattle and Portland, can be harmful to a community's image. "If you push too hard, you may poke out somebody's eye," Ezra adds descriptively. He has lived in the States since 1971 and seen the excesses to which some will go. "You must know how to stop and how to coexist with respect. That's what we need to learn. Every one of us has every right to live in this world, and if you don't respectfully see eye to eye, that's your own demise."

Most immigrants from the Horn who hope to make it in the United States know enough not to blow off steam in a public forum. "In Seattle, everyone is so PC," Mohamed concurs. "It's not that we Somalis in Seattle don't fight with one another," he explains, "but we try not to do it in public." A Somali Isaq and research technician in the Department of Medicine at the University of Washington, Mohamed came to Seattle as a student in 1986. He hoped to return to Somalia at some point, but the destruction of Hargeisa in 1988 forced his family to flee from there to one of Ethiopia's last refugee camps, Harata Sheik, and thence to Washington, D.C., and Canada.

Not everyone blogging or chatting on the Internet is as circumspect as Mohamed implies. Thus the undermining swipes found on many Horn sites breed anger and outrage. "How dare you spread a lie about Eritrea when my brothers and sisters died for its freedom?" asks Abraha, expressing what many Eritreans feel. The ongoing vitriol takes its toll, and beneath the surface, psychological wounds seep and ooze.

The newcomers thus arrive with a complex mind-set. While they appreciate democratic speech for themselves, accepting it for others requires considerable effort. That we cannot silence our enemies becomes a constant challenge, as all Americans know. For others to discredit one's voice, according to Alan Parry and Robert E. Doan, represents a form of terrorism, for it throws into question a person's judgment, leading to self-doubt and robbing him of his voice.[1]

IDENTITY OR NATIONALITY

"If you know your identity, then you know how to survive. It's that simple," Yosieph responds without hesitation when I ask him what his identity means to him. "My Eritrean identity helped me survive being a refugee and gave me the courage to make a new life for myself in America." His words are adamant, though he displays the easygoing smile that I noted in 1991, when he effortlessly opened doors for our University of Washington contingent in Asmara, enabling us to meet President Isaias Afwerki and his adviser Yemane Gebreab, once a student at the university. He explains now that he found his own personal answer to the importance of identity through reading Jacobo Timerman's *Prisoner without a Name, Cell without a Number.*[2] The book recounts the Argentine Jewish author's struggle to survive his thirty-month imprisonment under Argentina's military junta. "If *I* hadn't known my identity and history," Yosieph says, "I, too, would have been a prisoner without a name, a cell without a number." He jiggles his son Abraham on his knee. "That's why I want Abraham to know his identity. If he is a black man in America without any history, he's lost in this world."

At a dinner for young Eritreans at my home, I pursue the question of Eritrean identity further. For Esayas Mehanzel, who came to the States in 1984, identity emerges from "what you have in your heart." It's "the sense of familiarity that I felt when I returned to Eritrea in 2001 and saw people that looked just like me." He holds his fist over his heart. A slim, clean-shaven young man in a red sweatshirt and black jacket, Esayas frequently expresses nostalgia for the place of his birth.

For Yegizaw, something else besides birthplace holds relevance. About that, he is adamant, and he expresses his feelings in short, clipped sentences, as if making the point for the nth time. "Look, identity, for me, is not a place. I don't associate my identity with a land. For me, identity is the values instilled in me. I don't have that special need to go back to Eritrea in order to be Eritrean. I'm here, and I'm Eritrean, because it's in me. I take it with me."

Eritrean identity fills the local community with pride. They take great satisfaction in their people's courage and particularly in their staying power in the face of disappointments and setbacks. In fact, they judge perseverance to be one of their strongest characteristics. They say they keep the goal in sight and keep inching forward no matter how long it takes. Members of the community often refer to the narrative of the hare and the tortoise when talking about Eritrea's progress. It goes back to the days of the Eritrean People's Liberation Front, when the guerrilla fighters, like the tortoise of Aesop's famous fable, edged slowly but surely toward their goal. In the face of Ethiopia's faster advance, Yosieph explains, it looked like the Eritreans would never make it.

> Everything we did, we did so slowly that the EPLF became known as "the tortoise." It was not meant to be an insult because it referred to something else that is very Eritrean, namely, doing things on one's own terms— *abagobiye*. The Eritreans didn't compromise, no matter how hard it was for them to do it on their own, because we believed that eventually Eritrea would make up the difference, slowly, and in our own way.

"We Eritreans have our own Tigrinya word for what makes us Eritrean," Abraha tells me as we explore the notion of identity. "It is *nih*," he says pronouncing it with a guttural "gh'" sound. It refers to "the base of the soul. It is a kind of . . ." (he gropes around for the right word to explain the inexplicable) "oomph," he says with feeling, "a desperation for," a "hunger for," that is "the launching pad for everything we have achieved as a people." As he talks, he warms to the subject, his face displaying the feelings he tries to describe. A waitress leans over to take our orders, but Abraha barely notices. "It has nothing to do with government— governments come and go—or the country itself. It's about the people. *Nih* puts fire under your feet so you can jump hoops; *nih* feeds a hungry child because it gives you the ability to see beyond the hardships and suffering of the present. That's what Eritrea has got: *nih*." He leans back for a moment, secure in his pride. Then he takes me by the arm and says, "Look, the country is poor; we don't have anything, nothing, except our *nih*. During the bad times of colonialism, we lost everything except our *nih*." Then his pride swells again, and he says, "Our *nih* is with us always, and it will nurture our dreams for the next century."

The freedom to identify oneself as Eritrean assumes an importance not always understood by Eritrea's Ethiopian neighbors. David Makonnen, who does understand, still finds their fastidiousness about it frustrating. "They are consumed by identity," he explains, "and very particular about what it means to be Eritrean. Even if the majority of Eritrea is made up of Ethiopians who migrated there from Tigray and Gonder, they deny the heritage and emphasize their affinity with colonial Italian culture while making a distinction on Eritrean authenticity according to the number of generations of one's lineage. So even if a person is born and raised there and considers himself Eritrean . . ." he throws up his hands in a gesture of surrender. Still, with his more open outlook on identity and his ability to see the strengths and weaknesses of both peoples, he agrees that Eritreans have a sense of commitment and, especially, he adds, "consistency and passion." He remembers:

> I was here a couple of years ago when Senator Patty Murray was doing her half hour with the public. The meeting agenda wasn't related to East African issues, but there were two Eritrean guys from Seattle who wanted to talk to her about some marine fisheries research thing at the University of Washington that they wanted to tie to shrimp harvest on the Red Sea. I was so impressed. They were just two regular individuals. If you saw them on the street, you would never think they would be advocates of a cause in a faraway country. Things may have changed now, but at that time my observation was that they had so much love for their country that they were willing to use every single opportunity to lobby or do something for their government.

Besides their love of country, Eritreans say, they have self-reliance, endurance, and innovation to their name. So important are these qualities that the Eritrean government has memorialized them, creating an icon on Martyr's Avenue in the city of Asmara that captures the efficacy of these qualities in the heroic past and serves as a reminder of the country's continuing need for them in the present and future. This icon, a war monument standing in the capital of Eritrea, is not a bronze statue or marble obelisk like the ones other countries erect to glorify their war dead but a pair of black sandals the size of a house. The Shida monument, as it is known, memorializes those Eritreans who fell in defense of their country during its thirty-year war with Ethiopia, and many veterans of the war,

President Isaias Afwerki included, still wear black sandals as a reminder of them. Even in Seattle, most Eritreans own a pair, because, as Abraha puts it, they "bring us closer to those who can no longer wear them."

I ask him how the sandals' iconic status came about.

"Well, it was like this. When the EPLF conducted guerrilla campaigns in the countryside, they were fighting on rough mountainous ground, and so the stones and roots dug into their feet and made them bleed. But they couldn't afford boots. You see, the EPLF had no money, and no other country would come to their aid."

"So what did they do?"

"They realized they could not rely on the outside world; they would have to rely on themselves. So, using rubber from old discarded tires, they made simple black sandals for their *tegadelti*. Not combat boots, just sandals. They were sandals made to never wear out. They could be repaired over and over again just by melting and mending them with a cigarette lighter." He crosses his arms across his chest, an elder, proud of his people. But he is not through. When I express my admiration for what they had done, he adds his parting shot. "Do you know that it was while wearing these very sandals that the *tegadelti* overcame the forces of Ethiopia and in 1991 liberated our country?"

Of course, the objectification of cultural memory in public places represents one of the ways that governments go about nation building. Still, even if governments use public monuments along with the mass media and the educational system to instill nationalist ideology, the feelings such monuments provoke are genuine and sincere. Abraha and other Eritreans I interviewed take pride in their self-reliance and consider it, as Abraha says, "a measure of their self-confidence that they reach their goals on their own without anyone's help." They feel strong and autonomous. They are dependent on nobody. Others see this self-reliance as arrogance, and the government is often at the receiving end of criticism for its attitude. It refuses to allow nongovernmental organizations (NGOs) to work in the country, for example, unless they hand over control to the government. Abraha describes the situation differently and calls the government's policy one of "no angels." "Eritrea doesn't need people who, like angels, say, 'We'll go into Eritrea and do some good work and stuff,' and then tell us, 'We're taking 70 percent, and we'll give you 30 percent.'

'No,' he says, 'we'd rather be partners. Teach us along the way how to take care of ourselves so that you don't have to come back this way.'" He turns to me, "You know, most angels, they don't want to know."

Ezra Teshome bemoans the fact that even the Rotary Club is banned in Eritrea. "It is not functioning anymore," he says, "because [President] Isaias said, 'This is an NGO. You guys have to hand over or else dismantle.' So Rotary in Eritrea disbanded."

When I ask Ethiopians about their identity, they do not talk about a unique "Ethiopian-ness," as it were. There is the notion of *kinijit*, which refers to a spirit of freedom and of love and unity, but it's been appropriated by a group, mostly Amhara, who have made it the rallying cry of a political party, Kinijit-CUDP (Coalition for Unity and Democracy), which since 2005 has been dedicated to overthrowing the government of Meles Zenawi. David Makonnen says that Ethiopians just don't have the same sense of passion about their country or government because they've always been suspicious of whoever is in power. They'll volunteer to take on and support endeavors that benefit the community, he says, like getting involved in a project to promote Ethiopian coffee or to build a school for the disadvantaged, but only at an individual level, seldom as a large entity. "I haven't run into many Ethiopians here in the Northwest who want to do great things for the country that may end up also helping the Ethiopian government. People are just traditionally more skeptical, which in my opinion is also at times healthy. It challenges the government to work harder to reach out and earn the trust of the diaspora."

Perhaps it is their respected history that gives Ethiopians who have settled in the Pacific Northwest the confidence to be skeptical. They are able to criticize their government's actions without casting aspersions on Ethiopians as a whole. Thus, Ezra can say, "Occasionally we have a bad apple, but, in general, Ethiopians I know here and at home are wonderful, hardworking people and very frank individuals." Through Rotary, Ezra takes sixty to seventy people a year to Ethiopia. "It's amazing to see the look in their eyes when they first arrive, and you ask them, 'What do you think?'" They expect famine and starving poor people, but, as he points out, while it's true that some may be poor, "they are also so very rich. They have a rich culture, and they have great pride in who they are. They're honest, hardworking, dedicated individuals. Very poor people, if you go to their house, they don't come and tell you what they *don't* have; they want to give you everything they *do* have."

In Portland, where Green Cabs dominate the downtown area like brightly colored Bumper cars, I meet with Desta Wondwassen, who also attests to the work ethic of Ethiopians and their character. Desta, an Oromo Ethiopian who came to the United States in 1982 through the organization Caritas, works as a supervisor for City Parking, which employs "lots of Ethiopians." "They are responsible and hardworking people, and they're respectful and helpful, too," he says, explaining how they go out of their way to help people. "They're all just trying to establish a better life for themselves and their families. You certainly won't find troublemakers among them," he adds.

Another Ethiopian, Nuria Agraw, praises the generosity of the Ethiopians and their hospitality and warmness. "They always hug people and welcome them into their homes, even if they are poor." I have known Nuria for some years and vouch for her own warm and welcoming spirit. She works in my neighborhood, as sales manager at World Travel Services, an agency that frequently arranges travel for Americans who want to see Ethiopia.

Generalizations are questionable, and using them to describe an entire nationality leads into a miasma of contradictions. Sometimes, the descriptions refer only to people of the same particular ethnic group who, if asked about another ethnic group, might offer a different perspective. At the High Point housing project in West Seattle, for instance, where a number of Ethiopian families have made their homes, little social interaction takes place. Oromo, Amhara, and Tigray of Coptic Christian, evangelical, or Muslim faith live alongside one another in this lovely green community. Here, their homes with porches and energy-efficient windows, lighting, and appliances provide them with the most up-to-date green technology, but in their personal relationships, they live largely in the past. Even within each group, historic differences translate into separations. The Gonder Amharas from Gojjam, for instance, consider the Amharas from Shoa inauthentic and refer to them derogatively as "Gallas," a term usually applied to the Oromos, who have their own problems with the Tigrayans and Amhara. Amhara identity is in fact open to any Orthodox Christian in Ethiopia who speaks Amharic and accepts the link to the Solomonic past. But, as Matsuoka and Sorenson point out, taking on that identity can translate into cultural suicide, for once an Oromo becomes Amhara, he is forever cut off from the traditions and rituals of his original culture.[3]

The long-standing tensions between Amhara and Tigray Ethiopians, despite their common Semitic and Christian backgrounds, have given rise to separate community centers, separate churches, and, ultimately, separate identities in both Seattle and Portland. The cultural heritage of the priest, David Makonnen points out in relation to the church separations, dictates the ethnicity of his followers. "It has nothing at all to do with the priest's teachings." He explains, "Abba Haddis [Gedey, head priest of Emmanuel Ethiopian Orthodox Church] happens to be Tigrayan, but he is also a very well-educated priest, very kind, with a traditional Ethiopian classical orthodox training. He lectures at Harborview Hospital. I think he is a very good priest, but some people don't go to his church because they associate the Tigrayan heritage with being part of the ruling government in Ethiopia."

The Tigray-Amhara relationship has long been a competitive one, tracing itself back to each people's respective ruler in the late nineteenth century, Yohannes IV and Menelik II. The Tigrayans say that Yohannes in his largesse had made Menelik king (*negus*) of Shoa in 1878, only to have Menelik betray him to the Italians in order to oust Yohannes and become emperor himself. The Italians, angry about their defeat at the hands of Yohannes's troops at Dogali in 1887, offered Menelik five thousand Remington rifles in return for his neutrality in the impending conflict with Yohannes.

The Amhara dispute that telling. They claim that Menelik believed the Italians when they promised they would not annex Ethiopian territory and that was why, on hearing of Yohannes's death, Menelik signed the Treaty of Wichale with the Italians in northern Wollo on May 2, 1889. The treaty was signed at Sema Negus, an Ethiopian at the Mercato Ethiopian Market in Portland tells me. "That exact spot." We have just watched the movie *Adwa*, which waxes lyrical about Menelik's military strategies. Yet it was not Menelik but his wife who first noted the ambiguous Italian wording of the treaty and realized that it made Ethiopia an Italian protectorate.

"Taitu looked at the treaty," Sofi Mulugeta explains, "and said, 'Hold on! Are you telling me that we are going to be under you?' She was the one who saw around the subtle wording and realized what was going on. 'We would die first,' she's believed to have said."

So instead, Menelik signed away the Mereb Melash, and, on January 1, 1890, the Italians proclaimed the colony of Eritrea, with the port of Massawa as its capital. When they attempted to annex Tigray as well, Menelik, who was now Emperor and King of Kings, took his famous stand at the Battle of Adwa in 1896. The Amhara thereafter appropriated the Axum identity of the Tigray, making it their own and referring to the Tigray people as Weyane, an unflattering expression that, although taken from a traditional Tigrayan game and implying resistance and unity, has acquired derogatory connotations.

Today, the Tigrayans rule Ethiopia. Here in Portland and Seattle, however, Tigrayans still remember the stories about how Menelik called them locusts who destroyed the land, and when they speak to an Amhara Ethiopian, they recall that Menelik considered their language abrasive. They remember, too, how their fathers and grandfathers rebelled in 1942 and 1943 against Selassie's attempts to control their area and live off their labor. Using military arms left behind by the Italians, they fought back in numerous peasant uprisings that became known as the Weyane Insurgency. So successful were they that Selassie turned for help to the British, who savagely bombarded the Tigrayans from the air in October 1943, effectively putting an end to their rebellion. More than thirty years later, however, the Tigrayans once again assumed the emotive Weyane appellation, as the Tigray People's Liberation Front took on the Derg. The Amhara, the Tigrayans say, looked on impassively as the man-made famine of 1984–85 hit Tigray, and when Mengistu's air force bombed Hawzien, one of Tigray's main market towns, in June 1988, they never spoke out either. Helicopter gunships strafed thousands of fleeing civilians. Thousands more fled the country in search of refuge, some of them arriving in the Pacific Northwest, desperate and needy.

"They were *all* running away from the fighting and the famine," Ezra remembers, "not just the Tigrayans, but the Amharas and Oromo as well. And when they came to this area, most of them had no language skills and didn't have a clue about the country or the culture. Although I'm

Amhara by ethnicity," Ezra reminds me, "people know that I don't place any importance on ethnic background, and so I was able to help people and direct them to jobs, homes, and schools for their children."

Back home, however, hostilities between the Tigrayans and the Amhara continue. Many Amhara blame the Tigrayans, who, when the TPLF overthrew Mengistu and took over the reins of government as the Ethiopian People's Revolutionary Democratic Front, divided the country into a federation of ethnic regions and offered each the option of seceding, like Eritrea. "It's all very well to divide everything," Ezra points out, "but people are saying, 'Wait a minute. My mom is Amhara, my dad Oromo, so what region am I going to be?'"

"Some say it's the best thing that could have happened to Ethiopia," Haddis Tadesse explains, "and some say it's the worst." In his own experience in Seattle, he says, he has encountered a lot more people who believe the latter. "I wish there was a broader discussion about alternatives. If this is not the right arrangement, what is? We should be debating this and preparing for the transition when the time is right."

In laying out Ethiopia's identity problems, I do not mean to imply that the same doesn't exist in Eritrea. The fallout from the Eritrean Liberation Front–Eritrean People's Liberation Front clash has divided Eritreans here as well and created separate institutions. But as Eritrea is a smaller country with a diverse people who so recently united to fight for their survival, the problems of ethnic and religious identity have taken second place to nationalism. Identity has come at a bloody price, and many Eritreans bear the mental and sometime physical scars of the suffering they or their families endured in order to be able to call themselves Eritreans. Whether Tigrinya or Bilen, whether Christian or Muslim, the peoples of that area stretching from Ethiopia to the Red Sea struggled for the right to name themselves, and they hold fiercely to that right. They aren't easily going to give up their autonomy, their prerogative to make pragmatic choices that benefit them as a separate people in the diaspora.

The Tigray-Tigrinya relationship has been fraught with psychological and personal undercurrents. Many Ethiopian Tigrayans had Eritrean Tigrinya spouses, as those in Seattle and Portland do, and President Isaias Afwerki and Prime Minister Meles Zenawi have mothers who are Tigrayan and Eritrean respectively.[4] With a common ethnic ancestry and shared history, language, religion, and culture, these two peoples were bound by ties that made it impossible for them to consider the other their enemy. They had suffered together and fought together, and many had died alongside one another. But despite their cooperation, their alliance seemed more "a marriage of convenience than of romance."[5] Although the two presidents were once close friends, today that friendship is in tatters. Different Marxist ideologies led the EPLF to focus mostly on anti-imperialism, while the TPLF judged Eritrea undemocratic in that it wouldn't allow internal groups to secede as it itself had done from Ethiopia. Thus, when the TPLF turned to alternate Eritrean groups whose thinking more closely matched its own and formed new "work" relationships, the EPLF saw these actions as a betrayal. Coming right after the TPLF's withdrawal of its fighters from Eritrea, where they had been defending Eritrean positions, so that it could follow its own goal of moving the struggle south to Addis Ababa, it showed that the relationship was obviously on the rocks.

Talk of TPLF betrayal infuriates the Tigray Ethiopians in the Pacific Northwest who argue that the EPLF broke military and political relations. What is more, at the height of the 1985 famine, they say, the EPLF cut the TPLF supply lines that ran through Eritrean territory to relief depots in Sudan. In doing so, the EPLF effectively denied the Tigrayans access to food aid. The TPLF could not believe that the EPLF would do anything so savage, and its actions created a great residue of bitterness.

In Seattle and Portland, Ethiopians deny that their country colonized Eritrea, and David Makonnen questions what Eritreans actually mean by the term. He sees the Eritrean concept of Ethiopia as "the colonizer from hell who forced Eritreans to do this and that" as merely an interpretation that helped form an identity. "While I respect the right of Eritreans to choose their own destiny and I also don't claim to be an expert on colonialism," he explains, "the definition of the word suggests the presence of three things: first, a difference in rights of colonizers and those being colonized; second, a trade imbalance resulting in exploitation of the colony's resources to benefit the colonizer's economy; and third, an active cultural indoctrination of the colonizer's dominant culture." David has thought deeply about the issue and methodically checks off his arguments against colonization, among them, no documented evidence showing Ethiopians trying "to indoctrinate Eritreans into becoming something that they are not" and Eritreans holding key political leadership positions under both Haile Selassie and Mengistu and senior roles within the Ethiopian military and police. Finally, he points to the two regimes perpetuating poverty *throughout* Ethiopia, not just in Eritrea. He concludes his argument by suggesting that "the current Eritrean leadership who emerged from the Ethiopian student movement in the late '60s and '70s latched on to the 'colonial' label because it knew the strategy would provide international visibility to their cause."

"It's really no benefit to Eritrea to be alone and become a country," Ezra concludes. "I mean, if you look at it from the religion aspect, culture, and all that, they show that we have so much in common to unite us as one." Having been through so much, however, Eritreans take pride in their survival and carry their hurts, injustices, and vendettas in their stories.

For the older generation of both groups, as well as uneducated rural newcomers, their inherited narrative baggage is easily manipulated by political groups with agendas. The politicization of pain, not surprisingly, causes tension among some even as they themselves perhaps call attention to their own pain for political purposes. Even for those who prefer to bury the past and move forward, these stories remain deeply ingrained in the communal consciousness, which is sensitive to an incautious word or a perceived slight.

Here in the Pacific Northwest, Almaz Bahre talks of "long years of screaming bodies" that robbed her of sleep and how the sound of airplanes still terrifies her. She lives close to the southern end of Lake Washington, and as I watch her moving about her home, a smiling and gentle woman who delights in her small son, Abraham, I wonder what it must be like in this house when the Blue Angels jet across the sky during Seafair. I recall my own jumpiness after 9/11 and the upsurge of fear that shot through me at any sudden noise. It has been a long journey for Almaz to get to this place. When she was just seventeen, in 1987, she fled her home on the road to Massawa for refuge in Sudan. It took an eleven-day camel trip, with no food and no water, sleeping during the day and moving at night. Three years later, she arrived in the United States, where initially she worked at a gas station before using her keen business sense to start a Dollar Store in Seattle. Life has been good since then, but the past still haunts her, badly.

> Sandra, I remember during the fighting in 1977, every day between 4:00 and 5:00 A.M., we have to get up early to go underground. We have to work a long way from home, underground, for protection. But the time they bombed our house, because it was Saint Mary's day, my grandmother, she says she doesn't want to go underground that day. So she stays home and just makes coffee and prays to Saint Mary. My mom, she doesn't want to, but we have to listen to Grandma. So we were at home at eleven o'clock when there came two MiG planes, "Wooooooooooo" [*her arms trace the planes' trajectories*]. My mom, she screamed. We were all nervous, my mom, my grandma, me, and neighbors who came to visit. It was scary. "You see!" my mother said to my grandma. "We had to listen to you, and now this happens, now the bombs drop." My grandmother tells us, "Pray! Pray! Pray!" "Oh, no," says my mom, "let's go convert bullets into water and fertilize the soil!" And the bombs were coming on our house. Me and the other neighbors were in another room, and I didn't know what was happening or if the house was totally damaged. I hear my mom moaning and my grandma crying, "Oh, I've lost my daughter, I've lost her." And my mom tells her, "No, I'm alive, but I don't have my leg—I'm paralyzed." And my grandma's crying, but she tells her daughter, even though she can't see her, that her legs are OK. "Forget it, you're OK," she says. And then she starts calling for her son, my dad, and then, "Almaz, Almaz, Almaz!" But I can't see. I can't breathe for all the smoke. But I say, "I'm OK, I'm OK. I'm alive but I just can't see." So I walked . . . touch, touch, touch, until I reached my mom and my grandma, and we went to another place far away.

In an aside to me, her husband, Yosieph, says that after the bombing of Almaz's home in 1977, she and her mom searched the area for one of their missing visitors, a lady from Massawa. "They looked everywhere, and when they couldn't find her, they assumed she must have been killed. But weeks later, they found her severed head in a pail." Almaz went for therapy for six months because she couldn't sleep at nighttime, "not even for an hour," she says. Her sleeping has improved, but, like other Eritreans who experienced bombing raids, the images remain with her.

They remain with Ethiopians, too. So when Yosieph says, "War is a tragedy for everyone. It destroys innocent lives and causes death and misery to Eritreans and Ethiopians alike," I feel hopeful for the future of Eritrean-Ethiopian relations in the Pacific Northwest. It takes courage to go beyond the past and to acknowledge in retrospect the pain of others, especially in the face of his wife's suffering. Still, the violence perpetrated by the enemy always seems worse. Yosieph points to the more recent February 1990 bombing when the EPLF took Massawa and the Derg responded with cluster bombs that shredded both buildings and people. "Just the power that they have, the fact they killed so many innocent people, makes it worse. In the end, Sandra, numbers do make a big difference. When Massawa was inhumanely bombed—you've seen Massawa, some of the bullet holes . . . And there were kids begging for their lives and kids asking where their brothers were." He hugs Abraham to him. "That really hurts."

The struggle took many years and lives before the nation reached its current state and is seen as not yet won. President Isaias Afwerki's government remains on the defensive, claiming that Greater Ethiopia still has designs on the country and its strategic ports on the Red Sea. Yosieph agrees. "There are people who don't want us to exist," he explains, "who won't admit that Eritrea is independent. There are people who cannot tolerate to see an independent Eritrea."

While David Makonnen also says there are Ethiopians who "hate Eritreans and would like nothing more than to see the government destroyed," he adds that most do not feel that way. "Even the Ethiopian government, as a policy, does not have such a level of animosity toward Eritrea," he explains.

Many southern Somalis, like their Eritrean neighbors, believe the Ethiopians have designs on Somali land, too. That suspicion alone fans nationalism more than any attempt by politicians who must deal with the greater loyalty most Somalis bear toward their clans. As Somali history has shown, loyalty to the abstract concept of a unified state follows a shaky trajectory, which sparked only briefly at the beginning of Barre's reign. Even so, Somalis do speak of nationalism and dispute its origins, as the following conversation, overheard at a Somali restaurant on Pacific Highway South in Tukwila, attests.

Two Somali men twirl pasta in a spicy tomato sauce and speak in high-pitched voices. Although I cannot understand their Af-Maxaa Somali, the friend who accompanies me spent time in Somalia many years ago and so translates. He tells me they are discussing nationalism and two Somali heroes, the sixteenth-century Garey (Ahmad ibn Abrahim al-Ghazi) and the twentieth-century Mahammad Abdille Hasan. My friend, who was trained in England, calls Mohammad "The Mad Mullah" for his twenty-year guerrilla war against the British. We are the only non-Somalis in the restaurant, and I'm the sole female, so I try to behave circumspectly and not draw too much attention to myself. Still, I am keen to understand what they are saying. One man speaks of Garey and the Sayyid as uniters who introduced the concept of a Somali state into the consciousness of different clans who were feuding at the time, while the other insists that both men were more interested in upholding Islam against the infidels and that in fact both were associated with the Ogaden clan and area alone. "The Sayyid was interested only in the Ogaden," the latter says, punching the air with his fork. "He belonged to the Ogaden lineage of his father and the Dhulbahante of his mother." As my friend translates, I remember that the Sayyid's dervishes also came from the Dhulbahante tribe and that many of them had been his mother's relatives, who, in the course of their guerrilla warfare, had lost half their kin. I had earlier interviewed Abdihakim, whose family is connected with that history. He had told me that though the British were hated at the time, not many Somalis resisted them or refused to sign the protectorate treaty. "My tribe, the Dulbahantes," he had said, "was one of a few who fought many years against the British protectorate. My immediate grandfathers died in that war, which was led by Sayyid Mahammad and took almost twenty-two years." It was finally lost after Britain bombed the dervishes.

The conversation at the nearby table continues. "And Garey was also a Darod Somali," the same man says. Since everyone in the restaurant is most likely of the Darod clan family, nobody demurs. But if the same conversation had occurred at another Somali place farther along Pacific Highway or at the one on Rainier where other clans eat, the discussion might have been different. Those who had suffered at the hands of the Darod might point out with some satisfaction that Garey was the illegitimate offspring of a Somali woman and an Abyssinian priest. Or they might say that he was Oromo. And as for the poet-warrior, the Sayyid, if the critics were of the Isaq, Issa, Warsangali, or Gadabursi clans, who *did* sign the treaty with Britain and were considered collaborators and therefore enemies, the speaker might have been at the receiving end of even more pointed comments. Isaqs particularly have mixed feelings about Sayyid Mahammad, whose dervishes inflicted so much pain on their ancestors. Thus they do not claim the Sayyid as the originator of Somali nationalism. While they admire him as a poet—"I still read his poetry even though he calls my people collaborators," Mohamed Omer, an Isaq says—they also remember his attacks against the northern Somali clans and his burning and looting of their cities.

Given the absence of an accepted government that unites Somalis behind it, the question of Somali nationality and identity falls by the wayside. Large swaths of Somalia resist Sheikh Sharif Sheikh Ahmed's new Transitional Federal Government, and, although the United Nations brokered the meshing of the sheikh's Alliance for the Re-liberation of Somalia and the transitional government, most Somalis presume the new government will go the way of previous ones. Since nationalist pride, therefore, remains tentative, it would seem presumptuous to talk of a countrywide sense of identity. And yet, Somalis do indeed talk of *Somalinimo*. They don't, however, all mean the same thing.

In an ongoing conversation, Jamal explains to me his take on the question of identity in today's Somalia and in the process provides a glimpse into the politics of the south and the north. "To take *Somalinimo* first," he says, "we all belong to it. It includes everyone, all Somalis, no matter where they are, if they speak Somali. It could be Somalis in Ethiopia, Somalis in Kenya, in Djibouti . . . because they are all Somali-speaking. Whereas *Somaliweyn*," he makes the distinction, "refers to the irredentist policy of Greater Somalia, the political choice we made at a particular time in our history. You can choose to be part of *Somaliweyn*, or you can say, 'No, I don't want to be part of it. I want to have my own more specific identity.'" He checks to see if I'm following, then works logically to his point about his own home, Somaliland.

The problem is that some people conflate *Somalinimo* and *Somaliweyn*.
They say, once you are Somali, you have to be part of that bigger concept.

Otherwise they accuse you of being a separatist or a secessionist. But what I'm saying is, no, it's not necessary or imperative to belong to *Somaliweyn* if you are Somali. There are Somalis who live in Kenya, there are Somalis who live in Ethiopia, and they are not part of Somalia. They don't have to be part of Somalia.

"So," he says, leaning back, "the same thing with people in Somaliland, who have what I call *Somalilandnimo*. They can set up a different political situation and still remain Somali." He does not mention those Somalis who do not speak the state language but consider themselves Somali, like the Bantu. Do they have *Somalinimo*, I wonder?

Because Somaliland was ruled first as a British protectorate and then as a British colony, the people there consider their home to be separate and different from the south, which was under Italian rule. Thus, when the regime of the dictator Siyad Barre fell, the Somalilanders decided to go it alone and unilaterally announced their independence from Somalia in May 1991. Since then, they have been negotiating for political recognition from the international community. As a traditionally nomadic, Islamic people who have produced many of the great poets of old, these northerners pride themselves on their Somaliland identity while not forgetting their clan identities as Isaqs, Gadibursis, or Hartis. Since independence, they have managed to keep clan divisions under control and even to conduct a democratic election. "Instead of making civil war with one another," Mowliid Abdullahi tells me, "we came together. We said, 'OK, we live together. What's best for me is best for you. Are we going to go on fighting, or are we going to give it up and live in peace, happily with each other?'"

Everyone wants peace, of course, but only the Somalilanders have achieved anything remotely close. "What makes us different here from the people from the south," Mowliid continues, "is that what is going on back home in the south is selectively inserted in this diaspora. The divisions between the clans there become the subject of this whole diaspora society. Unlike us," he declares proudly. "When we came here, we declared a truce. We say, 'OK, I don't care who you are as long as you are a Somalilander.' That's what counts."

Like Somalilanders, Somalis from Puntland also take pride in their identity. They claim to be descended from inhabitants of the Land of Punt, the home of those biblical royals, the Puntite kings, who brought gold, myrrh, and frankincense to welcome the newborn Jesus. Their leader, Abdullahi Yusuf, became president of the transitional government of Somalia in 2004, and although he resigned in 2009, for most of those five years, he offered hope for the creation of a unified Somali identity. It was Koshin Mohamed who, belonging to the same Puntland clan (Majerteen) as Abdullahi, played a leading role in persuading the United States to support his clansman. Koshin explains:

> You see, I was traumatized by what was happening in my country, and I realized that unless the young people got involved, nothing was going to change. So I said to myself, "Well, what if you try to understand your community first?" That's how I got involved with the Somali Coalition in Seattle. And then I realized that the problem Somalis were having here in the U.S. is intertwined with the happenings back home. Because everyone, including myself, we were sending money back home to immediate family and relatives, and that was very significant. Imagine someone on welfare or making eight bucks an hour sending $400 to $500 a month back home. To me, it was just cra-a-zy. So, I said, "Well, are we going to give up our country to a warlord, or are we going to strive to fight for it back?" And so I tried to find out who was willing to fight for us.

He found Abdullahi. But it took him three years of flying back and forth and meeting with members of the U.S. State Department before he was able to convince the Americans that Abdullahi was their man. Washington realized after the shock of 9/11 that an unstable Somalia invited terrorist recruitment, but it considered Abdullahi at that time as just another warlord. I did, too, and when in 2003, Koshin attempted to bring Abdullahi Yusuf to the United States, I hesitated to invite him to speak on campus. At the time, I was aware of the controversy over Abdullahi seizing the Puntland presidency by force in 2002 from Jama Ali Jama, who had been elected by the elders, and also of the various killings of which he'd been accused.[6] When a group of Somali students, having heard via the very effective Somali grapevine that the African

Studies program was considering having Abdullahi address University of Washington students, they paid me a visit. Their delegation confided that Abdullahi's forces had been responsible for the deaths of their relatives and many people they knew and, what is more, had been the cause of their own flight out of the country. They were convinced that in seeking to give a lecture at an American institution of higher learning, Abdullahi simply sought American credentials so he could go back to Somalia and say, "See, the Americans accept me."

Abdihakim expresses skepticism when I discuss local Somalis' rejection of Abdullahi with him. "It's normal for Somali leaders to get a bad reception," he says. "A lot of people don't like Abdullahi because of his tribe, so they can easily target the guy."

Two years later, when I interview Koshin Mohamed, the young ambassador-designate is philosophical about the incident and our differences and puts it down to misinformation. "They say he was a warlord, but he wasn't; he was different. He was elected to his position in Puntland," Koshin insists.

As it turned out, Abdullahi Yusuf never did make it to the States that year, immigration authorities having found problems with his visa. Nevertheless, he was elected president of the TFG in 2004 and established his office first in Kenya, since he did not have enough support inside Somalia, and, in 2006, in Baidoa, his clan territory. From there, he attempted to promote reconciliation, even arranging, after the victories of the Islamic Courts Union in September 2006, to merge with the ICU in Khartoum. The latter, however, insisted on the departure of the Ethiopian army, and the merger fell through. With the help of the Ethiopians, TFG forces retook Mogadishu from the ICU and, by December 28, 2006, had control of Somalia. The Habr Gidir Somalis, one of the Hawiye clan family staged a fierce resistance in Mogadishu, and, in what must have seemed like déjà vu for Americans, they dragged six dead, burned, and mutilated soldiers through the streets. The *Seattle Post-Intelligencer* of March 22, 2007, described masked men shouting, "God is great!" while women "in head scarves and flowing dresses" pounded one charred body with rocks, before the men finally set the corpses alight. The men claimed to be part of an insurgent group known as the Popular Resistance Movement in the Land of the Two Migrations, which was linked to the ousted ICU.

Jamal, in an interview at that time, claimed to see no ideal answer to the situation:

> If the TFG tries to disarm the people, they will see it as one clan disarming
> another, rather than a government doing so. And they will ask themselves,
> "Why should we agree to this?" The elders in the community attempted
> to talk with the military but to no avail. The talks failed, and the two sides
> are at a standstill. What happens in the next few days will be crucial. Most
> likely the TFG will enforce their rule, using muscle and firepower, or else the
> Ethiopians will withdraw. Most of the Habr Gidir support the Islamists, but
> while the Islamists bring peace for some people, for others they are a danger.

With such a bloody history between them, the Ethiopians and the Somalis do not trust each other. On the one hand, the Hawiye in particular are suspicious of Ethiopian military support of President Abdullahi's TFG and fear that Meles Zenawi has designs on Somalia itself. The Ethiopians, on the other hand, claim they simply want peace along their borders and a stable country as their neighbor. Koshin makes light of their past history. "Ethiopia and Somalia used to be enemies. They are *not* anymore. OK? We have no quarrel with the Ethiopian people." He laughs. "We lo-o-o-ve them! We have property issues and want to have a border that is fair to us, but we don't have any other issues in that part of the world." Even the TFG expressed effusive emotions about the Ethiopians. After the Ethiopians assisted the TFG in retaking the country, Somalia's assistant prime minister, Hussein Mohamed Farah Aideed, announced at Villa Somalia in Mogadishu on January 2, 2007, that henceforth Somalis and Ethiopians will use one passport. In effect, the TFG would eliminate boundaries between the two countries.

"Abdullahi is so desperate for power," counters Jamal, "they are ready to sign on to anything the Ethiopians want. They're just interested in power. In any case, it is not Somalia that the Ethiopians favor—it is Somaliland. We are the ones who have a good working relationship with Ethiopia." He explains:

> We are diplomatically engaged, in that they have a liaison office in
> Somaliland and we have an office in Ethiopia. We do not have embassies

because Somaliland exists in an in-between state of nationhood, not yet an internationally recognized country. Ethiopian Airlines flies to Hargeisa several days a week, and Ethiopia also imports through the port of Berbera. There are no Ethiopian troops in Somaliland, and our relationship is mutually beneficial.

Somalia and Somaliland each contributes to the shaping of Somali identity, but yet another kind of identity has writer Maxamed D. Afrax concerned for the future of Somalis. He calls that identity *ragannimo*, by which he means the "theft, lying, hypocrisy, rape, and dishonesty" that have become "indicators of manhood" in the region. For this, he blames the military regime of Siyad Barre, which he sees as having reversed the traditional moral code of right and wrong.[7] His words are not lost on Somalis in Seattle and Portland, who also decry the eroded values they see among young men in particular. It's as if the *ragannimo* mentality picked up during the anarchic years of the civil war can reemerge at the slightest provocation in the new country. It disturbs the elders in the community. Abdihakim worries about their young people.

> Our crime rate is going up, and, although we don't have access to real statistics, there are a lot of Somali kids in the jails and in juvenile detention now. The number is high, and the community is very upset about it. We need Somalis in the police force who understand our culture and can talk to the kids. They have a lot of pressures on them in school, and they can't always deal with it.

There are Eritrean and Ethiopian kids in jail, too, story lines that don't always make it into the dominant narratives. Even so, all three groups wonder about the dissolution of values they have always considered part of their identities. Somalis possess an abundance of pride, for example, and face-saving behavior ranks high among most immigrants and refugees who cannot understand how their kids so easily slip into egregious behavior that reflects badly on their families. "Fear of gossip is intimidating," Rahel Gebreab explains about the Eritrean community, "and people are reluctant to discuss problems because they fear judgment, even though the problems in the other communities might be similar."

She shakes her head. "We are still a very reserved and complex society," she says, adding, "I appreciate that. Sometimes."

Islam is a major constituent of Somali identity, and for many Somalis, "Muslim" and "Somali" are interchangeable. "Islam *is* our culture," Portland's Amina Sharif responds when I ask her and her women friends about it. They admit they practice it a little bit differently from the traditionalists. "That's why," Amina explains, "Somali men go to Egypt and learn how the real religion goes. Then we adopt it all, so the Arabs won't think we're heretics!" She laughs apologetically and looks for confirmation from the other Somali women sitting around her, cradling babies or shooing their older toddlers away. The women live in a housing development in Tigard, near Portland, where the streets have woodsy, suburban names, like Ashcreek Park. Each woman has a home to which she points with pride. "Nobody's lived in them but us," Amina tells me. "Brand-new." The wooden houses wear pale shades of pink, green, and brown, colors that seem diminished compared to the vibrant hues the women are used to from back home. Inside the houses, the curtains are drawn, and it is dark and cool, the lightly painted walls providing a backdrop to floral-print sofas and dark wall-to-wall carpeting.

Many Somali women find comfort in their religion and speak of it with affection. Their lives center around Islam, and it provides the rules by which they conduct their lives in their new country. Not everything about Islamic law makes them happy, of course. For example, it bothers them, they say, that although most of them lost their husbands and the fathers of their children in the violence, they cannot remarry with American Christians, whereas Muslim men can, provided the women convert.

The Sunni Islam that gives most Somalis here in the Pacific Northwest their identity is not the same as the more extreme Wahabism imported from Saudi Arabia. The latter form of Islam, Koshin Mohamed claims, is responsible for the terrorism that has killed Americans and others in the West. It is not *his* Islam. Talking about their suicide bombers, he is adamant. "Islam doesn't allow the committing of suicide no matter what the circumstances. It doesn't fall under an exception to the rule, what we call *darura*, such as when your life is in danger or when you have no option."

"Who grants *darura*?" I ask.

"The Prophet Muhammad," he responds. "The ancestors decide if it's OK."

What becomes clear from our discussion is that most Somalis here are caught between an appreciation for the relatively free lives they can live in the United States, protected by inalienable rights that are upheld by the courts and defended by the American Civil Liberties Union, and the influence of fundamentalist religious groups back home. Koshin, who is nothing but straight talking on this issue, puts it more bluntly. "Somalis have been brainwashed so long about hating, about hating anything Western . . ." He hesitates a minute and then says to me, "Look, I like to give it as raw as possible. OK?" When I nod, he says:

> We hate America, we hate Jewish people, we hate this, we hate that. Yet we come to this country and we lo-o-o-ve America [*laughs*]. It's because of the conditioning we have right there. We have the best guy representing Somali people in Washington, Norm Coleman [U.S. Senator for Minnesota], a Jewish guy! Some of us don't mind that, because we're learning that all the brainwashing is basically bullshit; it's not true that Jewish people . . . When I was helping with the Somali community here, almost all the people who helped us were Jewish lawyers. And the people didn't mind. OK? So, they're learning that Americans, whether they are white, Jewish, black Americans, or whatever, are people. We were like animals in a little house, ruled by a dictator, and we had no chance to even think on our own. Somalis speak Somali language, live according to Somali culture, but are propped up by Arab brothers. And I'm not demonizing. I'm not saying Arabs did something bad in trying to . . . It was just the way it was. If you go to Iraq, there you find people who commit suicide to kill an American. But if you give that person, before he commits suicide, a one-way ticket and a green card, he will change his vision in no time!

These different perspectives on identity indicate the complexity of the word. What does it mean to say who you are? What does the word signify? Your sense of yourself or your family roots? Your clan or your nation? Or your religion? The word "identity" comes to us trailing clouds of meaning derived from earlier uses by earlier people, claims made in other moments of history, whether under political duress, in defiance of a colonial power, to win advantage over a rival, or simply to survive and feed one's family for another day. Identity construction often takes place in the most challenging of situations and, in many cases, within fields of power over which one has no control. As a result, people sometimes choose the identity that offers them the most leverage. Jamal, returning to the subject of the conflation of Somali and Muslim identities, points out that when Somalis are in touch with Arabs, they become more conscious of their Somali-ness and aware of the dichotomy. "If it's in their interests," he explains, "they may promote their ancient Muslim lineage. That's why Somalia joined the Arab League, for example." Arabs at the time were very wealthy because of their oil possessions. Sometimes, just knowing the circumstances that influence people to make decisions about their identities may assist others in understanding the choices that have been made.

BOUNDARY PERSPECTIVES

The Green Cab & Green Shuttle company on East Burnside in Portland employs forty-eight Ethiopian taxi drivers. Wherever you go in the city, you will see the dark green cabs cruising the streets, the drivers chatting to their passengers or listening to the company's radio instructions about where to find the next pickup. Although I tried numerous times to speak to Green Cab's owner to obtain his permission to meet with groups of his employees, I was never able to reach him. So whenever I needed transport, I would hail a cab whose driver looked Ethiopian and take the opportunity to talk to him. On one occasion, I brought up the border war.

"Such a tragedy, such a tragedy," the driver responds, shaking his head. He is a slightly built man with a quick smile that flashes suddenly from beneath his mustache and then is gone. He comes from a village in the Tigray area not far from the Eritrean border where much of the fighting has taken place. The members of his family who were displaced during the war have returned to their villages, he says, but still are dependent on food aid. And not just because of the drought.

"You see," he explains, "they're too scared to work in the soil. If they start digging and planting again, they might strike a mine."

"But isn't UNMEE clearing the mines?" I ask, referring to the United

Nations Mission in Ethiopia and Eritrea, the peacekeeping force that monitors the disputed border areas.

He shakes his head. "Only in the buffer zone," he says, meaning the fifteen-mile-wide strip between Ethiopia and Eritrea, "but there are mines everywhere, especially in northern Tigray. Ethiopia is one of the most mined countries in the world. And every day, a child loses a limb or an animal gets killed because it tripped over a mine." He glances at the picture stuck above his mirror, which shows a family group with three smiling children, one of them proudly displaying two newly emerged front teeth. "The Eritreans continue to kill us even though the war is over," he says softly and catches my eye in the mirror.

When I return home, I read at the Al Jazeera Web site, November 21, 2005, that the Landmine and Cluster Munition Monitor claims that during the border war, Eritrean forces laid 240,000 mines and Ethiopian forces 150,000 to 200,000. What is more, even now, long after the end of the war, tensions still run high and could spark into violence at the slightest provocation.

Ethiopian-Eritrean Border

Borders became an issue between Ethiopia and Eritrea only when economic competition made their delineation important. In the past, farmers had often clashed over the exact boundaries of their fields, but village elders on both sides had usually been able to sort out such disputes. Later, when members of either force transgressed the borders, their actions were seen as cross-border incidents that politically upped the ante. The disputed areas along the six-hundred-mile border were Badme (Badume) and its environs, Humera in the west, Tsorona and Zalembessa north of Adigrat, Altiena and Irob, Bada in the Afar depression, and Bure on the road to Aseb. The conflict hinged on the two country's frameworks for negotiation. For the Eritreans, the borders were those established by the Italians when Eritrea was separated from Ethiopia and colonized, whereas the Ethiopians defined the borders according to the treaties they signed with the Italians on July 10, 1900, and May 16, 1908.

The conflict began with a series of minor incidents and retaliations that prepared the way for the war that would follow. Then, in June 1997, the Ethiopians napalmed the Asmara airport; the pilot was an ex-EPLF prisoner, the same one who had flattened Massawa during the thirty-year war. In response, Eritrea dropped cluster bombs on a military airport, at the same time damaging a school and killing twelve children. Not surprisingly, tensions built up and finally exploded, reopening military hostilities between the two countries.

The day-by day developments of the war are described in Dominique Jacquin-Berdal's and Martin Plaut's *Unfinished Business*, for example, but for Ethiopians and Eritreans here in the Pacific Northwest, certain incidents stand out as bitter turning points.[8] When in 1988, on the one hand, the Addis Ababa government distributed new maps of the country to primary schools, the Eritreans say that the maps showed contested parts of Eritrea as being within Tigray. Since colonial-imposed maps can be transferred to official seals, posters, and letters and in that way absorbed into the popular imagination, the Eritreans became convinced of Ethiopia's duplicity. In fact, the new map confirmed it, they contend, since the year before, the Ethiopians had issued new currency featuring a small inset map that appeared to place parts of Eritrea in Tigray. Ethiopians, on the other hand, talk of Eritrean betrayal. At a May 7, 1998, meeting, they say, Eritreans had agreed to stay out of Badme until a final settlement could be reached, but even while the Eritrean delegates were participating in the meeting, President Isaias back in Asmara made the decision to use military force. The following morning, the delegates were gone, having fled their hotel room during the night in a suspicious act that indicated their lack of faith in the agreement.[9] The Ethiopians claim that they tried to negotiate with Asmara by telephone, but the latter wouldn't budge. On May 12, Eritrean forces took Badme and the surrounding area, having lost trust, Eritreans say, in Ethiopian promises of negotiation.

In Portland and Seattle, feelings about the border betrayals were keenly felt on both sides. While angry rhetoric ricocheted all over the two cities, those I interviewed were loath to be quoted for fear of exacerbating already strong emotions. However, I think this description, offered anonymously, accurately captures the sense of betrayal that many experienced:

> It's like this. Eritrea and Ethiopia are like a wife and a cheating husband. Once the betrayal occurs, she cannot return to the original relationship

because all trust has been lost. It is dangerous for her to forgive her husband, lest he betray her again. Even if she allows time to work its cure so that the pain of the betrayal might heal, she will always be suspicious of him, and paranoia will destroy their love. It is perhaps better, people say, to separate and form a new relationship.

Whoever betrayed whom, the Badme conflict led to an upward spiral of military aggression, with air raids and retaliation following one after another, some targeting civilians.

Back in Portland, where Sonya and her husband, Michael, attended their son's graduation with honors on June 13, 1998, she took note of "a rare moment of cooperation between different political factions within the Eritrean community." Eritrean students at Portland State University, where President Clinton gave the commencement speech, demonstrated outside and demanded that he intervene and stop the Ethiopian aggression. Five days later, the *International Herald Tribune* reported that phone calls from President Clinton to President Isaias Afwerki and Prime Minister Meles Zenawi, together with diplomatic efforts by an Italian delegation, brought an agreement from both sides to ban air raids.

A cease-fire was inaugurated on June 15, and the two sides, with the help of the Organization of African Unity, tried to come to a peaceable resolution, but by then, the conflict no longer concerned borders alone. Ethiopia felt that that it had been invaded and needed to reestablish its position as the major power in the Horn of Africa. So its forces attacked Badme and drove the Eritreans back. The Eritreans counterattacked but were unable to retake the town. It was only in July 1999, at the OAU summit in Algiers, that the two warring countries were finally convinced to accept an agreement. Neither was satisfied with the deal.

"Why should we return to pre–May 6 positions when the Badme areas are obviously Eritrean?" Eritreans in the Pacific Northwest asked, repeating the arguments from home, while local Ethiopians in touch with their compatriots through the Internet insisted, "Why does the Algiers agreement limit itself to Badme and its environs when there are other still-occupied territories?"

When no diplomatic solution appeared imminent, the Ethiopian government attacked other Eritrean-occupied areas in the west, destroying bridges, schools and clinics, offices and residences. The Eritreans then withdrew from battle, claiming that they were doing so for the sake of peace, but the Ethiopians saw their withdrawal as defeat and followed up on earlier victories by attacking Bure, Aseb, and finally bombing the military airport at Asmara and destroying a power plant. A cease-fire agreement was put into effect on June 17 in Algiers, and the United Nations Mission in Ethiopia and Eritrea was deployed under the auspices of the OAU. A temporary security zone separated the two forces while troops withdrew and populations returned home.

The border war lasted two years, with both sides finally signing a comprehensive peace agreement in Algiers on December 12, 2000. Two years later, the Eritrea-Ethiopia Boundary Commission awarded bits and pieces of the land between the two countries to each of the claimants. Badme, the source of the original conflict, which now stood as a symbol of their divisiveness, was acknowledged as belonging to Eritrea. The decisions thrilled neither country, and Ethiopia demanded a new inquiry. David Makonnen explains, "The Ethiopians feel that an arbitrary split that does not take into consideration the practical reality on the ground creates a potential security risk to both governments. That's why the Ethiopian government would rather see some villages go back to whomever the villagers have a historical affinity with."

The Eritreans, however, were prepared to abide by the commission's ruling. "Look, we're a small country," says David, summarizing their sentiments. "We went to an international arbitration committee, and we're entitled to all the territories we have been awarded. So if you want to continue to negotiate until you get what you want, then what's the purpose of going to court in the first place?"

More than seventy thousand people were killed during the two-year period, and today, the boundaries between the two countries remain tentative and under challenge.[10]

Sonya stirs her Ethiopian coffee and stares into its depth as she tries to understand the tragedy that the war has brought to local people on both sides. She was born in Asmara, and her educated parents, wanting to give her the best opportunities, sent her to private Catholic school. However, not long after the Socialist revolution started in 1974, the Derg started killing educated people, and so her family, concerned for her safety, sent the fourteen-year-old Sonya first to England and from there, in 1983, to the States. She continued her schooling in Salem, Oregon, and later married her Eritrean husband, Michael, and through him, she says, rediscovered her Eritrean roots. "I grew up as an international," she explains to me, "and so I spent a lot of time thinking about identity." Still, the border war of 1998–2000, or Second War, as it is known, has devastated her and others in the Portland community.

> The war did a lot of damage. No longer did Eritreans and Ethiopians attend each other's events and churches. Even mixed marriages broke up. In Portland, people demonstrated. On the Eritrean side, it was "We just want our country; we don't want anybody else's land." When President Clinton came to give the commencement speech here, the Eritreans brought their own separate video to show him. That kind of created a wedge between the two communities even more. It made it very uncomfortable. If you've always hung around with your best friend from the other community, what do you do? A lot of people chose not to go to community events and rather continued that relationship outside. Right now, there isn't a community relationship between the two groups in Portland, only individual ones.

Many community members in both Seattle and Portland had relatives fighting in this war, so emotions were raw, and when news of the numerous deaths started to roll in, each group simply turned its back on the other and withdrew into itself. Behind the closed doors of community centers and family homes, Eritreans cursed Ethiopians and vice versa. The rumor mill spread the vitriol. In Seattle, Abraha tells me, "the psychological warfare was devastating." All of this tension remained out of sight of the American public, who generally were oblivious of the war taking the lives of Eritrean and Ethiopian kin.

In the aftermath of war, suspicion continues to hound the Pacific Northwest communities and prevents Ethiopians and Eritreans from working together. Those of mixed heritage sometimes find themselves sidelined and not trusted by either side, and few people I interviewed talked about it dispassionately even five years later. "Neutrality is really hard to come by," Dawit Nerayo admits. But he feels glad that he has equal claims on both ethnicities. "It gives me a special right, if you will, to maintain objectivity. The whole debacle, in my opinion, was irresponsible, an embarrassing situation that could have been avoided in its entirety. Why couldn't they have discussed their differences at a round table or let the United Nations intervene early on, as it had offered to do at the start of the conflict?" He answers himself:

> Unfortunately, pride gets the best of both sides, and they commence a meaningless war to the detriment of the poor peoples of Ethiopia and Eritrea. So I hold both sides responsible for the suffering of the innocent women and children. Some argue that Eritrea was the aggressor and yet others that Ethiopia had no authority to be in that land to begin with. Regardless, war should have been the absolute last resort and not the first option.

Ethiopian–Somali Border

Back in Somalia, one particular boundary is the source of major tensions, and Somalis cross it at the risk of their lives. The intransigence of Ethiopia and Somalia when it comes to the boundary where the Ogadeni live results in frequent bloodshed. About 2.5 million Somalis live in the Ogaden, most of them belonging to this subclan of the Darod. They want independence from Ethiopia, but the government considers the Ogaden a strategic part of the country. The Ogaden National Liberation Front, however, sees Ethiopia as a colonial state and actively fights the Tigray-led government, which in turn has declared it a terrorist organization. One of its self-declared leaders was Seattle imam Abrahim Sheik Mohamed, whom the Puget Sound Joint Terrorism Task Force arrested in February 2005.

Ethiopians here base their claim to the Ogaden on Menelik II's 1887 conquest of that area and Haile Selassie's annexation of it as a lost province in 1948, but Ogadenis see the 1887 conquest as a land grab that was part and parcel of the European scramble for colonies in Africa. The ONLF home page of January 28, 2007, cites as evidence Menelik's letter to the Berlin conference, which states that "Abyssinia [Ethiopia] does not intend to stand idle while Europe partitions Africa" and that Menelik "demands his share, namely the south, stretching into Somalia." After

World War II and the breakup of the Italian colonial empire known as Italian East Africa, Haile Selassie made an impassioned plea for the Ogaden's return to the mother country. The British at first refused and offered instead to return Eritrea on condition that Ethiopia renounce its claims. In 1948 Britain finally transferred to Ethiopia parts of the Ogaden (Jijiga area) but withheld the Haud (northeast) and the Reserve Area (the corridor stretching from the Haud to Djibouti) until 1954, when it restored the whole region to Ethiopia.

"The Ogaden is like no other region in the country," writes Nega Mezlekia, an Amhara, who grew up in a number of different towns in the Ogaden. "There is no settled agriculture here, and only a very few buildings have the kind of foundations that promise longevity. No forests either. The sun's mirage over the horizon, resembling a periphery of ocean, is occasionally punctuated by acacia trees scattered over the landscape."[11]

In 1997 Jamal, a Somalilander, traveled by bus from Addis to Hargeisa along roads built by the Italians. He describes his experience in the Ogaden as like being in a different zone. "You become very conscious of the power of nature in the Ogaden because there is no technology and no amenities, just a vast open space, like virgin territory."

When Ras Makonnen, Haile Selassie's father, governed Harar at the end of the nineteenth century, his forces frequently raided Somali lands in the Ogaden and the Haud. Today, the Ogaden Somalis there "harbor a deep animosity toward the Ethiopians," Jamal tells me. They have never accepted or internalized their subordinate position in Ethiopia and continue to resist the military machine of the Ethiopian government. "They are fighting over land, and it's a fight for survival. It's like, either I live or you live," he says.

When the two former colonies, British Somaliland and Italian Somaliland, merged in 1960 as the Republic of Somalia, Ogaden became the focus of Somali irredentism. Somalia wanted its province back, and numerous clashes took place on the Ethiopian-Somali border between 1963 and 1970. Martial rule kept the peace, but after the Selassie government collapsed and the new Mengistu Haile Mariam regime unleashed the bloodbath known as the Red Terror in 1977, the Siyad Barre government decided it was time to get back the Ogaden for Somalia. Somali guerrillas infiltrated the Ogaden, and a full-scale war broke out between the two countries that same year, in 1977. Critics of the war were exiled to Kenya. With them out of the way, government forces soon took Jijiga but were unable to capture Harar, and in 1978, the Ethiopians, with Cuban and Soviet help, defeated them, thus putting an end to their hopes of achieving a Greater Somalia.

In Somalia's weakened state after its defeat, a group of Majerteen-clan officers tried to stage a coup d'état against Siyad Barre, who belonged to the same clan family as the Ogaden, but they were caught and executed. Barre held the entire Majerteen clan responsible for the betrayal. "My mother was Majerteen," Asia Mohamed says, "and at that time, my father, Mohamed Egal, was called by his uncle to a meeting of these Majerteens, where they said . . . you know, 'Come to our side; we're going to overthrow Siyad Barre.'" She continues:

> But my father had this allegiance to his country, he was a soldier, and he needed to do what he had to do. But Barre ended up finding out about the meeting, and my father was arrested afterward for treason and imprisoned for three years. My mother and I had to flee to Italy. Majerteen people were being executed all around, and every day of those three years, my father would never know whether it would be his last. You know, for three years! So then, my father's uncle, Osman Egal, very wealthy, very educated people, not active politically, were like, "You know, you can't do this, he's not the only person. The lawyers are us, the doctors are us, the pilots are us, this is who we are. You cannot kill our nephew." So my father was pardoned, but he needed to leave Somalia. I could never understand what happened. This entire thing didn't make sense to me as an eight-year-old. I remember my father and my uncles used to talk about Ethiopia with such hate and such animosity, and when I asked what the war was about, they would say, "It's about our land!"

There are still no answers. Abdullahi Yusuf, the Majerteen TFG ex-president, who was then a colonel in the army, managed to escape the executioners by fleeing to Ethiopia. Ironically, he had just returned from fighting the Ethiopian "enemy" in the Ogaden, but he formed a rebel group, the Somali Salvation Front (SSF), later to become the Somali Salvation Democratic Front (SSDF), to fight the military government of

Siyad Barre. He set up his base in Ethiopia. So many young Somalis joined his group that he eventually made his headquarters in a mansion outside Addis. Ayaan Hirsi Ali whose father was one of the SSDF leaders, notes in her 2007 memoir *Infidel*, that other Somalis in the camp saw Abdullahi Yusuf as arrogant. "He picked favorites," she quotes them as saying, "stocking high places only with relatives from his subclan." Almost all the men who were *not* Majerteen, she writes, were leaving because of Abdullahi Yusuf, and those who remained grumbled about him.[12]

Although Ubax's father, Abdullahi Mohamed, known by his nickname Gardheere (Long Chin or Beard), belonged to the same subclan as Abdullahi Yusuf, that didn't stop the colonel from getting into a conflict with him. Gardheere was also a member of the SSDF, but in 1977, he was exiled to Kenya. In 1991 he disappeared. His daughter assumes he is dead.

The café in the Horn of Africa Natural Food Store in Portland serves east Ethiopian food, a lot of it vegetarian, all of it organic. A young man and his date have just finished the main course, and they deliberate whether or not to indulge in dessert, particularly the sweet dumpling drizzled with orange blossom water. The owners mingle with the patrons and make this starkly decorated place look like a family dining room. Two older men at the table next to mine have just washed their hands with rosewater, and we strike up a conversation. They come from Dire Dawa, the new Harar, which they encourage me to visit. Although they don't know who I am, my questions about the old Harar lead them to the Ogaden, and soon we are discussing Ethiopia's relationship to Somalia. As patriots, they choose their words carefully. Their country has often given refuge to Somalis fleeing political persecution, they say, and also aided Somali opposition groups trying to displace their governments. We get into a discussion about various rebel groups, and one of them brings up the Somali National Movement (SNM), the anti-Barre movement formed by Isaq émigrés in London. When Ethiopia gave refuge to them in 1981, one of the men tells me, they had no idea that this would be the beginning of a Somali civil war that would explode out of control. When the SNM launched a military campaign in 1988, capturing the towns of Burao and Hargeisa, Barre's military regime responded with a particularly vicious reprisal, and

300,000 Somalis fled on foot across the border into Ethiopia. It was a time of disarray and bloody violence for the Isaq, and it would begin the first phase of the civil war.

Between 1988 and 1991, Siyad Barre, struggled to hold onto power. So savage were Barre's Red Beret forces and so brutal their treatment of Isaq women and children that the Isaqs realized the only way to insulate themselves from the violence in the rest of Somalia was to cut themselves off and declare an independent Somaliland, which they did in 1991. But other clans, even the Hawiye, whose members filled many of Barre's administrative posts, bore the brunt of his desperation as well. Civilians were massacred on the streets, and torture and murder became the order of the day. Barre, who had started out relatively idealistically, hoping to unite Somalis of all clans under a more egalitarian Marxism, now became hated and feared by all.

"In 1989 we were going to dinner at the president's house," Asia tells me as she adjusts her scarf and checks her text messages. She mentions it casually, as if everyone has dinner with presidents. She accompanied her parents, sister, and little brother. "I remember we used to call Siyad Barre *afwayne*," she tells me, explaining that the term means "big mouth." "I also remember that if you were heard calling him *afwayne*, then you would get shot, so this evening we were supposed to call him *ader*, or 'uncle.' And I was like . . . You know, nobody in our culture took the time to tell you, 'This is what's happening' and 'This is what you're supposed to do.' And I remember this one time, in 1989:

> Both my father and my mother became politically active to recruit the old
> SDF warriors, you know, to go and fight the northerners. So I remember
> this one occasion when they were talking politics, and somehow, we were
> not supposed to pay attention. And my sister, she asked me in Italian,
> "Who is this guy, and why is everyone being nice to him? I mean, look
> at mom and dad." And I'm like, "I don't know." And my little brother,
> the youngest in the family, he looked at us as if we were stupid. And he
> was just three, I swear to God. And he said, "Boy, you're idiots. This
> is the president." And I'm like, "Of which country?" [*Laughs.*] Because
> nobody took the time to tell us and explain. We didn't know this. And
> then he went, like, "Of Somalia." And then my little sister, she said, "This

is *afwayne*?" Suddenly, there was total silence in the room. And then my mother, she said jokingly, "Oh, stop teasing your brother!" And that was the first time I saw my mother lie [*laughs*].

"So, what was Siyad Barre like in person?" I ask Asia. "Do you remember?"

"He was charming, but also mercurial. One moment he was hot, the next cold. You couldn't let your guard down." She describes what happened afterward:

> I remember that after my parents left the meeting, they said, "I don't think he trusted us, he's going to check what we told him," and my mother, who was a very, very smart woman, she was saying to my dad, "Make sure that you remember everything he said." Because there was still this fear that he could come and do something. My father would be like, you know, "Why shouldn't I remember what he said?" She's like, "I know he's going to call you later and he's going to double-check, and then he's going to call me . . ." And then my father said, "Why's he going to call you? You're my wife." "Yes, but I also belong to the most powerful tribe at this point." And my parents actually ended up drifting, divorcing because of this, because there was a lot of money, power, and prestige involved, but it was done in a manner that was separatist, that was hateful, that was murderous.

"Since the collapse of Somalia," I say, "some Somalis think that Siyad Barre was one of the greatest leaders of Somalia."

"I think," Asia responds immediately, "*afwayne* was just a murdering bastard who morally robbed the nation."

Once Barre's government had been brought down in January 1991 and the second phase of the civil war ignited clan warfare in most of the country, Ethiopia disengaged from the rebel groups and from Somalia as a whole. Its borders were shut and defended against all Somalis, no matter what their origin or politics. "The border police came from the army," Mowliid explains. "They were there because the Ethiopians were afraid the civil war would spill over into Ethiopia and affect the Ogaden people. You see, they are Somalis, too, and can revolt against Ethiopia. The Ethiopians have to be on the watch. So they spread their military across the border wherever they think this might cause trouble." He reverts to his own personal story of flight from the Hawiye who saw his Biyomaal clan as collaborators. "We were lucky. We met one or two, but they didn't stop us." He continues:

> Some people weren't so lucky. They escaped from the Somalis, but when they met the Ethiopian army there, the soldiers did whatever they wanted. They raped women, they took everything of value from them . . . You see, we are of the same culture, so they know that our women should have a lot of gold on them. So they make you get down from the car and they strip-search you. Luckily, we weren't subjected to that. We personally didn't experience any trouble within Ethiopia.

The Ogaden National Liberation Front, however, did. At first, when the new Tigray-dominated government took control of Ethiopia, it seemed to the Ogaden Somalis that the Ethiopian People's Revolutionary Democratic Front at least acknowledged the colonial nature of the country by granting the various groups the right to self-determination through peaceful processes. But the honeymoon period was short-lived. The EPRDF divided the land into ethnically based administrative areas and maintained them like a colonial empire. Making use of a divide-and-rule strategy, it created "pseudo-organizations based on clan lines" and at the same time "spread its intelligence network and military garrisons" all over the Ogaden.[13]

When the EPRDF demanded that the Ogaden Somalis endorse a compulsory constitution that would have legalized their colonization by Ethiopia, they refused. It then disbanded the Ogaden region's parliament, arrested many of the politicians, and launched military offensives against ONLF positions until all resistance movements in the Ogaden were believed destroyed and a new surrogate party, the Ethiopian Somali Democratic League (ESDL), was established. The ONLF refused to participate in what it saw as phony elections, went into exile, and began conducting guerrilla campaigns instead.

Ethiopia accuses Somalia of supporting the ONLF as well as the Oromo Liberation Front (discussed in chapter 6), which seeks the Oromo people's independence from the EPRDF. "The Ethiopians just have an ingrained attitude against Somalis," Mowliid insists. "They have that hateful attitude because of the wars they fought with us." Suspicion characterizes both populations, and nobody wants to find himself on the wrong side of his country's border.

Whether borders were open or closed, while chaos reigned in Somalia, the country was helpless to stop the 1998–2000 Ethiopian-Eritrean border war from impinging on its own affairs. Refugees fled across borders in search of safety and employment, or simply to escape conscription into the warring armies. "Young Eritreans fleeing conscription turned up in Ethiopia," Ezra Teshome remembers, "and young Ethiopian men in Somalia." In Ethiopia's Region 5, the Somali region, the ONLF required the household of each Somali to "donate" an animal to the war effort. Those who could not afford to do so were obliged to send a son to the military. Needless to say, many young men fled to Somaliland or elsewhere in Somalia, for want of a goat.

Ethiopia and Eritrea conducted a proxy war in Somalia and tried to manipulate affairs to their own benefit. They actively participated in Somali politics by supplying weapons to the warring parties, each to opposing coalitions. Ethiopia had an incentive for doing so because involvement in Somali affairs helped it contain conflicts in its own Somali area in the Ogaden. Eritrea, in contrast, had no obvious strategic purpose in meddling in Somali business other than simply to cause trouble for Ethiopia in that part of its territory.

POSTWAR BANISHMENT AND RESETTLEMENT

The aftermath of wars sometimes provides the worst examples of persecution. When decency and humanity should prevail, power struggles and revenge for lives lost often lead to acts of unnecessary cruelty that become underlying sources of anger among the Horn diaspora communities. Soon after its successful march into Asmara in May 1991, the Eritrean People's Liberation Front established border posts and began expelling non-Eritreans who held sensitive positions in the administration. Within a few months, it was banishing resident Ethiopians, too. The Ethiopians, according to Harold Marcus, treated the Eritreans in Ethiopia leniently.[14]

The greater tragedy of Ethiopian-Eritrean expulsions, however, came during the struggle over the disputed territories, when more than 500,000 small farmers and nomads on both sides of the contested borders were displaced, 50,000 others were deported from Ethiopia to Eritrea, and 20,000 were sent in the other direction.[15] The Badme war, said to be the most devastating conflict ever staged between two armies in Africa, created a level of hatred, Michela Wrong writes, that was "unparalleled even during the Struggle, which found particularly mean-spirited expression." After June 1998, the Ethiopian government started expelling all Ethiopians with an Eritrean parent, even those who carried Ethiopian passports and considered themselves loyal to Ethiopia. Many of those expelled didn't even speak any Eritrean languages and were themselves married to Ethiopians and had Ethiopian children. "There was something of a spurned lover's fury behind the mass deportation," Wrong writes, as if they were saying, "You want independence? Here, take it, and get out."[16]

"I have cousins on my mother's side who got kicked out of Ethiopia because they couldn't prove their Ethiopian identity," David Makonnen tells me. His father is Tigrayan, and his mother Tigrayan-Eritrean. "And then, my uncles . . . some of my uncles were deported from Ethiopia because they carried an Eritrean ID card. . . ." He turns to me and asks, "What does the territorial boundary mean in this context?" His maternal grandparents' family migrated from Tigray and settled in Eritrea at the end of the nineteenth century. They owned a farm and city land there, and all of his uncles and aunts were born and raised in Eritrea. "My paternal grandfather is from Axum, my maternal grandfather from Gonder, Amhara. They both migrated to Eritrea over a hundred years ago. My grandparents met and married in Asmara. And all my uncles and aunts on my dad's side were also born and raised in Asmara." He looks at me as if to say, "So what's their identity? Eritrean? Ethiopian?"

Prime Minister Meles Zenawi claimed the expulsions were a security measure, but because Ethiopians and Eritreans had been intermarrying for years, many considered the expulsions violations of human rights. He also rid the bureaucracy of any Eritreans who held sensitive or high positions and deported those considered security risks, for example, anyone who had sent money to the Asmara government, held an Eritrean identity card, or voted for Eritrean independence. Marcus puts the number of those "forcibly" deported from Ethiopia at fifty thousand; Jacquin-Berdal and Plaut say seventy-five thousand were deported "without due process of law."[17] The deportees were often rounded up in the dead of night, jammed into buses without adequate water or food, and unceremoniously dumped at the frontier. Marcus notes they were not allowed to settle their affairs before leaving, and after they had gone, their property and goods were confiscated, sold, or auctioned off, supposedly to pay alleged tax arrears and bank loans. Their travel papers, Plaut writes, were stamped "Expelled, never to return."[18] Many of the first to be rounded up were the elite, who were educated and wealthy but now dependent on whatever money they might have accumulated outside of Ethiopia. Rural deportees were deprived of their homes and belongings, and their cattle were confiscated.

I express my dismay to David Makonnen at the unfairness of it all. Knowing that the expulsions affected his family, I expect him to feel similarly. Instead, he starts to explain the situation, trying to show me the logic in the government's actions:

> The Ethiopian government hadn't anticipated the Eritreans stabbing them in the back. So they had to take immediate action to break the Eritrean network that they thought that government had built in Ethiopia. Everybody was shocked by the social impact, and something that a lot of people don't know is that many Ethiopians hid Eritreans and saved them from being deported. You see, the government also had a legitimacy problem of their own. They said many Ethiopians felt the Tigrayan and Eritrean governments had a partnership and were making secret deals. Even before the war, when people were asking about their association, the Ethiopian and Eritrean governments' stories were always, "Oh, we're building a long-term partnership and the border will eventually disappear. We can't really talk about the details right now." And then, all of a sudden, when they found themselves in a war, Ethiopians felt a huge resentment toward their government. They said, "You must have made such a bad deal that your strategic partner is coming and making all these claims and taking land from your country. So what else is there that you are not telling us, what other deals have you made in secret?" So there was all this animosity building up everywhere, and they were concerned about the potential for

internal chaos. A lot of people tried to take advantage of the situation and settle scores with their next-door neighbor by laying accusations and saying, "Oh, he's Eritrean . . . he did this and that." And when the government officials tried to follow the rule of law and said, "Let's find out what really happened," people would then say, "You must be one of them. Why are you putting up all these barriers when I'm telling you the truth?" So they were caught in between trying to contain the political animosity and at the same time moving as quickly as things were developing. And they made a lot of mistakes. A lot of innocent people were caught. The objective was to break the network and contain the potential danger, but in doing so, the people-to-people relationship between the two countries was damaged.

The Eritreans, for their part, claim to have been merciful to the Ethiopian deportees. At the beginning of the conflict particularly, they took care not to blame Ethiopian residents for the war. But as the war heated up, Ethiopians increasingly became the targets of hostility, so the government initiated a program of internment and began preparing them for repatriation.

Unlike the thirty-year war, the new war seemed to be a personal battle between the Eritrean People's Liberation Front and the Tigray People's Liberation Front, in particular, between the two presidents. The war pitted brother against brother, two people with the same language, ethnic origin, and religion, and they fought with a fury that only family can understand. As I write this, I have a picture in my mind of President Isaias (I have not met Meles Zenawi), and I try to imagine the Eritrean man's fury. Although our meeting with him in Asmara in 2001 could not have been longer than forty minutes, my first impression of him was one of humility. He wore the trademark *tegadelti* sandals with his light khaki suit, and, unlike most people in power, he listened carefully to our delegation rather than dominating the session with his own presidential voice. When he did speak afterward, he was brief and to the point, responding to our ideas and asking pertinent questions before assigning us to others in his administration with whom we could follow up. Remembering the scene, I recall thinking at the time that he was particularly tightly controlled. He sat stiffly upright in his chair and folded his hands in his lap. Below his black mustache, his lips never wavered or broke into a smile that could show us a glimpse of the person behind the impassive face.

Whatever my thoughts about President Isaias, Ethiopians in Seattle and Portland say that Eritrea acted with a great deal of cruelty. While both countries generally tried to uphold humanitarian ideals in their treatment of prisoners of war, Plaut writes that according to the Eritrea-Ethiopia Claims Commission, Eritrea's behavior was considerably worse. Captives on both sides complained of intolerable camp conditions and being deprived of their shoes so that they had to walk miles over rough terrain barefoot, but Eritrea "sometimes inflicted brutal beatings and even killed Ethiopian prisoners," both at the front and during evacuation. In the end, Eritrea took 1,100 Ethiopians prisoner and Ethiopia 2,600 Eritreans.[19]

"I really am impressed by the fact that the Ethiopian government acknowledged its mistakes and was willing to move beyond them," David says. "In my limited experience of Ethiopian history, there is not any government prior to this that has come up and said, 'Look, I made a mistake, I screwed up.' Because when you say that, you are giving up the right to ask for forgiveness again. But at least there's some clearing for people to say how they feel and move forward," he explains, adding, "I haven't seen a similar willingness to be candid from the Eritreans."

As for Somalia's displaced peoples, the situation stretches the full spectrum from dire to desperate. Without a functioning state, it is every man for himself as clans take vengeance on one another for deeds carried out during Barre's long rule. The Bantu agriculturalists from the Juba river and Shabelle river valleys suffer perhaps the worst, as they do not have the clan protection afforded others and their fertile lands attract the militias of warlords who prosper from the chaos. Refugee camps for internally displaced people set up by the United Nations High Commissioner for Refugees as well as Islamic welfare associations, like Al-Ihsan, proliferate throughout the country but still are not enough to cope with the numbers needing assistance. Thus the internal camps overflow. In desperation, Somalis flee across the border to Kenya's Dadaab camp, now the largest refugee site in the world. Refugees International reported on its Web site that, as of April 2009, 1.8 million Somalis remain displaced within the country and throughout the region.

Although the UNHCR and various other refugee services do their best to feed and shelter the needy, the weak remain ultimately at the mercy of the hyenas with guns. Particularly vulnerable are the women, who, having lost husbands and fathers, come to the camps alone. On pages 151–58 of her book *Infidel*, Ayaan Hirsi Ali describes the scene at Dhobley, called the "Muddy Place," on the Kenyan border about a hundred miles into the desert, where desperate Somalis and their children squat under thorn trees, waiting for help. Somali women from minor subclans and lacking protectors are snatched by soldiers under cover of dark and raped. After having been shamed in this way, they are then abandoned by their communities. Hirsi Ali describes one such young woman:

> Her face was swollen and covered in dried blood, her clothes were torn, there were marks all over her legs. She was shaking uncontrollably.
> I touched her hand and asked if I could help her but she didn't talk. All she could say was *Ya'Allah, Ya'Allah*, "Allah have mercy on me."
>
> I went to get her more water, and all the people nearby told me, "You shouldn't be seen with that woman. She is impure. People will say you're the same." All I could see was a human being who had been abused, who was on the verge of death, but to them, she was an outcast.[20]

FIVE

CULTURAL AND ECONOMIC RIVALS

Yesterday's enemies are today's friends.

—MOHAMED OMER, SEATTLE, 2005

WHILE THE desire for the right to one's own land fueled both the Ethiopian-Eritrean and Ethiopian-Somali wars, it is not the sole cause of arguments among members of the three communities in the Pacific Northwest. Other issues most certainly also played a role, since territorial integrity in the form of secession, independence, or irredentism cannot easily be separated from other divisive matters. Class, clan, and religion, as well as economic power, all have a nasty way of interfering with who owns what and add their own challenges to the discord that riles Eritreans, Somalis, and Ethiopians here. As with territorial integrity, these issues, too, turn in part on the definition of identity.

CLASS FACTORS

On the sidewalk just outside a coffee bar on South Jackson in Seattle, I talk to a group of Somali men who have gathered for a smoke. They are young men whose crisp, starched shirts and ironed trousers with knife-edge creases distinguish them from other men in the area who dress in sweats or jeans. As we talk, a whiff of strong cologne mingles with the cigarette smoke and adds its own pungent note to the aroma of coffee. One of the men is chewing something, and I immediately assume it is khat, a mild stimulant leaf with a caffeine-like kick.

"No, no, no. Only the old men chew khat and only in the home." He is amused by my assumption and adds, "Anyhow, now they don't even do that."

"Not since the crackdown in 2006," says another, referring to Operation Somalia Express, when the Drug Enforcement Administration conducted raids all over the country in search of khat smugglers. In Seattle, nineteen men were indicted, although charges against fifteen were later dismissed. "Khat is illegal here." He twirls his keys on his finger.

"Now we just eat gum," the first one explains. "Like Americans."

The men are talkative, especially since few Americans ever ask them about their country. Nevertheless, they weigh their words carefully and do not say anything rash. But like young men everywhere, they are competitive, and when the conversation eventually turns to the causes of the mess in Somalia, the key-twirling Somali, who appears to be the oldest of the three, says, "It's all about land."

The first Somali jumps in and contradicts him. "It's all about money and power."

"The two are connected," I say.

"But some clans think they deserve it all because they are better than others," says the third Somali, jutting out his chin. "They think they are superior." He is the youngest in the group and looks not much more than a teenager. When I ask him to clarify what he means, he withdraws and changes the subject. Nobody answers me, and the question remains hanging.

Class is not something that most Somalis care to talk about. Nor do Eritreans or Ethiopians. But as the United States slowly discovers in its war on terrorism, beyond the desire for the material rewards of land, jobs, and security lies a greater psychological need, namely, a hunger for dignity and respect. This yearning for acknowledgment by those who have been demeaned aggravates the relationships among ethnic groups in each of the three countries. Even among countries, class resentments bubble. Though not explicitly expressed, their presence, communicated through subtle looks and gestures, can cool the room in seconds.

The relationship between Ethiopians and Eritreans, for example, balances precariously on issues of class, many of which carry over to the Pacific Northwest. Italian colonization of Eritrea (1881–1941) helped develop that country on a Western scale, and many Eritreans were imbued with a sense of their own sophistication. Italian architects created in Asmara a Modernist city that boasted daringly designed buildings, wide boulevards, and sidewalk cafés that forever after changed the way Eritreans perceived urban life in the highlands. Asmara became known as Little Roma. Technological developments, too, such as the narrow-gauge railway line running from the highlands down to Massawa on the coast, added to this modern urban setting. The Italians were fascinated by machines during the Modernist period, as was the rest of Europe, and factories and communications networks popped up all over the country. More than three hundred small workshops and industries dotted the areas around Asmara and the two ports, and such developments became part and parcel of the Eritrean landscape. Eritreans who had moved to the city adapted to this new life and took it as the norm. "The first thing my mother did when the Italians left," Abraha tells me, "was to dress up on Saturday afternoon and stroll down the boulevard like a real person. And then, when she was done," he smiles with satisfaction, "she sat at one of the small sidewalk cafés and asked the waiter to bring her an espresso."

When Emperor Haile Selassie annexed Eritrea in 1962 and Eritreans took jobs in Addis Ababa, they were astounded by the difference in lifestyles. To the Eritreans, Addis Ababa seemed like a huge village and the rural people uncivilized. "What the Eritreans saw in Ethiopia," David Makonnen explains, "were uneducated farmers who ate with their hands." Not surprisingly, they couldn't accept living under the yoke of the Ethiopians when, from their perspective, David says, "the colonizer was less developed than the colonized." He explains that many Eritreans identified totally with Italians and frequently mixed Italian words into their Tigrinya "as a symbol of their sophistication." Ethiopians, in turn, saw the Eritreans as "arrogant and pretentious."

In 1955 Eritrean hero Woldeab Woldemariam, broadcasting on Radio Cairo from exile in Egypt, played on these class sentiments. Using corn as a metaphor for the Eritrean people, he said during one late afternoon broadcast: "Corn grows a beard [silk] like an adult, and, like a child, it is carried away on [people's] backs." The words were understood by his compatriots, in wax-and-gold fashion, Alemseged Abbay suggests, as saying that "advanced" Eritrea had fallen under the rule of "backward" Ethiopia.[1]

For Ethiopian Tigrayans, brothers of the Tigrinya, the situation appeared even worse. Though the Tigray People's Liberation Front and Eritrean People's Liberation Front had fought side by side on the battlefield, undercurrents of class swirled beneath the surface of their relationship. The EPLF's longer experience of warfare led it to treat TPLF members as apprentices and to regard them, Harold Marcus writes, "as parochial country bumpkins and narrow nationalists, more interested in military struggle than the correct political ideology." He points out that Italian propaganda helped create the arrogance of the Tigrinya by asserting that they were "smarter, more moral and better disciplined" than their brothers south of the Mereb. He writes that the elite and even the Eritrean students at Haile Selassie I University stressed their superiority, claiming to speak a "purer and more original" form of the language than that spoken on the other side of the river. They showed contempt for the Tigrayans and made crude and tasteless jokes about them.[2] Such attitudes of superiority led to the demeaning of the Tigrayans, who held the low-paying, low-status jobs in Eritrea, such as laborers and domestic servants.

Alemseged Abbay denies the supposed sophistication of the general Eritrean population, suggesting that they developed a mythical perception of a superior way of life during the Italian occupation. In fact, they could *not* sit in the cafés, walk on the sidewalks, or live in the Italian residential areas and were mostly excluded from the main economy, which was handled by Arabs (Lebanese and Yemenis), Indians, and Pakistanis. Only "an insignificant section of the population, mostly in Asmara, would pass for being 'modernized,'" he argues.[3] Whatever the actual situation with the Eritreans at the time, the Tigray Ethiopians perceived themselves as disrespected and felt slighted by the haughty Eritreans. The latter's rejection of their common ancestry did not help matters either. And when the Eritreans also denied their common heroes and chose to create a brand-new history for themselves, the relationship deteriorated further.

Among both Eritreans and Ethiopians, class differences between rural and urban populations have been transposed to transnational communities in the Pacific Northwest. In addition, since those from Addis Ababa and Asmara were among the early immigrants who came to the States to further their education, their longer involvement with American culture has created even more distance between them and rural arrivals with little experience of the outside world and its functioning. "Class is not discussed much in the open," says Haddis, speaking of the situation among Ethiopians, "but it is very much there and applies mostly to those of us who come from the city. There's a tendency among people from the city, mostly Addis, to look down on people who come from the rural areas. And even in the city itself, class differences among those who have and those who have not is very visible."

In Seattle, middle-class Ethiopians, Eritreans, and Somalis now socialize more with American neighbors than with their less educated or less wealthy compatriots. Local movie theaters and tennis courts thus become their milieus, and for their kids, it's private schools. Marxism in the home countries, it seems, did not translate into classless societies despite attempts by both governments to level the playing field for all.

In Somalia, too, Scientific Socialism should have eliminated class differences and brought agricultural and manual workers into parity with the northern nomads and the city's businessmen, but it never happened. That's why, in Seattle and Portland, the pecking order continues to follow the old descending hierarchy of Darod, Isaq, Hawiye, Digil-Rohanweyn, Bantu, and outcasts.

The subtleties in the class-to-clan relationship in Somalia leave the outsider bewildered. Status among the different subclans and sub-subclans is even more complicated, as positions sometimes fluctuate depending on who wants what from whom. The nomadic Darod and Isaq of the north, who claim Semitic lineage through their Arab forebears, consider their pastoral, poetic culture more sophisticated than the mostly rural culture of the south, and Somalilanders, for example, claim to dominate the professions and the media and also to have taught the southerners the proper use of the Somali language. Thus the two clans consider themselves *landeer* or *bilis* (noble), nobler than the Hawiye, who are mostly small-scale traders and shopkeepers.

"Among Somalis, there are some big-time prejudices!" Abdihakim confirms. He himself is a Dhulbahante from the north, a member of the larger Darod clan family and therefore a *Samale*. To some *Samale* even today, agricultural and manual labor of any kind signifies as base work fitted only for lesser humans; thus they discriminate against the farmers and skilled workers whom they perceive as *langaab* (inferior). "They discriminate against people like shoemakers, haircutters, and metalworkers because of what they do, their jobs," Abdihakim points out, explaining that "there are specific tribes who do that. We call them Midgan and Tumal. 'Tumal' means 'smith,' like blacksmith, for example. They are the outcast groups, and we don't intermarry with them." The divisions remain because the northerners perpetuated this structure, which works to their advantage.

Colonization not only accentuated clan differences with its divide-and-rule ideology but also exacerbated class differences, particularly between urban and rural Somalis. When northern Somalia became a protectorate of the British Crown, the mostly urban middle class in British Somaliland gained a great deal of power. The colonial government, which was in the game for profit, encouraged Somali business operations in the towns and conferred middle-class status on those townsmen who owned property and paid taxes. Not surprisingly then, when the British left Somalia, the middle-class Somali businessmen, teachers, interpreters, truck drivers, and clerks took over the state. In addition, since the British had also given the clans communal identities so that they had legal and political authority over the individual, some of these businessmen who were traders in livestock were able to use clan kinship ties to set themselves up in business. But while the merchants in town grew wealthy, the nomads in the rural areas did not.[4] The traditional pastoralists saw their own status diminishing as the urban economy intersected with the rural. Townspeople took control, for instance, of the granting of licenses, tolls, and dues associated with livestock sales and land use, and in order to survive, clans had to vie with one another for control of resources. Thus did colonial privileges fan clan as well as class rivalry.

CLAN COMPETITION

At the Masjid Al-Taqwa on East Union Street in Seattle, Somali taxi drivers turn up at noon to say their daily prayers. Their cars used to carry religious leaflets and other objects that reflected their religious identity, such as Qur'anic verses or the Fatiha, but since 9/11, they carry only their prayer mats. They open their car trunks and slip their mats under their arms before entering the *masjid*, which is housed in a dilapidated wooden building on the south side of the road. Afterward, at Fatima's Café next door, the drivers bite into *sambusas*, the Somali version of samosas, or one of the café's spicy goat dishes before hitting the road once again. For many Somalis arriving in Seattle for the first time, taxi drivers perform a valuable service beyond driving, in that they direct them to Somali centers, restaurants, and stores, where they can feel safe and at one with their own. As newcomers, they still carry the divisions from home and do not want to find themselves overstepping invisible boundaries.

When Siyad Barre came to power in 1969, he promised to stamp out clan divisions and clan loyalties, which he perceived as archaic. So he encouraged the building of allegiance to a nation-state that would protect all of its peoples irrespective of clan. To many Somalis, nervous about losing the security blanket of their clan identities, the possibility of being brought into the modern world was appealing, and when in 1971 Barre directed a public spectacle in which effigies of the various clans were ritually burned, many perceived the act as discarding outdated structures that were holding the country back from competing internationally.

After Somalia's failure to win back the Ogaden in the 1977–78 war with Ethiopia, however, disillusion with the regime grew. Ordinary Somalis resented the National Security Service's heavy-handed enforcement of clan- and ethnic-free participation in the economic, political, and cultural life of Somalia. As the president's opponents multiplied, he abandoned his ideological aspirations for a society of equals and by 1980 ran the country with a select group drawn from the clans of his father (Marehan), mother (Ogaden), and son-in-law (Dhulbahante). These were the clans he also favored in distributing the state's resources.

Not surprisingly, members of the Majerteen and Isaq clans harbored resentment. Majerteen attempts to oust Siyad Barre failed, and bloody violence followed. When the Isaq also organized, with many young fighters joining the Somali National Movement at its base in Ethiopia, Barre's government tried to control the population through fear and intimidation. The clan had already seen violence at the hands of his forces after the Ethiopian-Somali war, when he settled almost half the Darod Somalis fleeing the Ogaden in Isaq-dominated areas. This time, he introduced the Mobile Military Court, which some Isaqs characterize as "Guilty or innocent, you will be found guilty," a Regional Security Council responsible for mass arrests, and the Hangash, a secret police unit that maintained surveillance and kept Isaqs in fear of their lives.

In the countryside, the situation was equally bad. The Isaq Exterminators, responsible for dealing with the Isaq nomads whom the government perceived as a fifth column for the SNM, confiscated the Isaq's cattle, taxed them double, and raped the women. But perhaps the most damaging and divisive of Barre's organs of control was the *tabeleh* system that designated a leader (*tabeleh*) to oversee twenty households and keep tabs on the movements of each member of every household. In this way, Barre forced neighbors to spy on neighbors, thus creating social and psychological divisions that prevented the Isaq from regrouping.[5]

In Portland, some of the older Somalis remember those years of *tabeleh* well, but circumspection rules what they say. So when they meet at the Hashi Halal Market on Killingsworth or at the Somali Community Service Coalition of Oregon's community center on Barbur, their conversation focuses on the future. They do not dwell on the past; they have enough problems just trying to adjust to life in their new country. Still, they haven't forgotten. It was the psychological intimidation, they say, together with the violence against students plus the economic war against the nomads, who were the backbone of the SNM, that brought things to a head. When the SNM attacked and captured the city of Burao and part of the port of Hargeisa in 1988, the Darod regime responded with its own violence, bombing the towns and sending more than 300,000 Isaqs fleeing to Ethiopia. The regime incited the Darod population to violence by telling them that the Isaqs planned to take over the whole country and destroy them. In retaliation, soldiers in Hargeisa robbed, looted, and killed, and SNM sympathizers were arrested en masse. Other towns followed one after the other. Even in Mogadishu, Isaqs were separated from non-Isaqs and detained.

That year, 1988, was a "year of negation," Jamal says. From Seattle, he followed the news, in utter shock at the tragic dimensions of Barre's massacre and at the United States' continuing support of the regime.

When Africa Watch called for an investigation, Assistant Secretary of State Chester Crocker rebuked the organization, saying it was better to trust that government to protect U.S. interests than to rely on a government of uncertain identity and character that might replace it.[6] The indifference of the world so amazed Jamal that he sat down and penned a poem, "The Year of Death," in the hope of bringing the destruction of his people to public attention. The poem makes clear, however, that despite the unleashing of "an orgy of bones and blood" and the digging of "a common grave as big as the sun," the world remained silent.[7] The fighting continued into 1990, until finally, in August, the SNM joined forces with the United Somali Congress and the Somali Patriotic Movement. Together, they attacked Barre's men in Mogadishu on December 3, 1990, and drove the dictator out of the city on January 26, 1991.

Barre's will to ensure his own position of power turned all the other clans against the Isaq, but more than that, in using clan rivalry and corruption to achieve it, he set the scene for the bloody conflagration that exploded in Mogadishu in 1991–92. Clans of the Hawiye clan family, the Abgal under Ali Mahdi, and the Habr Gidir under General Aideed struggled violently to establish their own empires and threw the entire area into chaos, resulting in widespread famine and the flight of thousands to refugee camps in Kenya.

With the fighting focused in the south, though, the north was able to recuperate and proceed in relative peace. Clan elders (*guurti*) helped midwife the peace, and on May 18, 1991, the former British Somaliland protectorate seceded from the rest of Somalia and became the Somaliland Republic. Although clan violence also flared in the north, Somalis in Somaliland were able to weather the strife.

When I ask Mowliid whether, given this bloody history, Somaliland will ever become part of Somalia, he laughs, as if I'm asking a ridiculous question, and then shakes his head with slow determination, "Over our dead body! No more! No more! No more Somalia!" He goes on to explain how Isaqs learned their lesson when, as an independent republic in 1960, they led the move to bring the whole area under one flag, including the Ogaden, the northern part of Kenya, and Djibouti. The gross injustices that the south meted out to them dispelled their illusions, but it was the state of Djibouti, he says, that "actually hit the nail in the coffin."

When they got independence, they said, "Let go our legs; we'll stand on our own." That is what cured Somaliland. Somaliland lost thousands of lives at that time. There were some Somalis who were saying, "We are coming, Djibouti, we don't know how long it will be, but we will come." And so we Somalilanders went into battle, and the others, they didn't come! We were alone. So that was the time our aspiration for a Greater Somalia died. It died in us.

"But I know there are Somalilanders in the TFG who support a national government," I say to him.

"We see them as traitors," Mowliid responds, "not as Somalilanders." He expounds further, hitting the table between us, "And they cannot, cannot, set foot on Somaliland soil. Never!"

When I ask Jamal about Somalilanders in the Transitional Federal Government, he replies diplomatically. "From their perspective, they think Somalilanders are on the wrong track and that history is going to prove them right and that what they're doing is in the best interests of Somaliland." Still, Jamal is part of a systematic national effort aimed at gaining international recognition for Somaliland as a separate country. The Somaliland Recognition Task Force facilitates discussions and conducts promotional activities to convince the world that there is a de facto state of Somaliland, which, unlike the rest of Somalia, has an elected government, a constitution, and a relatively peaceful and democratic society.

"I don't buy that whole package of independence rhetoric," Koshin says to me of Somaliland. He is Majerteen, and his voice drips skepticism.

I had the opportunity to meet with the chief spokesperson of the government in Nairobi, and he's from Somaliland, and I talked to the current foreign minister of the government—he's from Somaliland as well—and they both come from the prominent tribe, from a subclan. What I sensed from them is that all this rhetoric about independence, la . . . la . . . la . . . la. It isn't anything except hype. It's just hype. Because there is no central government, and it's not clear what clan owns the country. What matters more is that our Somali forefathers all fought side by side getting rid of this border. They wanted a Greater Somalia. We don't want to have less than what we have right now. When Mogadishu is in the hands of the government and they return Muslims to their houses, the whole thing is just going to evaporate. Nobody is going to want to be in Berbera when they can be in Mogadishu! [*Chuckles.*] Or Afgoi! Think of the climate! The place is hor-rible! It's hot! Nobody wants to be there, you know, especially when they have houses and apartments in the south. Those places are there because there is petroleum and natural resources. After unification, once we decompress—that's a word I like to use—there'll be no reason to fight over anything. That community will move in. And we will have one single voting system. After a year or two, people will realize, "Oh, Hadraawi," he was a pretty famous poet from Somaliland, but Somalia will embrace the Hargeisa poet as their own. So that's what we're thinking. The guy who is the president [of Somaliland] right now [H. E. Dahir Rayale Kahin], he is not a credible guy. He was a remnant of Siyad Barre. Nobody expects him . . . No, this whole thing will disintegrate on its own.

"But what if Somalilanders decide differently and really don't want to join the rest of the country?" I ask Koshin. "Are you going to use force?"

"Why would we have to use force when people are ready to join it?" he responds. "The ones who created the hype about the Somaliland thing, they are not credible people. Back at the time when there was a crisis, there were people who took advantage of them and they were telling them, 'Oh, we're protecting you, we're gonna have our own country, we don't want to . . .' No, no," he insists, "we will empower the right people."

By the time Siyad Barre fled to his seaside bunker near the airport and from there to Kenya and then Nigeria, his secret policies of divide and rule had turned clan against clan, even blood against blood. "People see Barre in different lights," Mohammed says, trying to explain Barre's role in the destruction of the country. "Some just won't admit the mess he made because clan lines, you see, are pretty strong, and many people jokingly forgive him. They say, 'At least it was a country then.' That's what they choose to believe. Others, of course, blame him for the loss of lives and livelihood."

In Seattle and Portland today, talk of "us" by Somali refugees inevitably refers to a narrowly defined clan group or, at most, members of the larger clan family. Nuruddin Farah calls such diaspora discussions "post-colonial realpolitik governed by the anachronistic sentiments of clannism."[8] Certainly, the actual experience on the ground here points in that direction despite efforts by many to break out of the mold that keeps them rigidly confined. Even as most Somalis I interview try to impress on me their aversion to clan rivalry, few actually mix socially outside of their clan group or cooperate in the work environment. Still, they bemoan the clannishness of others, particularly those elderly "sitting warriors" who reinforce one another's anger at past transgressions. "They are so narcissistic they think they're the only clan who are good and the rest are wrong," Ubax complains. "We need a tribal-blind people," Koshin pleads.

RELIGION

A visitor to Seattle and Portland, noting the number of mosques, Coptic Christian churches, and Oromo churches, might easily assume that Ethiopians, Eritreans, and Somalis are communities of long standing in the Pacific Northwest. At the Eritrean church on Seattle's Spruce Street, the sound of hymns sung in Ge'ez drifts gently out the windows, while inside, an electric Jesus with an LED halo radiates love over the white-robed women and the men in their best Sunday suits. In northeast Portland, at the corner of Skidmore Street and Martin Luther King Jr. Boulevard, pretty little Oromo girls, their hair braided with bright yellow ribbons, race out of the Oromo Evangelical Church at the end of services to play tag in the fenced yard outside.

When I talk to the members of the three communities in Seattle and Portland, many confirm the importance of their religion to them and especially to their sense of unity as communities. Whether Coptic Christians, Muslims, Catholics, or evangelicals, they find in their religions a source of deep spiritual comfort as well as a shared focus that draws them together. Furthermore, they say, their religions open paths into the larger community, in that their American coreligionists include them in the familiar rituals and make them feel at home. Before the Ethiopians built their own Ethiopian Coptic church, for example, the Greek Orthodox church brought them into the fold. "I was married in St. Demetrios Church on Boyer," Ezra informs me, "and my kids got baptized in that same church." The evangelical churches, too, opened their doors to the faithful from the Horn as well as to the potential converts they brought with them. These religions eased the way for newcomers who were transitioning into their host culture.

Generally speaking, the Amhara, Tigray, and Tigrinya practice Orthodox Coptic Christianity, while the Somali and Ogadeni adhere to Islam. The Oromo do not fit neatly into this ethnic-religious division, nor do the Bilen, who can be either Christian or Muslim. Some Tigrinya Muslims known as Jiberti also exist. By and large, however, direct ties link ethnicity and religion; thus, whenever events in the home countries take a turn for the worse, these ethnic and religious identities segue into each other. The politics of ethnicity lies just below the surface, and it entraps many of the new Seattleites and Portlanders from the Horn in ghostly webs from the past.

Local Religious-Political Schisms

"Ethiopia, Eritrea, and Somalia are all very religious countries," David Makonnen affirms. "Inside each country, faith not only unites them; they seldom think about a worshipper's ethnic heritage. But here . . ." he shakes his head, looking almost embarrassed to have to admit what he sees. In Seattle and Portland, the Coptic Christians who represent the largest religious group among the Ethiopians and Eritreans have split, with the result that each city now has more than one Orthodox Christian church. "Ethiopians don't go to church if some in the congregation are Eritreans or vice versa," he explains. "It's really sad. That's one of the reasons why a second Ethiopian church was built in Seattle. It came about because not even Ethiopians get along in sharing a place of worship. Now there's a 'Tigrayan' and an 'Amhara' church, with distinctions based on the cultural heritage of the priests, not their teachings."

At St. Gebriel Ethiopian Orthodox Tewahedo Cathedral, I sit in the vestibule, facing the Holy of Holies inside the church. I wait to meet Ezra, who has agreed to show me around. Incense wafts around me, and large, black, stylized Ethiopian eyes look down at me from the surrounding paintings that depict vivid biblical scenes. Throughout this weekday morning, worshippers drop by to communicate with their God. While a father kneels before the Holy of Holies and touches his head to the step, his children run in and out of the pews clad in Spiderman costumes, happily at home in this place of worship where the archangel Gebriel protects them.

Ezra speaks proudly of the church, which he was instrumental in getting erected back in 1999. "We built the church without owing anyone any money. Everyone in the community contributed." Ezra is State Farm Insurance's superintendent of claims for Washington State, his office prominently situated in the Capitol Hill neighborhood. A modest man, he has done well for himself and for his people. "The church was such a great, great project," he enthuses. "Everyone was involved, not only Christian Ethiopians, but even other non-Christians who were Ethiopians, like the Muslims." The project came about after the Tigray-dominated government assumed power in Addis in 1991 and the Patriarch and his assistant felt pressure to resign. When the assistant fled to Kenya, the Seattle Amhara community recruited him to be their religious leader here in the Pacific Northwest. Ethiopia appointed a new Patriarch, Abune Paulos, a Tigrayan, but when he visited the United States in late 1993, he was physically harassed by Amhara dissidents.[9] "People here associated him with the ruling government and its idea of creating divisions instead of unity," Ezra explains.

Today, despite St. Gebriel's public aspiration to welcome people of all ethnicities to its services, it also toes the ethnic line. Amhara dominate St. Gebriel, while Emmanuel Ethiopian Orthodox Tewahedo, the second church, is mostly Tigrayan, following the head person in Ethiopia. The third church, St. Michael's Ethiopian Orthodox, serves people who are not happy in either.

The Eritrean community also supports two different Orthodox churches in Seattle. At the root of the conflict is a similar politico-religious difference represented in the person of the priest, an Eritrean government–appointed representative. One church, the Eritrean Kidisti Selassie Orthodox Tewahedo, is located in North Seattle; the other, Debre Genet Kidisti Sellassie Orthodox, is in the Central District. While those Eritreans I interviewed hesitated to go on record, it appears that some members of the latter congregation rejected the priest sent to take care of their spiritual needs because they did not approve of the Eritrean government and believed him to be under its control. They felt so strongly about this government incursion into their spiritual lives that they went to court to rid themselves of him. Subsequently, they obtained their "proper" church paraphernalia from Ethiopia, so that services could be conducted in the "right" way. As a result of their actions, other members broke away and started their own church, under their own Eritrean patriarch. The split has been the cause of much sadness in the community.

"This is pretty awkward," Rahel Gebreab confides. "I don't like to talk about it because it's discouraging and sad. But on a positive note, diversity in thought is appreciated. As long as there are boundaries and respect for one another, then that should not hinder us as a people."

"In my opinion, religion should not be involved with politics," Bereketab Gebrehiwet adds. "Eritrea is not one religion. It should be separate from politics, something practiced in the home."

"A priest should not be considered a political representative," Yodit Tekle remarks. "If he says a prayer of praise over soldiers, he's not saying he's pro-war; he's not saying 'save the government.' He's saying, 'For the lives that are in this situation, please look over them.' But people thought that was a political quote."

Both Seattle church groups are now trying to separate themselves from politics.

Muslims from Eritrea and Ethiopia

Back in Eritrea and Ethiopia, Muslims number as many as, if not more than, Christians. Accurate figures do not exist, and the subject is a contentious one. Nevertheless, Ethiopia is believed to have the third-largest Muslim population in Africa, after Nigeria and Egypt, so it is not surprising that some Muslims resent the hegemony of the highland Christians. It is a sentiment that carries over to the Pacific Northwest as well, where Muslims say that though they contributed to the liberation wars in both countries, they have not always shared equally in the economic and political rewards of peacetime. In Ethiopia, the federated structure of the country further cements the isolation of Muslim ethnic groups like the Somalis and politicizes their identity, while in Eritrea, the desire to avoid partitioning the country along religious lines has persisted ever since the Christian and Muslim founders helped launch the country's struggle for independence. The United States supports this status quo, having no desire to see an Islamic caliphate in East Africa that could disturb the balance of power in the region.

"The Muslims in Eritrea are very hardworking people," Abraha, a Coptic Christian, confirms, "and during the struggle, they were with us. In fact, Islam is one of the pillars of Eritrea, and the country could not survive without it." On the surface, relations between the two religions in Eritrea have been good since independence, and, Abraha points out, showing his irritation at my questioning, "there's a mosque on every other block in Asmara" and "Christian and Muslim holidays are celebrated throughout the country." Nevertheless President Isaias Afwerki and the People's Front for Democracy and Justice remain wary. The government suspects Eritrea's Muslims, particularly those in the western areas bordering Sudan, of collaborating with armed opposition groups in Sudan. Young Muslim students and teachers suspected of ties to the Eritrean Liberation Front have been detained, arrested, or simply "disappeared," and when a Sudanese-backed plot to assassinate the Eritrean president was discovered in 1997, the situation for Muslims deteriorated even further. Yet, Eritrea threw its support behind the Muslims of the Islamic Courts Union in Somalia and helped them drive the warlords out of their cities when the Ethiopians, supported by the United States, sought to curb the ICU's power.

Here in Seattle and Portland, Eritreans hesitate to speak about religious divisions, since the state was founded on the acceptance of different religious groups: Coptic Christianity, Islam, Catholicism, and Lutheranism. "We are a society that formed through different churches," Yegizaw confirms. Yet, when I ask some local Tigrinya Christian Eritreans if they have Muslim friends, hardly any answer in the affirmative. While Eritrean Muslims of Tigre ethnicity, like the Beni-Amir, and others of Bilen ancestry do live in Seattle, not many have friends among the Tigrinya Christians. Abraha, for example, says he doesn't know any Muslims. He explains that because religious tensions are flaring now, "not only in the Middle East but everywhere, Muslims are pulling together and looking inward." He shakes his grizzled head. "That's not how the Muslims were when I was growing up," he says. His words suggest the kind of distancing that can occur in families when one sibling goes off on a different trajectory from another. The regret in his voice is palpable: "Now it's almost like they are foreigners."

A similar unease exists among the local Ethiopians, who are mostly Coptic Christians. When delegates of the Bedir International Ethiopian Muslim Federation representing the transnationals of Canada, Germany, Saudi Arabia, and the United States met with government officials in Seattle in April 2007 to discuss Ethiopia's millennium celebrations, they insisted that the festivities would be for *all* Ethiopians. That they had to stress "all Ethiopians" points to the problem.

"Not that long ago, Ethiopian Christians and Muslims were on much better terms," Ezra Teshome muses.

Still, locals aspire to better. Muslim Ethiopian Nuria Agraw, a lively and gracious young Seattle woman, works with members of all nationalities and ethnic groups. While living in Yemen, she says, she was employed by the United Nations High Commissioner for Refugees, and when she moved to New York, she had hoped for similar work with East Africans and Arabs. When that didn't materialize, however, she left in 1997 for Seattle, where her fiancé, Mustafa, lived. Together they run two building material businesses back in Ethiopia and supply their home country with cement to produce bricks and blocks. They are invested in the Ethiopian community both here and there. In Seattle, Nuria belongs to the women's group of the Ethiopian Muslim Association of Seattle and includes among her friends, she says, many Eritreans as well as Ethiopians of the Muslim and the Christian faith.

"Me, I don't see people in terms of their religion, only as people," Yegizaw tells me over dinner. "I don't talk to people about their religion. I just stay away from it. I don't ask them what they believe."

Somali Muslims have long been puzzled by the survival of Ethiopia's Christianity when so many other nearby areas ruled by Romans, Byzantines, and Persians fell to the Muslims in the early centuries of Islamic conquests. Even before the establishment of Islam, Abyssinia had been at war with the Yemeni, as the Qur'an sura "The Year of the Elephant" recounts. But long after that elephant expedition, in the early days of Islam, the Prophet saw things differently and set the relationship with Ethiopia on a special footing. "One of the reasons why Ethiopia was not attacked and Islamicized," Jamal explains, "was that when Muhammad and his followers were being persecuted in Mecca [in the seventh century], he told them to leave Mecca and go elsewhere." In an aside to me, Jamal says, "So you see, Muhammad was actually blessing migration! He said, if you have a problem somewhere, then go somewhere else." We both laugh, and he returns to answering the question:

> One of the places that the Muslims went was Ethiopia, and the Ethiopian king [Ashama Ibn Abjar], who was Christian, let them in and said they could stay. So when the *nejashi* [or *negus*, meaning "king"] died, and Muhammad had become successful, he held official days of mourning for this Christian king who was helpful to the Muslims. That's one of the reasons given for the injunction by early Muslims not to attack Ethiopia.

The Prophet considered a land ruled by people who believed in God to be more protective of Islam in its infancy than pagan Arabia, so his companions and relatives flocked there to avoid persecution. The religion spread rapidly south of the Axumite kingdom, and by the fourteenth century, there were seven Islamic sultanates—Yifat, Dawaro, Arbabini, Hadiya, Shakara, Bali, and Dara. This is why, historically, Ethiopia has been known to Muslims as the Haven of the First Migration (or Hijra).

Despite their original welcome by the Negus Al-Asham and the subsequent expansion of the Muslim population in Ethiopian lands, Christians and Muslims have been at each other's throats since then as each group has pursued its own interests in land, trade, and souls. The Ethiopian Christian Church's influence on state leaders in the past has not been good for Muslims, and holy wars in 1332 and 1527, interspersed with numerous smaller wars and battles over the centuries, have further increased suspicions on both sides. Most Ethiopian kings, with the exception of Lej Iyassu, have been at the beck and call of the Coptic Church. Haile Selassie, for example, installed Christian governors over Muslim populations, a move that led to the resistance that eventually toppled the King of Kings.

The secularization of the state in the post-Selassie era, during the Marxist-Leninist rule of the Derg, seemed to bring Muslim and Christian closer. In 1974 they joined together in a mass rally to demand equality between the two religions, and for a while, calm seemed to prevail between their followers. The calm continued with the ascent of

Prime Minister Meles's Tigray rulers, and in 1993, the U.S. Department of State's Human Rights Report on Ethiopia notes, Muslims for the first time in that country's history were able to participate fully in Ethiopian political, economic, and social life.[10] But when members of the Somali al-Ittihad al-Islamiya mounted several bomb attacks in the Ogaden in 1995 and attempted to assassinate the leader of the Ethio-Somali Democratic Movement, Prime Minister Meles sent his armed forces to destroy AIAI bases in the Ogaden. Since 99.5 percent of Somalis are Sunnis of the Shafi'i sect, they view non-Sunni Muslims with suspicion. Thus they fear this violent Saudi Arabian form of Islam as much as Ethiopian Christians do. The Wahabis have been connected to reported mosque burnings and are seen as introducing intra-Islamic divisions into an already volatile ethno-religious mix.[11]

Most Muslims in Seattle and Portland say they have no interest in the extremism of those who push violent agendas and political control. "The Somalis here are not religious fanatics; they are not out to destroy American Christians," Abdihakim assures me. "They like it here. They just want to get on with their lives, make a living, educate their children, and practice their religion in peace."

At the Dur-Dur Café on Seattle's East Cherry, where Somali taxi drivers hang out and play games while they wait for calls on their cell phones, the conversation often turns to Islam because it is inseparable from everyday life. Amid talk of gas prices and the dangers of picking up rides after midnight in certain areas, one of the drivers lifts the common thermos to refill his cup of smoky-flavored tea, *shaah harwash*, and then leaves his money on the counter. It is the honor system here, and nobody even checks. It's what Islam teaches, after all.

As the scents of cardamom, cinnamon, and ginger waft from the kitchen and linger over the tables, the men talk, too, of incidences of disrespect. At one of the tables by the window, a patron pushes aside his dish of goat meat and bananas to recount what happened to his son at school when the teacher wasn't looking. Another man, old enough to have known Italian colonialism firsthand, twirls spaghetti on his fork and waves his hand to imply that it's nothing, just boys being boys. When the clock calls the men to *salat*, they clean their hands and pull out their prayer rugs. They are an observant lot.

And yet, in February 2006, when Muslims all over the world raised angry fists about the publication of a Danish cartoon of the Prophet, Somali voices at the Dur-Dur and elsewhere in Seattle were more muted. This in itself does not suggest that local Muslims feel less angry about the insult to Muhammad nor that they have assimilated the democratic freedoms that allow the ridicule of religion in this country. More likely, they merely fear the long arm of the law in the persons of the Puget Sound Joint Terrorism Task Force. Somalis define themselves by their religion, which is the basis of most of their cultural traditions, and as they feel themselves more targeted for attention by the Christian majority, they turn even more to Islam for comfort and security.

When the ICU moved into Mogadishu and for a while brought some peace and stability to the area, many local Somalis felt grateful. Even though they disagreed with many of the social restrictions the ICU imposed on Western cultural influences in terms of female dress, music, and soccer, they were grateful for its imposition of Islamic law, which calls for the amputation of thieves' hands and the execution of murderers and rapists. Widespread rape, even of children, has made women the chief victims of the warlords' roving gunmen and elicited public revulsion. The sisters and cousins of many Portland and Seattle Somalis still live in Mogadishu, and their overwhelming feeling on hearing the news of the ICU's successes was relief at what they believed would be the end of an epidemic of sexual violence. Nevertheless, most kept their feelings to themselves. They maintained a low profile and discussed the possibility of an ICU-ruled Somalia only among themselves.

Nuruddin Farah writes that in spite of Somali identification with Islam, he doubts very much "if there are more than a handful of [his] countrymen who are prepared to lay down their lives for Islam." He continues, "Many a Somali might not hesitate to die for his clan family or for financial gains, but not for an abstraction, which is what, in the final analysis, religion is to the barely literate."[12]

Nevertheless, the continuing war on terrorism keeps Muslim communities in the Pacific Northwest on edge. The images of themselves they see reflected in the eyes of their American neighbors do not fill them with confidence. In the early months of 2007, while the Islamic Courts Union and Transitional Federal Government battled for control in Somalia and Ethiopians arrested fleeing ICU fighters and transported them back to Ethiopia for questioning, Somalis avoided talking to me on the record. In Portland, even with introductions and referrals, they did not return my calls.

Other Religions

Religious freedom is part of both Eritrea's and Ethiopia's constitutions. Article 19 and Article 27, respectively, confirm that the peoples of each country have the right to practice their religion. Back in Eritrea, however, religious persecution of Jehovah's Witnesses and evangelical Christians arouses international complaints. Church members have been detained, and, since 2005, human rights violations have intensified. Amnesty International reported on its Web site on December 7, 2005, that churches have been shut down and members tortured in an attempt to "force them to stop worshipping and to thereby abandon their faith." The government argues that national service is mandatory for men and women over eighteen and that if Jehovah's Witnesses cannot bear arms, then they have no right to the fruits of other Eritreans' sacrifices. "What do you expect?" Abraha says to me. "The country became independent by the gun, so if you can't serve it that way, then you have no right to live there and take its food as well."

In Ethiopia, Article 11 of the constitution confirms the separation of state and religion. There is no official state religion in Meles Zenawi–led Ethiopia. But back in 1980, the Mengistu government targeted those religions that were understood to have connections to the United States or Israel, namely, the evangelical and Baptist churches as well as the Beta Israel religion (Falasha). "'Falasha' is a derogatory word," Michael Damtew tells me. He is of Jewish lineage on his Ethiopian father's side. "It means 'Wanderers,' people without land." Although their origins are not known for certain, these Ethiopian Jews who maintained their Jewish identity for possibly two thousand years are thought to be either from the lost tribe of Dan or of that lineage of Jews who left Israel for Egypt after the destruction of the First Temple in 586 B.C.E.[13] Others say they are descendants of Menelik I, believed to be the son of King Solomon and the Queen of Sheba.

"No," Michael dismisses those explanations and offers his take on their origins. "The Beta Israel were those Jews who did *not* cross the Red Sea with Moses during the exodus from Egypt to Israel." He goes on to explain:

> They stayed on the eastern side of Egypt, and everyone was disagreeing with Moses. At this time, there were lots of followers who were frustrated, and when Moses returned from getting the Torah, the Ten Commandments, they complained, and he told them that they were giving up on the one true God. So some of them wandered down the banks of the Nile and made their way down to Ethiopia.

Whatever the origins of the Beta Israel in Ethiopia, their lives have been ones of hardship and persecution ever since Christianity arrived in the area in the fourth century. They have suffered forced conversion, persecution, and the appropriation of their land in Gonder. A brief respite occurred during the tenth century when Yodit Gudit (Queen Judith, as she is known in English) led them in a popular revolt that succeeded in overthrowing Axum. For the next three centuries, they exerted a modicum of influence on Christians and Muslims, but when the Axum dynasty returned to power, they were once again forcibly baptized or sold into slavery.

As they were an isolated community, their situation did not attract international attention, and only in the twentieth century were they formally accepted as Jewish brethren by Israel, whose chief Sephardic rabbi in 1973 declared them the descendants of the Tribe of Dan. Israel's Operation Moses in 1984 and the United States' Operation Joshua a year later relocated many of them in Israel. It was Mengistu's own economic problems at the end of that decade, however, that helped set the stage for the largest airlift of all. In 1989 Mengistu, needing help from Israel against the Tigray People's Liberation Front, "more or less barter[ed] the Beta Israel for unspecified military assistance."[14] His regime was fast falling apart, but before the TPLF reached Addis Ababa, Israel airlifted 14,325 Ethiopian Jews in Operation Solomon on May 24, 1990. In 1991, with Meles Zenawi in power, some of the last Jews from the remote area of Qara were able to leave; those who had undergone forced conversions followed in the mid-1990s. To Zenawi's credit, he returned the money

Israel had paid Mengistu's Ethiopia for the Beta Israel, money the administration desperately needed after the war, noting quietly that Ethiopia would not accept "blood money." Today, few Beta Israel or Jews of any kind remain in Ethiopia. Even the Adenite community of Sephardic Jews in Addis was forced to leave in the 1970s. The Derg appropriated their land, their property, and their factories, leaving them no option but to flee.

The situation is much the same in Eritrea. Michael grew up in Asmara when a Jewish community still existed there. Under Haile Selassie's rule, he claims, they did not practice their religious beliefs openly. Thus they didn't go to synagogue for fear that people would know they were Jewish and ostracize them. "But it was a community that worked hard and thrived financially," he remembers. Today, there is only one Jewish family to be found in Eritrea, and it is in Massawa. "It is the family of a rabbi, by the name of Cohen," Michael says. "He came from Egypt." About five years earlier, I had visited the old synagogue. It was closed up and locked with chains.

In Muslim Somalia, "other" religious groups fare far worse than they do in Ethiopia and Eritrea. The small Christian community depends on the goodwill of the governments and warlords of the different regions. In Somaliland and Puntland, where Islam is the official religion and its adherents practice sharia law, proselytizing by non-Muslims counts as a criminal offense. In February 2000 the government arrested nine Ethiopian Christians in Somaliland on charges of proselytizing, and in February 2006, when the Danish cartoon of Muhammad sent the Muslim world into an uproar, thousands of Somali demonstrators took to the streets of Mogadishu in a stampede against Christians that brought out the city's police.

In spite of the various religious divisions in the local communities, both Ethiopians and Eritreans in the Pacific Northwest claim to see religion as a unifying force. Even in 2003, with Amhara, Tigray, and Oromo tensions high, the *Seattle Post-Intelligencer* on January 7 quoted a St. Gebriel member, Girma Haile-Leul, as saying that even people who are different politically and who have not talked to one another previously are ready to serve and worship at the church. In the same article, the Reverend Girma Desalegn at the Medhane-Alem Ethiopian Evangelical

Church also spoke to religion's unifying force when he said, "All groups are working together—Protestant, Orthodox, and communities." The previous summer, four Protestant congregations—two Amharic churches, an Oromo church, and an Eritrean church—joined in a Christian conference, meeting at Lake Sammamish, near Issaquah, to talk and picnic. While such sentiments of religious unity may omit more than they claim, they speak to the communities' desire to find common ground and a way of working together for the common good.

Hope for the future cooperation of Muslim and Christian in the Pacific Northwest still holds. A precedent for working together can be found in the early Eritrean resistance group, when, in 1941, Muslims and Christians broke their religious traditions of not eating the meat of animals slain by religious outsiders in order to show their good faith and determination not to let religion prevent them from working together for unity. Muslims felt strongly the prohibition against eating *sga kistan*, while Christians felt the same about eating *sga islam*. They were determined, however, to bridge their differences and join hands in creating an all-inclusive, cooperative narrative of liberation that would move them and their followers into a more peaceable future.

ECONOMIC RIVALRY

Although class, clan, and religion all play a part in the rivalry among the communities in the Pacific Northwest, ultimately the larger goal of economic power fuels competition most. It leads communities to squabble over who gets grants, for example, and encourages a secretive mentality that tries to protect access to monetary sources for each group's own benefit. A community's desire to hoard the spoils for itself alone is hardly surprising, since wealth provides the wherewithal to improve its standing in the diaspora while also enabling it to bring its influence to bear on events back home. If all three countries were not so dependent on diaspora money, perhaps things would be different, but each lives in a state of impoverishment in which the majority of its people struggle for daily survival. For each, the competition for power in the form of wealth has brought warfare and strife in its wake.

Ethio-Eritrean Economic Conflict

It is difficult to separate territorial hunger from economics. Ethiopia's economy certainly was slashed when Eritrea gained its independence in 1991 and took with it not only its land but also the seaports through which Ethiopia conducted much of its trade. Economic distrust had been a fact of life between the two countries, and the border war of the late 1990s did nothing to resolve that rivalry. In part, economic distrust and rivalry themselves led to the war.

The steps that precipitated the economic and military showdowns began in 1993, after Eritrea had become an independent nation. Although the two rebel forces–turned–governments already had misgivings about each other, in a show of cooperation they agreed to share a single currency, Ethiopia's *birr*, so that they could synchronize their economies. One of the significant parts of the deal signed at Asmara enabled nationals of each country to make investments in the other country. Thus, "After 1993," David Makonnen says, "a lot of Eritreans preferred to invest in Ethiopia instead of Eritrea because it was a much larger market." Two years later, Isaias Afwerki and Meles Zenawi went even further and announced a free trade area.

On the surface, economic relations seemed harmonious. Ethiopia imported and exported goods through Eritrea's ports, while Eritrea earned about $90 million a year from the provision of services and port duties to Ethiopia.[15] Eritrea also exported many of its products and services to its neighbor. Behind the scenes, however, dissent and disagreements were rife. Landlocked Addis Ababa complained that its goods were being held up at Assab and that Eritreans undercut them with Ethiopian coffee in the international market. Eritrea had a huge trade surplus with Ethiopia, which the latter resented. "From Ethiopia's perspective," David says, "it seemed like Eritreans saw Ethiopia as their own private market whereby they could export whatever they wanted. They didn't have any obligation or commitment to the government, so they could come to Ethiopia and destabilize the market by undercutting prices or doing whatever they wanted."

To complicate matters further, both parties used proxies to invest in companies that were supposed to be private and not state-owned. Such para-party activities were difficult to prove; nevertheless, suspicion itself undermined economic cooperation between the two governments. In Tigray, especially, the Ethiopian government feared that investments made by the Eritrean People's Liberation Front would be in direct competition with its own, made by the Tigray People's Liberation Front. The Eritreans say that the Ethiopians built their own factories in Tigray so that they could supplant Asmara as Ethiopia's supplier of manufactured goods.[16]

The Tigrinya had been the major economic players when they were still the Mereb-Melash, but their colonization by Italy together with the subsequent marginalization of Tigray by successive Amhara rulers had impoverished the Tigrayans, and they were eager to revitalize their area and return it to the prosperity it had once known. Mistrust grew on both sides, and each introduced its own investment and tariff regimes as well as independent exchange and interest rates.[17] It was Eritrea's introduction of its own currency, the *nakfa*, in November 1997, however, that finally helped push matters to the brink. "We thought the *nakfa* would be on a par with the Ethiopian *birr* and that we could use the two currencies in both countries," Portland Eritreans say. But Ethiopia, feeling slighted by not having been consulted first about the move, refused and required the Eritreans to conduct trade with Ethiopia in hard currency. In order to do this, the Eritreans had to borrow currency from Ethiopian banks, a situation that proved untenable and reduced trade between the two countries to a minimum.

Eritrea's introduction of its own currency made the delineation of these borders a subject of urgent attention. Without knowledge of exact borders, the government could not regulate cross-border trade, taxation, and foreign exchange flows, a situation that led inexorably to the border war of 1998–2000. After the fighting at Badme and Eritrea's attempt to bomb the Tigrayans' pharmaceutical plant in June 1998, the Ethiopian government accused Eritrea of deliberately trying to impoverish its brothers south of the Mereb.[18] The United Nations then placed an embargo on all trade between the two countries and halted Ethiopia's use of the Massawa and Assab ports for foreign trade. The two governments failed to resolve currency, trade, and investment disputes, and the economic losses they sustained, together with the crippling costs of the war and of resettlement, left both countries devastated and distrustful.

With coffers bare, they turned to their transnational communities for financial help, appealing to these communities' nationalism and encouraging them to support their homelands. Abe Demisse, president of Oregon Ethiopian Community Organization, confirms what other Ethiopians have told me, namely, that the country cannot survive without the money people send from outside. "It's close to $300 million a year!" he says, adding that Ethiopians can't even afford to visit home anymore because they have to contribute so much. "The country needs it," he says. "The Tigrayans cleaned us out with their war. Everything. We have no buffers left."

While Ethiopia certainly needs that financial support, Eritrea relies even more on remittances from its transnational communities. Eritrea's smaller economy and financial reserves do not allow it to draw on domestic sources of taxation, so it tithes its countrymen and countrywomen abroad. Here in the Pacific Northwest, Eritrean immigrants and refugees have regularly sent a percentage of their incomes back home, but during the border war, the government demanded greater contributions than ever. In Seattle at that time, an Eritrean fund-raising effort brought in $1 million within a few hours. Hidaat Ephrem, one of the Eritreans who took part in the campaign, fueled the Eritrean spirit of sacrifice with her poetry. Because of her successful efforts, she earned the moniker Million-Dollar Poet. As the war dragged on, however, and locals became disillusioned with President Isaias's handling of the border struggles, remittances dropped off.

Unsettled economic and territorial questions spill over into Eritrean and Ethiopian neighborhoods of the Pacific Northwest, where they wedge themselves between Eritreans and Ethiopians, pushing them further apart. When I ask the group of young Eritreans sitting at my dinner table whether, given such subjects of estrangement, they ever actually mix with Ethiopians in person, Yodit Tekle responds, "Not really." Then she adds as an afterthought, "Except if there isn't an Eritrean available."

Her words make Yegizaw uncomfortable. "I understand that some Eritreans distance themselves from Ethiopians because of their history," he tries to explain, "but for me, since I was raised in Addis Ababa, I understand both histories and cultures, and I don't appreciate disrespect no matter which side it comes from."

In both countries, postwar programs of rearmament continue to consume what resources are left.

Ethio-Somali Economic Conflict

Economics is also pivotal in fueling competing versions of events among Ethiopians and Somalis. In the Ogaden, for example, economic factors are responsible for much of the tension that has kept Ogadeni and other Somalis at Ethiopia's throat. The Somalis living in Region 5 find themselves increasingly isolated economically and feel that the present Ethiopian government continues, like its historic predecessors, to neglect and marginalize development of the area. In fact, some Somalis call it the "leftover" region. When the civil war broke out in Somalia, Ogaden's main trading partner, it reduced traditional exchanges between them and had a major impact on Ogaden's economy. As a result, the Ogaden National Liberation Front came to rely on al-Ittihad al-Islamiya for financial assistance and arms.[19]

The Ogaden Basin is believed to be rich in mineral resources, including natural gas, hydrocarbons, and petroleum, but while Ethiopia's ownership of the Ogaden remains in dispute, many Somalis are reluctant to support mineral excavations and drilling that might result in economic rewards that would inevitably stuff Ethiopia's coffers and not those of the Ogaden. Nevertheless, the drilling and excavations continue, particularly in the Calub and Hilala areas, where 135,000 square miles of natural gas reserves have been found. Since 1999, Gazoil Ethiopia Project, a joint-venture partnership between the Ethiopian government and Texas-based Sicor, has developed the reserves in these two areas. Despite armed conflict between the ONLF and the Ethiopian government over control of the basin, international companies from other countries, among them the Netherlands, Sweden, Hong Kong, and Malaysia, have engaged in petroleum exploration and development activities there.[20] On April 24, 2007, the *Seattle Post-Intelligencer* reported, two hundred Ogaden rebels attacked a Chinese-run oilfield at Abole, a small town seventy-five miles from Jijiga, killing nine Chinese oil workers and sixty-five Ethiopians. Wary Americans take a watch-and-see approach and in the meantime stay out of the area. Nevertheless, many Ogaden Somalis believe that the

United States is trying to establish a foothold in this area through oil, so that it might better position itself to oversee the Red Sea traffic of oil tankers and warships.

Seattle's Koshin Mohamed is not so sure. "There's a bunch of jihadists in the ONLF," he says. He expresses skepticism about the ONLF's claims, saying that if it was just Ogadenia that mattered to them, they could gain their independence through democratic means. "Why fight a country whose constitution allows you to be elected by your people and to secede, if you choose?" The question is pertinent because the Ogaden zone is like any other zone, with its own leaders and police. "If the ONLF held elections, you see, they would lose. Most Somalis in the Ogaden don't want to secede."

Within Somalia itself, although the civil war turned on clan rivalry, such rivalry had at its core the struggle to gain control over the resources that supported the Somali political economy. The most important of these resources were the fertile riverine lands that fed the country and were in the main owned and worked by the Somali Bantu. But in addition to these lands, other economic resources collected by the ruling government, such as foreign aid, currency, and remittances from overseas workers, also spurred clan rivalry because they could be dispensed by the state to favored members of the ruler's clan. As de Waal points out, ever since Siyad Barre divvied up the spoils to his clan brethren, the dominant Somali perception of government rule today is winner takes all.[21] The sovereign leader and his governing elite can bestow wealth, land, and opportunities on the clan family. Given these conditions, businessmen, for example, have no incentive to work together across clan lines to increase production or sales and thus do not generate the resources needed to enlarge the economy. The whole system becomes parasitic, relying on such handouts and on the *actual* labors of, for example, those in the agricultural sector, who generally remain outside of the main clans and power structures of the country.

This winner-takes-all mind-set percolates into the Seattle and Portland communities, too. Somali men frequently want to start their own nonprofit organizations under the mistaken belief that the owner has access to monetary rewards. "A lot of them," Koshin says, "wanted to be on the board of the Somali Community Services Coalition, the nonprofit

I was with, and I had to explain to them that in a nonprofit, just because you're on a board doesn't mean you're going to get any money out of it." He laughs at their misapprehension and goes on to repeat what he told them. "If you want to get paid, I can't give you money that belongs to the community. I can only give money to people who earn it. You have to be an employee."

When I ask how they responded, he replies, "They don't want to know. They have it all wrong. They don't understand that you have to do research and train to run a nonprofit, you have to have lawyers . . ."

Somali businessmen here, too, see the handling of remittances from the diaspora as a monetary jackpot. When the Somali state collapsed and with it the formal financial sector, brokers in the private sector established a money transfer system so that Somalis in the diaspora could wire money back home. With Islam and clan as its base, the system functioned on trust and became so successful that it produced major wealth and political power for the businessmen operating it. While no major clan controls the flow of remittances, the businessmen who run the system, as de Waal points out, align themselves politically, or at least they did until the U.S. government, in the wake of 9/11, started investigating Al Barakaat on the grounds that diaspora money was being channeled through this system to support terrorist organizations at home. Since then, bankers have lain low.

With many Somalis in Somalia dependent on remittances from their diaspora families, however, the Somali community here in the Pacific Northwest was at a loss as to how to get money to their families back home. Many were panicking. "So I tried to help by exploring how to set up a new system that would be transparent to the U.S. government," Koshin says. Afterward, he opened Asli Financial Services, a money transmission store. "I got a group of experts including the former director of the Washington Financial Institution, John Blaine, to participate in the company and check compliance for me," he explains. "We also had Bank of America participate, and they allowed us to open an account and also to use their banking system. Thus, we had the capacity to capture money from all over the United States into our account."

When I ask about the name, he says it's his mother's. "That way," he chuckles infectiously, "I am reminded not to do anything wrong!" An image of a stern middle-aged Somali woman shaking her finger at her son creeps into my mind. When I ask how the business fares now, his face falls for a moment. "It didn't go well because of the heavy investment I needed. I was trying to raise at least $10–15 million to cover transmissions all over East Africa. But the Americans didn't trust that." I express my sympathy. I can't imagine any American investing in a Somali money transfer system with U.S.-Somali relations as they are right now. When, months later, I drive to the address of Asli Financial Services, I find the small store vacant and barred. Outside the store, newspapers blow down Twelfth Avenue and catch in the doorway, lending a dilapidated air to this banking service that started out with such enthusiasm and hope.

In March 2007, returning from the Tigard community to downtown Portland, I am caught in a traffic jam. My mind is in the Horn of Africa, and I ruminate on how economic developments there affect communities here. As economic conditions deteriorate in the Horn, family members struggling in the tightening vise of poverty demand ever-increasing amounts of money from people who themselves can barely get by. But as I drive along Barbur Boulevard, crawling along at ten miles an hour, I observe yet another economic narrative taking shape on the paths alongside. As I watch, I see the teenage children of Somali immigrants waiting at bus stops or entering stores. They look as American as any other young person on the street, and whether they have any inkling of the economic chaos in Mogadishu or Kismayo, or whether their parents discuss such things in front of them, I do not know. No doubt, like all teenagers, their minds are filled with more pleasant things. More bling, perhaps. I notice that the young Somali girls jazz up their modest headscarves and trim them with glitter or choose vibrant colors that flatter their skins and emphasize their dark eyes. They wear them with American blue jeans that bear fashion logos I can't make out from my car, but their gait is spirited, and they clutch their cell phones to their ears. I also see them through the windows of McDonald's and Starbucks, where they huddle around tables, their heads together in animated conversation. As they sip their Cokes, I think about the contributions these young Somalis are making to another economy, that of the United States.

SIX

THE
CHALLENGERS WITHIN

If the nose is injured, the eyes will cry.

—ERITREAN PROVERB

*T*HE OPPORTUNITY to influence generations of schoolchildren through their history textbooks represents a prize that local Somalis, Ethiopians, and Eritreans have been quick to appreciate. Their readiness to speak out in order to establish their versions of "the truth" testifies to their awareness of story's importance. When the challenge comes from *within* their own communities, however, from members who say, "I, too, have a story, and it doesn't jibe with yours," it is seen as a betrayal that exposes the community's dirty laundry. When Philip Roth published *Portnoy's Complaint* in 1969, for example, members of the American Jewish community expressed outrage. Struggling for acceptance and still faced with anti-Semitism in many neighborhoods, they felt they couldn't afford to be represented by one of their own in an unflattering light. During the early Harlem Renaissance era, African Americans, too, reacted angrily to black writers who created characters who drank, swore, or womanized. It wasn't until a black middle class arose and achieved standing in the larger American community that unflattering individual portraits could be tolerated.

Members of the new communities just settling into the Pacific Northwest remain unsure of their own standing here, so they feel understandably nervous about the unguarded word. At stake is their image, the way they are perceived as a people, which ultimately can translate into how well their neighbors, bosses, and lending institutions accept them as individuals.

Yet, as their adopted country preaches, democracy requires tolerance for dissenting voices. "We also have a right to our stories," say Somalia's outcasts and Bantu; "We also want our voices heard," say the Ethiopian Oromos. Members of these groups have been treated as second-class citizens in their own countries, sometimes even as slaves, and now that they stand on the verge of new lives in the United States, they want to clear the record. Some seek redress for their exploitation at home, while others hope merely to discard their old class labels and gain acceptance into mainstream society here. To the credit of the Horn of Africa communities in the Pacific Northwest, sections of it move stoically and with resolve in the direction of tolerance.

THE SOMALI BANTU

At Portland International Airport, a group of Somali Bantu men, women, and children pass through the doors of the baggage-customs hall and step into their new lives. They have been prepared for this moment by the refugee service agency under whose auspices they emigrated to escape the violence in their homeland. They have undergone medical exams, security checks, literacy training, and cultural orientation, so they know what to expect. Still, the size and bustle of it all overwhelm them. They look around in wonder at the many people and the number of restaurants. Despite their weariness, they take it all in and stash it with the many other bits of information about America that they accumulated in their Somali-Kenyan border camp while preparing for this day. The sudden boom of a jet taking off startles them, and some of the women jump, then smile apologetically at an elderly white couple who have turned to stare as if trying to make out from the women's looks where they have traveled from. With their dark skins, the Bantu could easily be confused with Kenyans, Tanzanians, or even Ugandans. The host families move forward now, and the arrivals break into small family groupings and wait expectantly. A carefully practiced "Hello, my name is Abdi. How are you?" reaches across the void and is met with hearty handshakes, smiles, and even a tentative *"Salaam."* The agency leader checks off the new arrivals' names on her long list, and, one by one, the groups pair off with their receiving families and trail out to the parking garage The men lug baggage and boxes tied with string, while their children struggle to keep up and hang onto the long corners of their mothers' familiar shawls.

The Somali Bantus' appearance on the public radar has taken many scholars in the area by surprise. For years, they've considered Somalia a homogeneous country where everyone is of the same ethnicity, speaks the same language, and practices Islam. Somalis in the Pacific Northwest, too, generally speak of themselves as homogeneous. But when I talk about Somali sameness to Portland's Omar Eno, himself a Bantu, he throws back his head and laughs. "Right!" Omar is a big man, and his laugh reverberates as if bounced off a tightly drawn drum skin. "No, no, no," he puts me straight, "we are way different. Like any society in the world, Somalia is diverse. There's nothing wrong with being diverse, but the Somalis think that if we are different," he feigns a look of desperation and throws up his hands, "oh, the country is going to collapse!"

He and I, each with a colleague, sit on opposite sides of a conference table at Portland State University's Mark O. Hatfield School of Government. Omar leans across the table and asks rhetorically, "If we *are* so homogeneous, if we have everything in common—same culture, same religion, same language, same everything—why did the country collapse anyway? If we are all the same, why are we so irreconcilable? What is the Somali problem?"

While class distinctions prevail among the major clans—the Darod, Isaq, and Hawiye—an even more pernicious one separates those clan families from the rest of the population that serves them. From the bottom up, the groups most discriminated against are, first, the so-called outcasts, followed by the Somali Bantu, and then the coastal fishermen, like the Benadiri, and the Bravanese traders. The mostly agricultural Rehanweyn (Reewiin) sit uneasily between the major nomadic groups and the others.

This discriminatory class system, based on occupation, relegates 40 to 60 percent of the population to second-class status. "Forty to sixty!" Omar repeats, "yet the major clans call us a minority!" Omar has researched and written about his people's oppressed situation, and he explains that after 1956, which was the last time the United Nations provided statistics, each leader who came to power claimed his clan to be the largest. Since the noble clans known as *Samales* measure their wealth and standing in camels, cattle, and goats, they consider farmers who work the soil as inferior. They call the Bantu farmers and all those with Negroid features *jareer*, or "kinky hair," as opposed to themselves, the *jileec*, or "straight hair."

"That is how they distinguish between us; they think they have better hair!" Omar mocks the *Samales*. He laughs infectiously and goes on to explain that the basis for Somali discrimination lies not in skin color, since everyone is black, but instead in hair texture. "Theirs is soft, and ours is kinky," he says, fingering his own curls before adding proudly that he believes his kinky hair to be better than any other. We smile at his attempt at a joke, but it is obviously a painful subject. Still, he is fortunate because, empowered by the security his education affords him in the United States, he can laugh at the notions of superiority held by the dominant pastoralist Somalis. In fact, Omar is full of jokes about his people's erstwhile oppressors. "Do you know the Somali proverb 'The camel is for all men'?" he asks. When we shake our heads, he explains: "Today, the camel is yours, tomorrow I steal yours, and the next day my neighbor steals mine!" He chuckles. "You see? That's why the camel is for all men."

Not all Somali Bantu can see their situation vis-à-vis the *Samales* with the same humor. Besides calling them *jareer*, clan Somalis sometimes will refer to them as *boon* or *adoon*, meaning "slave," or *habash*, a term previously used for Abyssinian slaves. The Italians knew them as *ooji* after the Italian *oggi*, meaning "today," based on Somali perceptions of the Bantu as unable to think beyond the present moment.

Omar, together with Daniel Van Lehman, now co-director of the National Somali Bantu Project in the Hatfield School, spearheads the project, which assists refugee service providers to better understand Somali Bantu culture and history and works directly with Somali Bantu community organizations to promote them at the local and national levels. Most important, it aims to expose racial discrimination before it becomes entrenched among Somali refugees. Van Lehman, who worked as a field officer for the United Nations High Commissioner for Refugees in the Dagahaley refugee camp in Kenya from 1992 to 1994, was instrumental in getting the United Nations to persuade the U.S. government to accept more than twelve thousand Somali Bantu refugees for resettlement in approximately fifty sites in thirty-eight states, including Oregon and Washington.

These days, the term "Bantu," which originally merely signified a human being, functions in the United States as a catchall term for Somalis of black African heritage who do not resemble the ethnic Somalis. Some of these Bantu have settled into the suburbs of Portland and Seattle. They enroll their children in schools there and enjoy the same civil rights as all U.S. residents. But having found relative freedom in the United States, they demand a cessation to the continuing discrimination they experience from clan Somalis on U.S. soil.

"I am so disgusted with some of these caseworkers and the way they refer to their clients as *adoon*," Van Lehman recalls a Somali American caseworker once telling him. Some Isaq and Darod Somalis working in Seattle and Portland social services are said to act dismissively toward the Bantu. They provide them with less help than they give their clan kin and speak to them rudely. The Bantu resent this treatment, and leaders of the community work to bring such discrimination to the attention of American service providers. Their job is cut out for them, since many Bantu hesitate to express their resentment and anger publicly.

"I don't know how many meetings I attended at the refugee camp where I said to a Somali Bantu, 'Now is your opportunity to speak out publicly about your mistreatment,'" Van Lehman tells me, "only to have him say, 'No, no, we and the other Somalis are brothers.'" In private, however, it was an entirely different story. They'd tell Van Lehman, "I have to go to sleep tonight. I don't want to speak out against the Somalis because they'll kill us in the refugee camps." In the United States, the intimidation continues. "If a dominant-clan Somali caseworker mistreats a Somali Bantu, it's hard for them to speak out because they've been told by the case manager, 'Your relatives [in Somalia] will pay [if you complain to the case manager's American supervisor].'"

Omar explains further that the Bantu have to walk a fine line because the Americans don't understand. They listen to the *Samale* service providers who dismiss the complaining Bantu as just an angry man. However, everywhere a Somali *Bantu* caseworker is hired, Omar says, the problem immediately drops 50 percent. Somali caseworkers and advisers of *Samale* lineage have great influence on the American organizations with which they have contact, and since the Bantu avoid confrontation, many dubious assertions can find their way into mainstream knowledge. For example, despite what some *Samales* say, there are *two* Somali languages: Af-Maxaa and Af-Maay, more commonly known in the United States as Maaha and Maay or Maay-Maay. Maaha is the language imposed by the government, the official language of written Somali, but Maay-Maay is the predominant language of the south, spoken by 80 to 85 percent of Somali Bantu. Many Bantu also speak Kizigua (or Mushunguli, as the Somalis call it). Although many Maay-Maay speakers cannot understand Maaha speakers and vice versa, Omar says, a Somali caseworker who speaks only Maaha will convince his American boss that they are all Somalis and there's nothing to worry about. In fact, the first Maay-Maay dictionary is already out and being sold on the Web.

Not everyone buys the story that the Somali Bantu don't understand Maaha. Bob Johnson, regional director of the International Rescue Committee, which provides generous support services to the Bantu, expresses skepticism. "We found that 99 percent of the Bantu spoke Somali," he tells me when we meet at the IRC offices in downtown Seattle.

Haji Shongolo, vice president of Somali Bantu Community Services of Washington (SBCSW), however, says that language confusion is rife. When his wife, Fatuma, gave birth in a local Seattle hospital, she and the Somali translator struggled to understand each other. "Even her name," he tells me, "appeared on the paperwork as a Somali name rather than a Mushunguli one." Haji Shongolo, a tall, friendly thirty-two-year-old, spent eleven years in the Dadaab refugee camp in Kenya before coming to Seattle in March 2004 under the auspices of World Relief. "I was only the second Bantu Somali in Seattle, and within three months, I was fully employed." He remains so today, supporting his wife, three sons, and three daughters on his salary as a forklift operator. Although he now speaks excellent English and could easily convey medical information for his wife, the mistakes the translator made then obliged Fatuma to spend months correcting all her identity forms and clearing up the confusion.

Along with the language question, Johnson queries the accusations of class discrimination. "Among the Somalis we were working with, I didn't see any difference in the way the Somali Bantu were treated. When the Bantus arrived, the Somali guys were all welcoming," he says. "They brought clothing and showed them where the mosque was."

To be fair, many of the Somali service workers do acknowledge the bad treatment meted out to the Bantu. Nevertheless, like Johnson, some take the narratives of discrimination with a pinch of salt and look with suspicion on claims about the Bantu. Abdihakim recalls how they were told that the Bantu didn't know how to use a restroom, or the Bantu didn't know how to do this and that. "But it wasn't true," he insists. "The Bantu make up the skilled community in Somalia. They are the engineers and house builders, the farmers and fishers. They are more civilized than the other Somalis who don't have those kinds of skills."

"You only have to look at Omar himself," says Bob Johnson, who goes further in questioning the accusations of discrimination. "He's getting his Ph.D., so, right there, he's living proof that the stories of discrimination may not be so true. He's the one going around saying that the Bantu are uneducated, but I've been told that his family had an English school in Mogadishu." Omar, however, claims that the Somali Ministry of Education twice "robbed" him of scholarships because of his ethnicity and that eventually he used his own resources to study in Italy.

In Seattle, the president of the SBCSW, Abdi Madey Ali, recounts Somali Bantu experiences that confirm discrimination. Speaking in Maay-Maay, which his colleague Mursal Abdullah translates for me, he tells the story of Bantus unceremoniously elbowed aside by *Samales* at the job site so that the latter can get employment for their own kin first. Further, when the Bantu workers speak Maay-Maay to one another at lunchtime, the *Samales* upbraid them, saying, "Why are you speaking that language when you are from Somalia?"

"You see," Mursal explains, "they want all Bantu in the United States to speak Somali. That's why when the Bantu answer back, they threaten them. They say they'll cause trouble for the Bantu with their American bosses. Because the *Samales* have lived in the States longer, they believe they know the system and how to get it to work to their advantage."

It is not only intimidation that prevents the Bantus from speaking out about their treatment at the hands of local Somalis here. Shame, too, holds them back from being the masters of their own narratives. Acknowledging their identity is tantamount to admitting their slave ancestry, something they do not want to broadcast in their new country if they can possibly get away with passing. The situation is complex, because many ex-slaves, especially those who were enslaved as children, adopted local clan affiliations and began to identify themselves as Biyomaal or Hawiye, for example, rather than by their tribal names. Clan affiliation supposedly offered them certain protections, but they held a lower status within the clan, and the clan itself was considered by others in the lineage system to be inferior because of its slave component. Nevertheless, clan affiliation offered the Somali Bantus the protection of double identities when they came to the States. Their ancestry, however, is easily detected by the dominant-clan members, hence the continuing race and class discrimination.

The Bantu derive from two separate groups, each with its own foundation narrative: one tells of a slave community, and the other tells of an indigenous people who lived in the Horn. The members of the first group claim descent from slaves captured in the area between Kenya and Mozambique. In the late 1830s, when several years of drought left many East African families starving, parents became easy prey for Arab slave dealers who tempted them with better times and wages for their children in another country. Thinking they were providing their offspring with opportunities for a comfortable life, they gave them to the Arabs, who instead sold the children once they arrived on the Somali coast.

"You know who brought them into Somalia?" Abdihakim fills me in, saying, "Said Barqash, a king who ruled a long time ago from Zanzibar to Mogadishu." Abdihakim knows the story well, and he informs me that the slaves spoke Swahili and that they still haven't forgotten their language. "We call them Mushunguli," he adds. Between 1800 and 1890, these young slave girls and boys, totaling between twenty-five thousand and fifty thousand, were absorbed into the Shabelle river valley, where they labored on the plantations. Their only break from heavy toil came at night, when they performed subversive narratives in dance and vented their frustrations with the plantation owners.

The story of their eventual escape has become part of Somali Bantu mythology, and it is a story the Bantus in Seattle and Portland want every American to know. It centers on a female hero, a Somali Bantu woman by the name of Wanakhucha (or Wanakooka), who led the runaway slaves from the plantations to freedom in the lower Juba Valley in the 1840s.

"I'll tell you how they were able to outwit their masters." Omar leans over the table and recounts their story with some glee. "You see, in order to keep the slaves from organizing, the slave masters kept them in separate slave villages and did not allow them to visit each other." Little did they know, however, that the slaves were speaking to one another through the rhythm of their drums. "They were playing the drums, and their masters were thinking they were just dancing, but that's the way they did all their planning, through their drums, and thus knew when to run away and to where. On one particular morning," he continues, and we lean forward eagerly, "when the slave masters woke up, they found every villager gone, and they wondered, 'How did they organize this?'"

> Well, it was Wanakhucha's plan. She was the one who planned it so they could leave under cover of an all-night dance. And she is the one who led them to Gosha, which in the Somali language means "forest." They had intended to go back by foot to their ancestral homes of Tanzania, Malawi, and Mozambique, but again, Wanakhucha realized—some say she saw an earthquake-inspired vision—that it was a long trip and that it would be too dangerous, because they would not make it. So she said, "This is where we will settle."

The slave masters pursued them into the Juba river forests, but by then, the Gosha settlers had armed themselves and resisted recapture. By the early 1900s, thirty-five thousand to forty thousand ex-slaves had settled there and established village communities based on their East African tribes. Known to the Somalis as the "people of the forest," they are more generally called Mushunguli. Although they became a relatively stable farming community, they still lived in fear of slave traders. Even after slavery had been abolished in southern Somalia, Italian authorities attempted to reconscript the Bantu into labor brigades for the colonial government's plantations. The settlers had no interest in distinctions between different groups and lineages, and they considered all black Africans in Somalia one and the same, lumping them together as a Negroid labor force they hoped to exploit. To make matters worse, they co-opted Somalis of pastoral origin, who then subdued and secured this African labor for them. In this way, the Italians supported the pastoral Somalis in their system of class differentiation based on occupation and further strengthened the dominant-clan Somalis' disdain for farm labor and the black laborers themselves. Which is why, after the Italians left and the Somali republic came into being in the 1960s, the dominant *Samales* continued to see race as intricately linked with agriculture, thus allowing them to exclude the Bantu from the running of their country and the sharing of its wealth.

The Bantu have another foundation narrative that dominant-clan Somalis would like to see disappear because it undercuts their own origin story of Arab-Somali ancestry. Somali Bantus of the second group believe themselves to be descendants of the original inhabitants of central and northern Somalia who settled in villages around the Shabelle River long before the *Samale* Somalis arrived. Italian diplomat Enrico Cerulli, as early as 1957 and in the face of racist Italian scholarship about the peoples of the area, concluded that these were indeed the original inhabitants of the Shabelle river valley who were later overwhelmed by the Oromo and then by the Somali pastoral populations.[1] The Somali upper class (*bilis*), however, didn't want to know. They simply lumped together the descendants of both the indigenous people and the slaves and referred to them all as commoners or *sheegad*, descendants of slaves.

"Among Somali scholars themselves," Omar explains, "nobody wanted to write about the Shabelle because it would have contradicted Somali notions of homogeneity." And even in the United Nations, Van Lehman notes, nobody wanted to touch the subject of slavery.

Catherine Besteman claims that it was Omar Eno himself who helped open the floodgates of revisionist studies of Somalia. Identifying himself as a Somali Bantu, he presented a paper about his people's grievances as part of the panel "The Invention of Somalia" at the 1993 International Congress of Somali Studies. His words "shocked the audience" of scholars who reacted "with a mixture of embarrassment, silence, uncomfortable laughter, awe, and pain." Besteman quotes part of Omar's address:

[The Bantu in Somalia] have been suppressed and oppressed, robbed, raped, and killed. We have been deprived of our civil rights as Somali citizens, from independence by every Somali regime until the present. We have been stigmatized and undermined as inferior to other Somalis; yet we are never given any eligibility for opportunities in the Somali society. . . . My experience in Somalia has been [this]: we [Jareer] did not need to commit a crime of any kind, because being a Jareer itself is a crime.[2]

These terse and direct words give us an idea of the degree to which Somali Bantus feel they have suffered at the hands of their fellow Somalis. Yet the IRC's Bob Johnson took exception to Omar's words. "Why say something like that at a public conference and upset everyone? I mean, maybe there was discrimination, but to bring it up and perpetuate it doesn't do anyone any good." While this book certainly attests to the importance of moving beyond historical resentments, the problem with Johnson's argument in relation to the Bantu is that many *Samales* still deny that the Bantu were ever treated as slaves and second-class Somalis, and some still treat them as such here in the diaspora. During the twenty-one-year rule of Siyad Barre (1969–90), despite Scientific Socialism's claims to enact egalitarian measures preventing the hierarchical privileging of the clan system, Somali Bantu constantly endured humiliations and indignities. For example, the state military frequently kidnapped the southerners and conscripted them into the Somali army. It deployed them in the front lines of battle in Ethiopia, where they suffered huge numbers of casualties. Furthermore, Barre's government expropriated their land. After the introduction of the Land Law in 1975, a mad land grab of the Gosha people's property ensued.

Shongolo, who used to live in Gosha, explains that because few Bantu were literate, they were unable to obtain titles to their properties. "The government wrote the Domain Law just for us Bantu," he laughs. His friends join him, their laughter tinged with irony as he explains how the government would send the Bantu away when it wanted their land and in their absence grant it to *Samales*. The fertile muddy land known as *dhooboy* is extremely productive and provides Somalia with most of its staple stocks, which include maize, millet, sorghum, sesame, beans, cotton, rice, vegetables, and fruits. "It was known as the food basket of

Somalia," Mowliid informs me. "That's where all the agriculture was," he says, "just outside Mogadishu."

That was also the place where the fighting first started in 1990 as the Barre regime came to an end and demand for land in the fertile valleys of the Juba and Shabelle intensified. As Somali civil society broke down and normal networks for food collapsed, people starved and bandits and militia attacked the Bantu for their food stocks and ultimately their land. The Somali clan networks excluded them, so the Bantu had no protection and began fleeing the "triangle of death" between the rivers for refugee camps in Kenya and northern Tanzania.

"It was not a civil war," Omar Eno argues. "It was a regional war, because it was utterly confined to the south. This is a war about resources," he insists, "a struggle for the agricultural land and the river water." With confirmation from revisionist scholars like Besteman, Cassanelli, and Ahmed Samatar, the Somali Bantu are convinced they've been victims of a twenty-year land struggle with the state.[3]

"Thank goodness scholarship now is much more competitive," Omar claims. He explains how, in earlier times, scholars could say anything and get away with it because nobody challenged them, which is how the old thinking on Somalia perpetuated misinformation. "You see," he says, "American and European reports built on this misinformation, which was fed to them by Somalis who were exploiting the situation for their own benefit."

When I ask about the future of *Samale* and Somali Bantu relations in Seattle, Hamadi Hassan of Somali Bantu Community Services of Washington shakes his head. "The *Samales* are never going to be honest with the Bantu," he says. "In the presence of other communities and organizations, they act cooperative, but when everyone leaves, they revert to their usual attitudes." For that reason, he and Shongolo are rewriting history based on what they saw and experienced between 1991 and 2009. "We're writing our story . . . actually, it's history," he laughs.

"History *is* story," I say.

"You're right," Hammadi agrees. He left Kenya's Dadaab refugee camp for the United States in December 2004. "So far, we have 140 pages."

"It's a gift to our community," Shongolo adds.

OUTCAST GROUPS

The Somali Bantus, however, are not the only ones exploited by the *Samale*. The hunters, blacksmiths, metalsmiths, shoemakers, and potters, the so-called outcasts of Somalia, have an even harder time of it. Like the Bantu, they are considered ritually inferior on account of their occupations and suffer the ingrained biases of the pastoralists even though they are often indistinguishable from *Samales* in looks.

"The most beautiful and well-mannered women come from the outcast groups," Omar informs me, "and the most handsome men." Among them can be found the Midgan, Yibir, Galgala, and Tumal, whose origins, despite their external similarity with the *Samale*, remain vague. In *Aman: The Story of a Somali Girl*, the eponymous Aman recounts one version of the Midgan origin story. It tells of a man and his two sons, one of whom he disowns because the boy breaks the law that forbids Muslims from eating an animal that has not been prepared ritually. Though Islamic law allows transgression for the sake of survival, the older of the two starving brothers goes beyond what is permissible and indulges greedily in the flesh of the dead animal they find on their path. What is more, he does not throw up after other nourishment has been given to them. His sibling therefore refuses to eat from the same plate, as he now considers his brother dirty. When they return home, the father's shame at his older son's transgression leads him to disown the boy and kick him out. That, according to the myth as Aman understood it, is how the older brother and his descendants became outcasts—the Midgans—and why at weddings, even today, it is believed that couples state their lineages back thirty generations in order to prove that they have no connection with the Midgans.

When I ask Amadu about breaking the dietary law, he responds, "So what if my great-great-grandfather ate dead meat? Look at the circumstances under which he did it. Somalis need to think about the situation realistically and ask themselves: Was this really a crime that merited imposing such a weighty punishment on future generations?" The speaker chooses to be quoted under a fictionalized name, so I cannot say more about Amadu, other than that he actively investigates the history of the outcast groups. When I tell him I cannot find anyone in Seattle who acknowledges being a Midgan, he expresses no surprise.

"You should never ask 'Are you Midgan?' but rather 'Are you the man of the arrow?'" he says, explaining the offensiveness of the former term. He suggests "Madhiban" instead, although that word also trails connotations. He says it means "harmless" and applies to all the outcast groups because they are really just one large intermarried group.

Still, each of the groups claims its own story of origin. The Galgala, among whom are animal slaughterers, shoemakers, and also talented woodcarvers, for example, consider themselves descendants of Mohamud and Omar Mohamud, subclans of the Majerteen. The Yibir metalsmiths, however, claim Israelite roots. Their somewhat violent legend begins with them enjoying an easygoing lifestyle in what is now Somalia. With the arrival of Islamic newcomers in the area, however, disputes arise, and the sheikh accuses their king, Bu'ur Baayr, of living in luxury and being a bad influence on both his subjects and the Muslim community. The king is found guilty and sentenced by the sheikh, who, wanting to undermine his influence, challenges him to bring down a particular mountain in two separate parts. When the king of the Yibir successfully performs this act, the sheikh, desiring not to lose face in front of his own people, challenges the king to repeat it and then stand between the two split sections of the mountain. When the king does so, the sheikh, feeling his own humiliation at this double act of faith but also the shame of his envy, prays to Allah for forgiveness. Immediately, the ground trembles, the sky turns black, and the two parts of the mountain collapse, killing the king of the Yibir where he stands between them.

Despite the different origins of the various outcast groups, Amadu speaks of them all as one. "We Madhibaan are the descendants of the original Cushitic inhabitants of Somalia, an ancient people who were there even before the Nubians came," he asserts. "We were the owners of Punt, and long before Islam arrived on the scene, we controlled the area. These people now, the ones who call themselves Somalis . . . in the twelfth century, they were just a lot of different ethnic groups. They were not of Arabic origin, nor were they descended from Muhammad."

"What made them come together then?" I ask.

"They wanted to defeat us. After we fell to them at Hargeisa, they enslaved us and converted us to Islam. Ever since, we have borne their insults and denigration. Even their proverbs demean us."

Today, these groups constitute the "untouchables" of Somalia. "If they drink from this glass," Omar points to an ordinary water glass on the table between us, "it is considered broken. Nobody else touches it anymore. It is broken." The four of us at the conference table at Portland State University all stare at the glass. An image from South Africa many years ago flashes through my mind, of a Xhosa house maid given her own separate glass and the white children of the household forbidden by their parents to drink from it.

The cultural stigma associated with the work of these outcast groups limits their ability to buy cattle or land and prevents them from ever gaining political power. Since they are also few in number and do not have their own militias, many have assimilated into other clans in which they have a client-patron relationship that provides them with some protection when disputes lead to financial or even blood debts. President Siyad Barre tried to emancipate the outcasts as part of his attempt to rid the country of its archaic clan system and, to that end, banned the use of words that inferred race (like *jareer*) or occupation (Midgan and Tumal). But while his purpose may have been admirable in the beginning, the absorption of some of the occupational castes into the military implicated them in Barre's violence, and they were held responsible for it after he ran away in 1991. After his fall, brutal reprisals took place in Mogadishu, including a savage roundup and massacre of Galgala in Mogadiscio Stadium.

"The crimes that we have committed against Yibir as well as Midgan, Tumal and Bantus are a mountain high," writes Somali critic Ahmed Ismail Yusuf. On the Midgan Web site, he claims, after reading the novel *The Yibir of Las Burgabo* by Mahmood Gaildon, that there is "no way to compensate their loss of dignity and the psychological trauma they suffered for centuries." In the novel, a young Yibir boy, Ali, tries to find his way out of the "vicious current of social bias" in which he is blamed for his own situation. Ahmed ends his review by suggesting that the novel be taught in every Somali classroom.

In Seattle and Portland, the words "Tumal" and "Midgan" still pop up in Somali discourse. Many of the so-called untouchables, hoping to start afresh in a democratic environment, try to pass as members of other clans. They do not want to be identified and thus choose to live covert lives. Amadu refers to them as "integrationists" who seek assimilation so that they might be protected from class prejudice and hostility. The "separatists," on the other hand, work toward a separate but equal relationship, one that demands respect from the Somali tribes and recognition of the rights of the outcasts as human beings.

"I mean," Amadu asks rhetorically, "what did we do to the Somalis that they hate us so? We are a hardworking people whose labor should be acknowledged and respected. We are in building and construction, shoemaking, and cutting meat." As one of his first jobs after he arrived in the United States, Amadu tells me, he worked in a "beef factory" (slaughterhouse).

In an ironic turn of events, now that the diaspora Madhiban have their own organization to protect their interests, members of other clans have begun claiming Midgan identity. "For the last nine hundred years, the clan Somalis have insulted us, but now they pretend to be Midgan so they can claim persecution and thus gain refugee status!" Amadu laughs at the ridiculous situation that has arisen and then points out reassuringly, "Look, I don't hate anyone. All I want to do is educate the clan Somalis so that they will change their behavior. I want to tell them that America is a free land, a free country, and you cannot do here what you did at home."

Omar, too, tries to be the dispassionate scholar. Even so, he cannot resist expressing his feelings. "The Somalis claim brotherhood with us, but they are two-faced and behind our backs dismiss us as slaves." He points to Somalia's division of the population by a four-and-a-half-clan rule that bundles together all of the minority groups like the Bantu, Benadiri, Bravanese, and the outcasts into half a tribe, with the main four being Darod, Isaq-Dir, Hawiye, and Digil-Mirifle. With more than a touch of sarcasm, he goes on to explain that since those labeled as a half tribe did not initiate any of the chaos and destruction caused by the so-called major tribes, they did not qualify to be recognized as fully represented Somalis. Then he regales us with a joke making its rounds at that time suggesting that since the outcasts constitute only a half tribe, perhaps they should only pay half taxes, fight for the country half-time, and work half-time. Beyond the laughter, however, real anger simmers, for the discrimination continues to fester in the new country.

THE OROMO

In Portland, an Oromo evangelical church stands on the corner of Martin Luther King Jr. Boulevard and Northeast Skidmore, its parking lot packed with cars. Farther along King Boulevard and Broadway, Ethiopian restaurants, such as the Queen of Sheba and Blue Nile, plus Ethiopian markets like Selam and Mercato offer the American outsider an appearance of Ethiopian uniformity, which the Oromo church, with its large imposing sign, undercuts. Like the Somali Bantu and the outcasts, the Oromo of Ethiopia also have a story that sits uncomfortably within the national narrative. Despite what the history books say, namely, that the Oromo were "predatory" invaders with a "predilection toward warfare" who migrated from the south into present-day Ethiopia in the fifteenth and sixteenth centuries in search of new land and pastures, their oral history suggests that they are the original Ethiopians.[4]

They are a Cushitic or Hamitic people who speak Oromiffa (Afaan Oromo) and claim to be the native inhabitants of the kingdom of Cush. Cush was the son of Ham, son of Noah, as related in the Bible, and his kingdom rivaled that of Egypt in the second millennium B.C.E. Shigut Kumera, a Portland Oromo, proudly testifies to the size of the kingdom. As we walk to the car with his brother Tesfaye, he holds his arms out wide and explains with expansive movements how Cush's lands stretched for thousands of miles, all the way from northern Sudan to the Red Sea and even to the southern edges of Nubia. "We are his descendants," he says with pride, "and we know we are Cushitic because our language has many of the same words as the languages of other Cushitic people, like the Afar and Somalis."

"You see, we no longer look like pure Hamites," Tesfaye explains, "but that's because of intermarriage and assimilation. The Axumites, whom the Tigrayans and Tigrinya consider their ancestors, destroyed Cush, and being themselves more Arabic, they introduced the Semitic strain." We arrive at a café in northeast Portland, and Tesfaye opens the car door for me. "That's how the whole Horn of Africa got mixed up," he adds.

Tesfaye and Shigut Kumera are Arsi Oromo whose people have resisted the Amhara appropriation of their land ever since the 1880s. They finally lost what was left of their traditional homeland, the area around Lake Langano, about a hundred miles south of Addis, in the 1960s. "You know this area?" Tesfaye asks me as we finish our cups of strong black coffee. He purposely chose not to drink the Ethiopian blend and instead asked for Sumatra. When I indicate that I don't know Lake Langano, he explains that it was a very tough area. "No one came through it; they didn't dare." Tesfaye's voice, unlike his older brother Shigut's more resigned one, barely conceals his resentment. Shigut tries to explain that Langano was a low-lying lake area where most of their family lived and where he was born and raised, but Tesfaye, anxious to get to the point, interrupts to tell me how in 1963 it was totally subjugated. "The place was completely burned," he says, biting down on the first part of the word, then dismissing the rest with a sideways chop of his hand. Shigut looks at his brother as if he expects an outburst, but Tesfaye continues in controlled fashion to describe how, years later, they used to dig up pages written in Oromo, just lying there in the dirt. "All those books," he shakes his head. "We tried to read them—we read, you know, in Oromiffa—but gradually, as time went on, people forgot how to speak it. Even the Mass they forgot."

"So, everything that was written about the Oromo . . ." Shigut adds, "now, you don't see anymore in the libraries."

Until the 1990s, finding anything about Oromo history in books about Ethiopia was like finding the proverbial needle in the haystack. Even though the Oromo make up approximately 30 million of the total population of 60 million, readers were hard pressed to come across their story at all. Instead, what they found was the derogatory term "Galla," used formerly by the Amhara for those who lived in the southern lowlands of Abyssinia. The word itself translates as "River People" and is believed to have derived from the Oromo's mythological creation narrative, which represents their origins as the emergence of the first Oromo being, their founding father Orma, from water.[5] In Amharic parlance, however, "Galla" denotes inferiority and signifies "savage," "slave," "barbaric," "uncultured," and "ignorant." Its use effectively removed the Oromo peoples from any role in Ethiopian history.

The othering of the Oromo actually began with the Amhara scholar Abba Bahrey, whose *Chronicles of the Galla*, written at the end of the sixteenth century, set the tone for writers who followed.[6] One Amhara account after another depicted the Oromo as brutal and bloodthirsty, so when Western scholars started writing their histories of the area, they uncritically repeated the denigration of the Oromo and the valorization of the Amhara. Further, the racialized images of the Oromo presented by Amharas who were claiming Semitic ancestry for themselves fed into Western racism and led to increasingly physiognomic descriptions.

Oromos in the Pacific Northwest dismiss this scholarship. In particular, they criticize the narrative of the Oromo's fifteenth- and sixteenth-century arrival in Ethiopia. Three elderly Oromos who have overheard my conversation on the subject with another Oromo outside their community center on South Jackson stride over to set me straight. It was, in fact, neither an invasion nor a migration, one of them argues, as his two friends murmur their support. It was a national movement, they say, to stop the Ethiopians from grabbing all their territories and destroying their culture, including their religion and their *gada* system of social and political organization.

Later, I ask Tesfaye about the *gada* system. He describes it as a carefully organized age-group system that uses its members' age-defined abilities and skills to the advantage of the community. That way, he says, "each member has a chance as he passes through various stages to gain the skills of each, be it herding, fighting, or ruling. And no group has a greater right to the community's resources than any other. Instead, the community's wealth and its property and other assets are used whenever and for whomever they are needed. Like during war, or famine, and also marriages." He saves for last what I consider to be one of the best attributes of the system, namely, the eight-year nonrenewable limit of rule that precludes aging men holding onto office. If only the Zimbabweans had a *gada* system, we joke. We throw out the names of various aging despots whose communities could have benefited from such a limit, and with each one, Tesfaye thumps the table. He is proud of *gada*, but today, little remains of its symbols and rituals.[7]

Like Eritreans, the Oromo see themselves as having been colonized by Amhara rulers. Such talk of colonial occupation, however, exasperates many Ethiopians, as the conquest occurred in precapitalist times, when Ethiopia was a feudal empire. Besides, even if one calls it "colonization," the typical Ethiopianist approach has it, by establishing Ethiopian rule over the conquered areas, the Ethiopians solved serious intertribal wars, eliminated slavery, and protected all the people of Greater Ethiopia from the European imperialists. Local Oromos bridle at these arguments, but what irks them most is the claim that Oromo primitivism had kept Ethiopia underdeveloped.[8] Tesfaye counters that both the Selassie regime and that of the Derg promised democracy, but "neither was prepared to allow the organized existence of a people who actually practiced a democratic system, *gada.*" What they really wanted was absolute power.

"That's why our Oromo language [Oromiffa or Afaan Oromo] also became a casualty at the hands of the Amharas," Shigut adds. Oromiffa is second only to Swahili as the most widely spoken language in Africa. Despite its use by more than 20 million people, it has been ignored by the world, and the literary inheritance of the Oromo has been lost.

Portland's Gelete Gemechu explains to me in her calm and even voice that the loss of language has meant the loss of most of Oromo history prior to 1970. "Histories, storybooks . . . these books that were written in Oromiffa, you can't find any more in Ethiopia. Basically, they just burned them up," she says. "Now you have to go to other countries, to Germany and Britain, to find out about our people. It has all been eradicated, and the history books today paint us all black."

"No wonder we Oromo are so full of resentment," Tesfaye murmurs under his breath. "Even though Selassie was half Oromo, and Menelik, too," he explains, "when people talk about Ethiopian history today, they mean Amhara history because that is what past governments pushed. There is absolutely no Oromo history there."[9]

The little written about Oromos by scholars relying on Ethiopian, Kenyan, or Somali sources does not correspond to the oral narratives still alive in Oromo communities. "The Oromo are not, for example, heathen, despite what the Amhara Christians think," Gelete informs me. We sit in her living room, and, as she gently but adamantly talks about the faith of her people, she keeps an eye on her sleeping baby, who lies on the sofa, his small fists clenched. On the wall above the sofa hangs a picture of Lej Iyassu, the only Ethiopian king who defied the Coptic Church and tried to help the Oromo. "We are *waqafata,*" Gelete explains to me, "worshippers of one God, the creator God, Waqa. And we had temples, including one to Mary. I only remember bits and pieces of the religion"—

she smiles apologetically—"but what I know is that the Oromo have their own priestly tribe, the Alujana, and that people thought the tribe had supernatural powers and could affect you in such a way as to bring about forgiveness."

"Was it a theology?" I ask.

"No, but it was some kind of organized belief. But not like voodoo," she adds quickly, as if to reassure me, "it's different. My father was a high priest at one of the temples, *galma*, we call it. It means, 'where God lives,' and it had several sections, the Holy, the more Holy, the most Holy, etc., etc." We both laugh when she gets to the Holiest of the Holy, and she explains that on the High Holy Days, the priest would pray his way through all seven sections and on the seventh day walk out completely transformed and in need of a translator. There were also numerous rituals, she says. At the beginning of Holy Week, for example, they would butcher a lamb and "put the blood on the door of the church and on the foreheads of individuals who come through it as a blessing, a kind of cleansing." She goes on to describe other ceremonies that sound hardly different from traditional Christian ones. "And people bring young children to the priest, and he puts them on his lap and gives them a beautiful name of the blessed one, he who is according to the heart of God." She turns to me and adds, "Just meaningful things, really."

Oromos were forced to convert under threat of losing their property, and successive rulers have generally continued to impose religious uniformity. "The old rituals have all died away," Gelete tells me, her eyes betraying her apparent calm. "The government just erased them."

"How did the government do it?" I ask.

"For one thing, they confiscated my father's drums and drumsticks. Usually they are used in the rituals, but they were taken away by the city government. And so in this way, you know, they tried to discourage the religion." Not surprisingly, the people resented the government's actions, and so when they did convert, rather than join the Coptic Church, they became Seventh Day Adventists or Catholics.

Jalata argues that by dismantling Oromo religion, the Amharas destroyed the Oromo worldview that connected the spiritual with the natural and encompassed an ethical and moral code. By destroying *both* the religion and the *gada* system, he writes, the Amhara demolished the entire underlying structure of Oromo society.[10] Ethiopian administrators eliminated Oromo prophets and oral historians and built churches on Oromo cultural centers.[11]

Decades of religious, linguistic, political, economic, and cultural oppression have left the Oromo with skeletal pasts, skimpy narratives full of gaps. The onus for filling them lies with diaspora Oromo, who by and large represent the intellectual elite and whose research must recover the lost identities. Their job is huge, for in addition to uncovering those stories that have been erased or suppressed, they must rectify the misinformation of past records and retrofit the whole. Menelik, Selassie, Mengistu, and Meles Zenawi, they say, have all distorted the Oromo story.

"For example," Shigut says, focusing my attention, "let's get the Shoa-Amhara relationship straight!" The Shoans were originally an Oromo group, but Shigut explains that Menelik bribed them with guns and in that way subjugated them and appropriated their land. Then, once he had converted them to Christianity, he used them against other Oromo who traditionally used spears. "The Shoans knew the Oromo language and culture," he explains, "so when the other Oromo came out to negotiate rather than shoot, as was the Oromo custom, the Shoans could defeat them." In return for the weapons, the Shoan Oromo paid taxes to Menelik and spoke Amharic. As Christian Amharic speakers wielding guns, they expanded Amhara power in the southern states and then in the north, finally assuming Amhara identity themselves.

Many of their countrymen, however, resisted Menelik's attempts to unify Ethiopia by force, the bravest among them the Arsi Oromo, the group to which Shigut and Tesfaye belong. "Our horsemen were known as the Germans of Africa for their ridership." Shigut squares his shoulders. "They were very, very, very powerful horsemen, warriors who were naturals at horseback riding. When they were fighting, they would just swing under the horses and let the enemy go by."

The battles of Arsi, Gulalee, Abichu, Chalanqo, Wallo, Meta, and Borana are alive in the oral stories that recount the heroism and feats of bravery performed by those Oromo warriors of old. At Asala, for instance, the Amhara were so desperate, Gelete informs me, they even resorted to biological warfare. "They gave the warriors smallpox," she says, referring to the epidemic that raged in Oromia from 1886 to 1887.

In the end, however, the Amhara had their way, and "after two decades of plundering and terrorizing us and reducing us to poverty," Tesfaye explains, they finally succeeded in conquering the Oromo people, annexing Oromia, and incorporating it into the Ethiopian Empire. Only those Oromo who were prepared to support the Coptic Christian Church, pay taxes, and otherwise show their loyalty to the emperor managed to hang onto their lands.

To keep the Oromo subservient and dilute any resistance, Menelik practiced a policy of divide and rule. "I tell you, the Amhara were vicious," Tesfaye bridles, "cruel killers and looters. Those captured were massacred or sold as slaves, and the elderly and children burned alive." Menelik's successor, Haile Selassie, continued his policy of cultural oppression alongside an active campaign of Amharanization. He incorporated the vast majority of the Oromo population, banned their *gada* system, and forbade the teaching of Oromo history. The state denied official recognition to the Oromo language and culture and suppressed the Oromo alphabet that was invented in the mid-twentieth century. As a result, many Oromo were obliged to assimilate if only to obtain employment and access to modern education for their children. Those who lost their language, Tesfaye informs me, and are no longer able to speak Oromiffa are called *grassali*.

"So, does that mean that in order to be treated as equals in Ethiopia, Oromos had to become Amharas?" I ask Tesfaye.

"Except in jail," he responds. We both laugh, and his brother Shigut elbows him and shakes his head. However successful Oromos became, they say, they were never accepted as equals by the Amhara. Their class status remained a persistent obstacle to their standing in Ethiopian society.

It was during this period that Oromo nationalism first emerged as a movement. Many young people and students went underground, circulating samizdat, such as the "Voice of Oromo against Tyranny," which dispensed with the name "Galla" and instead began using "Oromo," with its connotation of "brave people," to challenge the Ethiopian historiography that had wiped out the word. The name instilled pride and unified the people, changing their perception of their own standing. Study groups turned into underground political movements, and in 1974, an armed pan-Oromo movement, the Oromo Liberation Front (OLF), emerged, intent on creating an independent state.[12]

With the overthrow of Selassie in 1974 and the rise of Ethiopian socialism, many Oromos took hope from the Derg's pronouncement that all peoples in the empire would be considered equal. They soon learned, however, that all that had changed were their masters. Like their predecessors, the Derg settled thousands of Ethiopians in Oromo territory, but they went further, displacing the Oromos and settling them in experimental "socialist villages" where they could be better controlled and their labor managed. With the socialist appropriation of the land, the 80 percent of Oromo people who had tilled the soil for their livelihood lost not only any right to the land but even any guarantee to its sustainable use. The Derg demanded hefty taxes for the land the Oromos plowed as well as involuntary military or other unpaid services. Oromo society fell apart, and more than a million Oromos became refugees in different parts of the world. Poverty and servitude faced the Oromos who remained, so they joined the Oromo Liberation Front and were instrumental in bringing down the military regime in 1991. With its collapse, the Oromo again dared to hope that now, finally rid of the Amharas, they would be able to recoup their losses and rebuild their culture. But the Tigrayans, who make up about 10 percent of the population, felt threatened by the numbers and power of the Oromo and reneged on their promises. Like their predecessors, they practiced a policy of divide and rule, and to that end created a puppet Oromo organization, the Oromo People's Democratic Organization (OPDO), which led the Oromo Liberation Front to withdraw from the government.

"The TPLF-EPRDF were out to destroy OLF leaders and rebel forces," Tesfaye explains, speaking of the Tigray People's Liberation Front and the Ethiopian People's Revolutionary Democratic Front, so they banned their political organizations and free press, arrested and tortured political dissidents, and threw others into camps for reorientation. The Tigrayans monopolized the economy, and once again the Oromos were sidelined.

After being forced to leave Ethiopia in 1992, the OLF reorganized in the diaspora and formed numerous committees to carry on its work. Seattle and Portland each have its own committee around which the local Oromos rally, raising money and awareness in the hope of affecting developments at home. When heavy-handed actions by the Zenawi government's security personnel resulted in the deaths of more than one hundred protesters during the May 2005 elections in Ethiopia, the Seattle Oromo community requested in a public letter addressed to Senator Maria Cantwell "the immediate involvement" of the United States to avoid "further bloodshed" in Ethiopia, according to a December 21 report at the OLF Web site.

While some in the OLF are convinced that the Ethiopian government seeks an ethnic cleansing of Oromo, others do not support the OLF position at all. Many Oromos benefited from the expanding Ethiopian Empire, and assimilation often translated into the acquisition of social and economic status. They thus look with suspicion on the OLF's efforts to destabilize their position. Intermarriage also complicates the picture, and it isn't always easy to distinguish who is Oromo.

In Portland, the president of Oregon Ethiopian Community Organization, Abraham Demisse, acknowledges his Oromo ancestry, but first and foremost, he insists, he is Ethiopian. Abe, as he is known, has lived more years in the States than he has in Ethiopia. He is a dynamic and passionate speaker who feels strongly about Oromos separating themselves from Ethiopia. "Usually, it is the fringe element among the Oromos that push things," he says, adding cynically, "perhaps because they make money out of it in this country." We sit alone in a huge empty restaurant in the middle of the afternoon. The shutters are down because the restaurant doesn't open until five, but Abe seems to be a regular here, and the smiling waiter brings us coffee anyway. Abe holds strong opinions, which he proceeds to share with me. "I tell the Oromos," he says, "you can be Oromo and have some history, but when you put Ethiopia behind it, you have a *lot* of history that you can talk about. And the truth of the matter is they all know that." He goes on to explain:

> Look, the Oromos think they are going to be just like Eritrea, that they, too, can be a separate country one day. But that's something they need to eliminate from their minds. This kind of thinking was started by the current government. The previous military government never negotiated their nationality. They did not offer autonomy to the point that people could do what they wanted to do. Why? Because it threatened their society. This new group from Tigray comes in, it's a guerrilla organization, a Communist organization, it's not even capitalist, and it's still a baby

government finding its feet. They're hurting us internally because they are only 12 percent of the population, and they come from the north and they have no idea of our administration. Just like the conquerors of Africa used the Bible to divide the people, this government is doing the same thing now. They've divided us all, and the rulers are playing once again the game of *apartheid*. That's why the Oromos forget they're Ethiopians.

Unlike Eritrea, Oromia is not separate from Ethiopia and cannot simply be sliced off. Oromos live everywhere in Ethiopia; thus the exact boundaries of Oromia are a matter of speculation. Some say Oromia exists wherever Oromo live in Ethiopia, while others describe a 375,000-square-mile location between latitude 3° and 15° north and longitude 33° and 40° east. "It's just not practical to have an Oromo state," David Makonnen argues. He believes there are people in the local Oromo leadership who understand this. "But they know, too," he says, "that realizing secession is a guaranteed right in the Ethiopian constitution and could fundamentally alter the territorial integrity of current Ethiopia. So they effectively use the leverage they have in being the largest region with most of the natural resources to address the iniquities Oromos have always suffered with Amhara and Tigray leadership of the central government."

Although many Oromos in Seattle yearn for their own homeland, they concentrate more on reestablishing their Oromo culture for their children. The Oromo community center on South Jackson provides lessons in Oromiffa, and many older Oromos, discarding the Amharic names they were forced to assume back home, have reverted to their Oromiffa ones. The center also teaches English as a second language, and tutors help children with their studies after school. Education is their priority, and the Oromo Community Organization commits itself to improving women's and children's education especially. It also focuses on health and job training, stressing sports as an alternative for young men who might otherwise get drawn into the destructive activities of urban life. To that end, they support Seattle's Oromo soccer team, the Madda Walaabu, which took fourth place at the 2009 Oromo National Soccer Tournament and is fast establishing a soccer tradition in the Emerald City. A women's soccer team plus a track-and-field program are in the works.

The community numbers approximately three thousand, and those in need receive assistance from the Oromo Community Organization of the Seattle Metropolitan Area (OCOSMA). They live mostly in the Rainier Valley and in Holly Park, although some families have also settled in Ballard, West Seattle, Kent, Edmonds, and Bellevue.

"The Seattle Oromo community is very strong," David says. Having worked with them, he has also seen how they form coalitions with the local Somali and Eritrean communities. One of their best leaders, he says, is Abubakar Ali, who teaches at South Central Community College and also works for the YMCA. "He is well versed in the challenges that face the Oromos, is well respected in the Oromo community, and is very open-minded and pragmatic. Most importantly, he understands the value of working together."

Portland's approximately one thousand Oromos have settled in the northeast part of the city, near MLK Boulevard and Broadway, and also in the southeast. Like the Seattle Oromos, they came to the States as refugees mostly during the late 1980s, fleeing famine and bloodshed, though some, like the Kumeras, arrived earlier, in the 1970s, hoping to study and improve their situation. Many of the Portland Oromos also are involved in resurrecting their culture and are helped in the recovery of their identity by a nonprofit group, the Portland Oromo Community Association. The two diaspora communities are well organized, and although not everyone shares the exact same dream for Oromia, all agree that Oromos themselves should be allowed to decide what they want.

The young in particular are angry. "There's a new generation of diaspora Oromos coming up with a growing resistance and resentment," David points out. "They believe Oromos provide most of the natural resources that fuel the Ethiopian economy and they are not getting a fair deal in return. This young generation feels strongly about their identity and is increasingly prepared to do anything to fight for the secession of Oromia." With the creation of an intellectual elite in the diaspora and discussions on Oromo culture available to any Oromo with access to the Internet, local communities have become extremely well informed. The OLF's radio station, the Voice of the Liberation of Oromia, also helps keep the community abreast of developments. The Oromo American Citizens Council guides the local organizations in forming alliances and educates them in the workings of the U.S. political system so that they can influence American public policy and foreign policy to their benefit. Every July or August, a national Oromo congress meets to discuss issues of interest to the community as well as political events in the home country.

Despite the best efforts of Oromo leaders like Abubakar Ali to work across ethnic and national lines, many Oromo in Seattle and Portland will not mix with Amhara or Tigray. They eat at separate restaurants, worship at different churches, and go their own ways. If they are part Amhara, Tesfaye says, they claim they want to be only Ethiopian and dismiss the separation at the local level as just a "natural division." It just happens, they say.

Still, it's sad that the division exists. In Portland, Gelete argues for a better future for her people and expresses her hope that Oromo and Amhara eventually will appreciate each other. Her democratic sentiments echo those of most other local Oromos who claim to want to work together through cooperation and consensus.

The situation between Oromos and Somalis is equally complex, and I have observed the avoidance strategies Somalis use to sidestep any obligatory fraternizing with Oromos. Seattle Somalilander Mohamed Omer tells me that Somalis have no contact with Oromos in that city. If they attend the same mosque, he says, they may interact, but they do not discuss anything political.

Their relationship wasn't always so fraught. Though tensions over pastoral land have plagued the two sides since the late nineteenth century, many Oromos after the 1960s considered Somalia their country of refuge when things went wrong. Now, however, their relationship challenges the best intentions of each side. While historically Muslim Oromo groups such as the Arsi did maintain friendly interactions with their Somali neighbors, the new federation of post-1991 Ethiopia has poisoned relations.

Within the restructured federal Ethiopian state, the Oromos and Somalis have each been assigned their own areas with their own regional administrations, but the new borders have simply intensified the long-standing territorial competition between the two peoples. The OLF's militant agitation for self-determination in the Ogaden has sometimes put it at loggerheads with the Somalis and Ogadeni in the area, who also seek the right to decide their own future. Since they live in contiguous areas, the Oromo Liberation Front and the Ogaden National Liberation Front sometimes coordinate the actions of their guerrilla movements, but, as Jamal reminds me, "the OLF is only one section of the population of the Ogaden." What is more, they are "sometimes not reasonable in a situation that is difficult," thus making it even more so for the local people.

"The OLF recently attacked an Isaq vehicle," Jamal reports. OLF cells in Somaliland had been sneaking across the border, so "Somaliland, which cooperates with Ethiopia in terms of not allowing groups fighting against it to cross through the Somali border, cracked down on them and gave them over to Ethiopia. In retaliation, OLF attacked an Isaq vehicle in the region and set it alight." From Jamal's viewpoint, they created even more hardships in doing so, "since the vehicle was moving goods from one part of the Ogaden to another."

Further complicating the Oromo position, the Zenawi administration has labeled the Oromo struggle for self-determination and independence as terrorism. The OLF Web page calls the administration's action "mislabeling" and claims that this designation simply provides cover for its efforts to wipe out the OLF altogether. Since the December 2006 Ethiopian "invasion" of Somalia, the OLF claims, "another terror front" has been opened on the Oromo people, and they are being hunted down by members of the Somali militia and handed over to Ethiopian security forces for bounty. The Oromos' narratives about their Somali neighbors have become as bitter as those about the Ethiopians.

For most of their lifetimes, the Oromos interviewed in this story have been presented to the world as characters in stories spoken and written by other people. Now, with their own story out and revisionist scholars actively engaged in uncovering further information that might have been suppressed, the genie cannot easily be returned to the lamp.[13] Ethnic massacres may attempt to wipe out oppositional stories, but suppressed voices have a way of making themselves heard.

SEVEN

WOMEN
SPEAK OUT

Traditional behavior is learned behavior.

—RAHEL GEBREAB, SEATTLE, 2004

A S WE have seen, criticism from within can rend the social fabric of a community and present a divided face to neighbors and the world at large. When those internal critics also share one's bed and home, personal and political tensions can undercut everyday life and threaten the basic relationship on which all others depend, namely, that between man and woman. Nothing remains the same, narratives diverge, and male and female stories compete with each other, causing tensions in the home and sometimes in the larger circle of the community.

Women who challenge the status quo in this way have generally undergone a gradual sea change that has transformed the way they perceive themselves and in turn influenced their role vis-à-vis the opposite sex. Their new selves were often forged in the crucible of the liberation wars themselves, the very struggles that in Ethiopia and Eritrea heralded freedom and democracy for all people. Women took the liberation message to heart and threw themselves into the struggles alongside their brothers and fathers. As equal participants in the wars, many saw action and experienced injury, torture, and death, just like their male compatriots. Women soldiers in Eritrea constituted one-third of the Eritrean People's Liberation Front army. Even Muslim women, though forbidden by Islam to fight, donned uniforms and went into the field. There, along with their Christian sisters, they worked in every sphere of the struggle, from commanders to tank drivers, acquiring new skills and self-assurance along the way. Some of this new confidence eroded, however, after they returned to their rural homes and, once again, to the dictates of patriarchal expectations. Even some of the male fighters, men whose very lives had sometimes been protected by these same female soldiers, once home, wanted more submissive partners. The divorce rate soared.

"It was equality with a small 'e'," Michael Damtew explains, a cynical smile on his face. His wife, Sonya, a professional woman who holds her own with ease, nods in agreement. Michael proceeds to tell me an anecdote about an Eritrean man in Portland who "went out and bought a car without even discussing it first with his wife." His face expresses amazement, and I am loath to tell him that some American men have been known to do that, too. When he repeats the story to another Eritrean, "one of the Red Flowers, one of the 'Bearers of the Torch,' as the EPLF used to call them," he is again taken aback by the regressive attitude, he says. "I mean, this guy is born to the idea of gender. When the EPLF were giving them all this political education, they were told that women are equal to men. I mean, this is a very liberal way of looking at it." In an aside to me, but within his wife's hearing, he adds mischievously, "Of course, they were mistaken!" His wife and I smile indulgently, but he doesn't notice. "I mean, what happened to all that acceptance?" he asks.

Much of what was taught for the purpose of conducting warfare was forgotten when people returned home. In the privacy of his own place, the man once again picked up the reins and resumed his traditional role, forgetting everything that had happened in the field, when male and female fought alongside each other and depended on each other for safety. It was a big issue with the *tegadelti*, Sonya confirms. At the Immigrant and Refugee Community Organization, she worked with many Portland women who had experienced such change. "Some ex-fighters actually divorced," she says. "In the field, there had been no formal marriage; they just loved and were committed. But when they got home, their roles often reverted to the traditional prewar ones, where men went out to work and women stayed in the home. As a result, many of the marriages broke up."

In Eritrea, many women retained their hopes for a better and more equal role at home and in the public sector, where new laws appeared promising. Women now had the right to own land and to vote, feudal marriage laws were banned, bride prices and dowries were restricted, female circumcision was criminalized, and citizenship was granted to women and to children born out of wedlock. The government, however, chose not to enforce the new laws in the rural areas and relied instead on education and social influences to bring about gradual change. In the cities, some of the luckier female veterans who came from Asmara were able to start small businesses such as shops, hotels, and gas stations or won positions in local and regional governments.

For those women who fled to the United States, the knowledge of what they were capable of stayed with them. In the more feminist milieu of the Pacific Northwest, many refugees flourished as they returned to school, found jobs, and proved that they could stand on their own two feet. But these challenges were not the end of their problems. What really tore them apart emotionally and psychologically were grievances and resentments that are more difficult to discuss.

At the small storefront office of an Eritrean women's resource center in Seattle, a number of female refugees sit quietly drinking coffee and chatting with their neighbors. They are mostly middle-aged women, and they speak about practical issues. One complains softly about the myriad forms her doctor requires her to fill out when he knows she still struggles with English, while another seeks advice on how to deal with the housing authority that won't give her a bigger apartment despite the fact that she's had two new babies since arriving. Yet another woman shares a story about her teenage son's increasingly "American" behavior, which she feels helpless to control. While the women show no obvious reluctance about speaking of such subjects, they do not talk about themselves in a personal way. They keep buried the unpleasant images from the past and their own resentment about opportunities lost. They fear being ostracized as unpatriotic if they speak out about their wartime experiences, disloyal if they disparage their husbands, and shamed if they admit to being raped during the war.

Lette Hadgu is very cognizant of the problems facing Eritrean women and has been counseling them and offering them support through the Seattle chapter of the National Union of Eritrean Women (NUEW) ever since she became president and chair on June 15, 2000. While she sometimes speaks of NEUW's role in terms that seem to come straight out of the organization's leaflets—"NUEW aims to empower women and help them move forward with their lives through the discovery and recognition of their strengths, talents, and abilities"—in practice, she is a warm and gracious woman who has extended a helping hand to many. "We try to create a sisterly atmosphere at NUEW where women can feel safe and welcome," she says. "We believe that it is only when we openly share our ideas, thoughts, and concerns that we begin to make sense of our lives and find solutions to our many challenges."

The women who gather at NUEW or at some of the other resource centers that also counsel women, such as the Eritrean Association of Greater Seattle or the Immigrant and Refugee Community Organization in Portland, want to claim the respect and dignity they feel are often denied them. They have their own war experiences to recount and want to ensure that women like them also have a place in the histories of their countries. They want control over their own bodies and sexuality, the right to say "no" and to marry when and whom they want. Moreover, they desire the rights to their own productive labor, to be able to work and consider the money they earn as theirs. And finally, they want equal respect within marriage and relationships.

It is what most Eritrean women in the diaspora want. It is also what most Ethiopian and Somali women here desire, too.

CHANGING RELATIONSHIPS

Not all immigrant women make it, of course. Like raisins in the sun, the deferred dreams of many young mothers struggling to find their feet in the Pacific Northwest dry up as they are obliged to take menial jobs to support their families and put food on the table. At Mary Gates Hall on the University of Washington campus, Ethiopian, Eritrean, and Somali women move barely noticed through the washrooms on each floor. The laughing and chattering female students spritzing their hair or applying lip gloss in front of the mirrors do not acknowledge these women's presence. The women are not that much older than the students, and as they wipe down the counters or replace the toilet paper rolls, they study the students' gestures and memorize the way they wear their clothes and how they arrange their hair. After finishing with the bathrooms, they take a break in their "office," the small room where the cleaning supplies are kept, and often, peals of laughter followed by effusive talk in one of the Horn languages can be heard from behind the closed door. The women, who are uneducated and unskilled, make up a large sector of the janitorial staff who scrub floors, clean bathrooms, and generally pick up after messy students. In a February 21, 2004, *Seattle Times* article, "An Immigrant's Fate: From American Dream to 'America's Dirty Work,'" Mary Andom, an Eritrean student at Western Washington University in Bellingham, writes that her mother has done this for ten years, eleven hours a day, five days a week. She has accepted her fate, her daughter says, because she has no education. But there are days when exhaustion and the "lingering chemical smells" on her skin leave her depressed, and her daughter imagines her thinking to herself, "This is no life." Still, she is proud of her daughter, the first member of the family to attend college, and accepts that, like other first-generation immigrants before her, her own dreams have to be put on the back burner.

Despite the hardships of immigrant life—the menial jobs, sometimes two or three of them to make ends meet, and the juggling of home and work responsibilities—such women now enjoy freedoms they never experienced in the Horn. They participate in the public sector and earn their own money. The really lucky ones also attend high school or college, catching up on education interrupted by wars and poverty or never offered to them in the first place. Among the more urban intellectuals, a university education is seen as the gateway to the American Dream. "Do you know, we have more Somali female university graduates here than male?" Ubax Gardheere tells me as we sit talking in the small library at a mall in Tukwila.

"Really?" I say, impressed.

"Yeah, and the men rationalize it by saying it's because they have to work!" Then, in that global female gesture of amused exasperation, she sighs, "Men! There's an excuse for everything." A Somali man looks up from his Somali newspaper, but she barely notices. Ubax, when I first interviewed her in March 2005, worked full-time while also studying for

her master's degree in public administration at Seattle University. Five
years and two children later, she is getting a management certificate in
fund-raising so that she can pursue her activist goals.

Back home in Somalia, in 1975, when Siyad Barre introduced family
law based on sharia, Somali women initially benefited with regard to
property rights and inheritance. However, as the government increasingly
curtailed civil rights, only educated urban women profited. Some city
women succeeded in climbing business ladders, but they often had
to submit to certain indignities in order to hold onto their wage jobs.
Women tried to organize to protect their rights and in 1977 formed the
Somali Women's Democratic Organization (SWDO), which by 1985
had attracted a membership of sixty thousand. As income earners and,
increasingly, participants in the public sphere, these women became
politicized, and the SWDO ultimately became the women's branch of the
Somali Revolutionary Socialist Party.[1] Later, as civil society deteriorated
further and infrastructure collapsed, some women were able to take over
trading in the towns and assume other tasks usually reserved for men.
A few even resorted to becoming warlords themselves, although Ubax
argues that they weren't in it for the money and had "basically organized
to protect themselves." At the time, women were always in danger from
men who saw them simply as a means of getting even with the women's
clans. By attacking, raping, or killing a woman of an enemy clan, a man
could easily score a victory for his own clan.

"The older generation of men in Somalia, they are all like dinosaurs,"
says Koshin. As always, he is blunt and to the point. He has no time for
people living in the past. But while he accepts that Somalis are prejudiced
against women in the public domain, he considers Abdullahi Yusuf of
the Transitional Federal Government an exception. "Even twenty-five
years ago, he tried to let women have a say in politics," he enthuses about
Abdullahi's record. "He is one of the leaders who doesn't put them down,
who listens to them and likes them. Any woman who has met him will
tell you that, even Jendayi Fraser, the U.S. Assistant Minister of State
who was so impressed by him that she made many trips to meet with him.
You know," he says to me, "she sees in him an African baroque."

In Seattle and Portland, Horn women do not want to be held back
by old ideas and traditional behavior, and while some struggle under the

burden of schizophrenic lives at work and at home, others renegotiate their relationships with their husbands. Many of them came to the States before their husbands or as single unmarried refugees and, in some cases, widows. Armed with minimal education, scant English-speaking skills, and little knowledge about negotiating the American system, they had few resources with which to fend for themselves. With the help of church organizations and the guidance of friends or countrymen, however, they began the process of surviving on their own in a foreign country. Senait Habte, an Eritrean student at the University of Washington who hopes to study law, has nothing but praise for such women, women she sees all around Seattle doing whatever they have to do to get by.

"They have gone through so much," she says, "but still they have all this love in them for their families and friends and the community at large. What my mother went through, for instance, would make a bitter woman out of anyone." Her mother came to the States in 1981 as a young woman of twenty-four, with her one year-old baby, Senait, cradled in her arms. She had gone to school and then to college and worked her way up into a managerial position before her husband arrived. Such women have to overcome all kinds of obstacles and adapt constantly to the changing needs of their situation.

"They're flexible in the best way," Mehret says of her own mother, who also had to bring up and support her family single-handedly, both in a refugee camp in Sudan and then in Seattle. Reinforcing Senait's observations about women's love, Mehret talks of how these mothers manage to keep "a smile on their faces for their children," no matter how hard the circumstances of their lives. At a Seattle Art Museum Eritrean evening in 2003, Mehret, who is also a poet, performed a moving tribute to her mother by reciting a poem about the older woman's *netsela*, the traditional shawl that she wraps around her shoulders and head. For Mehret, who wrapped the *netsela* around her body onstage, the shawl also stood as symbol of the many things Eritreans mothers do. The *netsela* provides shelter over her child's head, a face cloth for her child's dirty face, a tablecloth on which to put their food, a covering on the earth to sleep upon . . . The list goes on and on, counting out all the ways the *netsela* helps the child feel forever safe.

Such independence struggles, with their failures and successes, have bred strong women, which is not to say, of course, that Horn women have not always been strong. Life for most women in the three countries, but especially for those in the rural areas, has always been challenging.

"When I look back to nomadic life in Somalia," Abdihakim says, "the way women care for the animals, like cows, and the kids, and the food . . . and then the guys," he shakes his head, "they just go into town in the morning supposedly to look for information—what's going on—and then return home in the afternoons." For a moment he remains silent, staring at the women busily working behind the counter. "I may be biased, but African women are much more productive than men."

"Well, Somali women have told me that, too!" I tell him.

"I'm sure, I'm sure! So when they come to this sort of society, they take more advantage." He points out the workers around us, all women. "That doesn't mean there are more women in Seattle than men, just that they are more employed."

Being away from home in a foreign environment, using a foreign language, and negotiating new systems and new values certainly build competence and confidence, qualities that are not invisible to husbands when they eventually join their wives. Also, economic power begets personal power in relationships, and when the chips are down, the partner who earns the higher income usually has the final say. For local women who have become used to wielding control, the arrival of husbands who expect them to take second place, to walk behind them, or to cook and remain in the home causes family disruptions. For example, Senait says of her parents that "the dynamics of their relationship changed" when her father's lack of papers initially prevented him from getting a job and he was obliged to stay home and be supported by his wife. Role reversals brought their own tensions. "Your mom is not the woman I married," Senait remembers her father telling her, "Not that I don't love her any different; it's just that she's very much not the woman I married."

"It's taken my dad all of three years to come to terms with my mom not doing the housework and not being that same subordinate person anymore. I know that sounds kind of negative, but that's what she was. My dad drove, while she didn't drive until she came to America. She was a secretary at the school; he was a teacher. That was the dynamics of their relationship. And now it's different."

While love may remain, husbands and wives have to work at this new relationship, and in time, men must adapt to the new sensibilities. Their host society does not tolerate physical abuse of women by their husbands, although some men have found ways of inflicting harm without leaving tell-tale signs. Horn of Africa women in Seattle and Portland, however, no longer keep silent about it. Finding themselves in a society that encourages women to speak up, they are making their voices heard like never before. And what they have to say often contradicts the images their male counterparts present to their American neighbors.

Nevertheless, the situation is usually better for women than for men. This is particularly true for educated men, who have found themselves in a spiral of downward assimilation. Many remain underemployed, working as janitors, taxi drivers, and garage attendants, after having held posts as teachers or civil servants at home. Some are working at what traditionally would have been considered women's work and are also helping out at home.

"Men are not men anymore," complains Abe Demisse. "Women wear the pants. They are the movers and shakers today."

Reasons for women's empowerment vary. "Women have found themselves in America," Sonya suggests, because of "their ability to connect with others and communicate better. Many of them have never held jobs before, but now, even if the positions are low level, they provide them with confidence and the independence to make decisions about their lives."

To Yodit Tekle, women are successful in Seattle because "they have a way of turning challenges into opportunities." Yodit, who came to the States from Eritrea when she was just ten and now studies with the Seattle Business Institute, explains, "I feel as a woman that it is easier for me to adapt to someone else. I'm not so adamant about the way I conduct myself that I won't conform in order to get ahead. But men!" she laughs. "To request even the slightest change from men is like asking them to change their anatomy!" Her Eritrean friends, both male and female, laugh at her ridicule, but the women agree. They understand what she means. In the many conversations I've had with Eritreans, Ethiopians, and Somalis about women's success in the United States, the discussion inevitably turned to the differences between men and women and the changing dynamics of their relationships once they started living and working in the new country. Men are just reluctant to give up their dominance, Rahel Gebreab concludes. It is easy to see why.

"When we were children," Yegizaw describes to the eight of us, including Rahel, sitting around my dinner table, "when my father came home from work tired, we would remove his shoes and kiss his feet before our mother washed them. I used to fight my brother to do it. My father didn't ask us to do it—we kids wanted to."

"And today?" I ask. "Is there still the same kind of reverence and respect?"

"Today, of course, if I had to ask my daughter to wash my feet, she would roll her eyes and tell me to wash my own!" He smiles at the incongruous scene in his head, then qualifies the statement by explaining that Bilen expresses her love in different ways.

Such tender devotion to a man's comfort is no doubt hard for males to resist, and the older generation, particularly those from the rural areas, have more difficulty in letting go of these traditional signs of respect. But exposed to television and the behavior they see around them, men inevitably will have to move with the times, if only to keep up with their wives, who may assimilate faster and want them to act more like the romantic heroes of the screen. Many of the women I spoke to in Seattle echoed the complaints of those in Portland.

"There are double standards governing men's and women's behavior," Yodit says, shaking her head, and Rahel agrees.

"You hope to have equality in household chores with men who have been raised in the diaspora, but . . ." The men smile self-consciously, for they are a younger generation of Eritreans who want to appear sympathetic. "As it is with women in the society as a whole," she continues, "we Eritrean women still have to find that work-life balance."

"My boyfriend has no feelings of sympathy," Yodit complains. And, transferring her experience to *all* Eritrean men, she concludes, "They are unable to relate on an emotional level."

One of the men at the table, Bereketab Gebrehiwet, a student of multimedia and graphic communications at Eastern Washington University at Cheney, decides to stand up for his side and says that men just express their love differently. "For instance, my grandfather would gather leafy wood and bring it to his wife so that she could cook and also so she could have a 'tish' sauna."

"A 'tish' sauna?" I ask.

"Yes, you stuff herbal wood and roots in the ground and then you make an African smoke sauna. It sweats impurities from the body." He goes on to describe how his grandfather would also read his Bible to his wife, "particularly the stories of David and Moses, and the love passages," and how his own parents would sit together and talk over coffee or tea. "While they had a kind of quiet togetherness," Bereketab explains, "they were not overtly affectionate. But we, this generation, are influenced by the media and the American people to expect *big* emotions."

The conversation continues in this vein, about love and relationships, and most important the respect that both Eritrean men and women, like their counterparts of other ethnicities in Seattle and Portland, seek from each other. "You have to respect your family," Mehret points out, "even if it is sometimes challenging . . ." Her sentence trails off, and her husband, Yegizaw, sitting across the table, assumes a faux stern look. He shakes his finger at her. "Don't joke like that or I'll take it personally," he says. The table erupts into laughter and leaves me feeling hopeful for this twenty- and thirty-plus generation.

SEXUAL AUTONOMY

It is the area of sexual autonomy, however, that produces the greatest divergence in male and female narratives. At home, men traditionally had control over women's bodies, and women did not own their sexuality, their reproductive rights, or even the living products of their wombs, their children. Young girls were married off as soon as they became pubescent—sometimes at even younger ages—their bodies given to older men for safeguarding and use. Abraha, while disapproving of the practice, explains that Eritrean families believed that if they married off a young girl before puberty, "then, when her hormones came into play and with them feelings of romance and love, she would naturally focus those feelings on the one man who was part of her life and associate them with him." Since she wasn't exposed to other men, "he would become the center of her attraction, and she would make a contented wife."

The tradition is ancient, and during colonial times in Somalia, for example, the Italian regime reinforced it by giving the agriculturists they brought in as forced labor the right to choose the women they wanted, without the consent of the women or their families. Fathers had no choice but to cede their daughters under threat of their sons, or even they themselves, being conscripted.[2] Ever since, the practice of giving young girls in marriage for the financial or social benefit of the family, or to fulfill an outstanding debt to another clan, has continued to undermine women's power over their own bodies. The notion of women as exchange commodities has been part of the socioeconomic structure of most countries until relatively recently, but in the Horn, it remains a destructive practice with few supporters among the female population.

A tradition that hasn't changed with modernization is the expectation of female virginity. Even communities here still expect their young girls to be virgins, and the girl's words attesting to that state do not suffice. "A potato or wild fruit is used as a virgin tester," one of the Eritrean men at my dinner table informs me. The women with us look away, perhaps embarrassed at such an undignified and helpless image of young womanhood presented to me, an American. Families place a very high value on the virginity of their daughters, and in Somalia, brothers are known to murder sisters who allow their passions to get the better of them. Even if they have been raped, the stigma of lost virginity lasts a lifetime. Young Muslim girls have to protect their virginity fiercely. In *Aman: The Story of a Somali Girl*, the eponymous young woman describes how, in order to remain intact, young Somali girls would allow men to "paint" them by "brushing." "You didn't allow them to go in," she explains, "just held your legs together" while "they did their thing between your legs—like that uncle did to me when I was a little girl. It's filthy, and your clothes would smell horrible. But many of the girls were doing it."[3]

As in the United States, the narratives of sexuality and politics easily intertwine, both carrying within them the issues of power that try to conceal themselves by referencing traditions and thus making everything seem "natural," "the way God intended," or "the way it has always been." The situation is the same in most Muslim countries. "It is simply a male power issue that allows men to blame women for their own victimhood," Ubax notes. She reports matter-of-factly, although I can see the anger simmering just below the surface, that she stopped her own attempted rape in Dubai. When she tried to press charges against her assailant, she says, she was beaten up and imprisoned by the Dubai police. "Only when they discovered I was an American citizen did they release me," she says.

Traditional expectations of all kinds die hard. For Yodit, who chose not to marry, the communal pressure has been difficult. "I am a single parent of two bicultural children, which is out of the realms of experience for most Eritreans and is considered abnormal. I made a conscious decision not to marry, but that isn't common, and it was received negatively by the community."

In Eritrea, sharia law still governs the behavior of Islamic men and women, and the government is unlikely to push too hard on behalf of Muslim women's rights. The People's Front for Democracy and Justice fears that Islamic opposition groups might press their advantage with traditional Muslim groups, so instead it drags its feet on women's rights and might even sacrifice them to counter such opposition.

In Somalia, where the fragility of the current transitional government makes binding national legislation unfeasible, women's roles are defined by religious leaders, and wives remain physically the chattel of their husbands. Few people outside of Somalia know the extent of women's suffering, except perhaps for a handful of scholars, like Kapteijns. Women's treatment came to the forefront of Western awareness with the brave advocacy of two famous Somali women living abroad—supermodel Waris Dirie and Ayaan Hirsi Ali, then a Dutch politician—who spoke out on behalf of women and continue to do so, despite the threats to their lives.

Waris Dirie's autobiographical book *Desert Flower* describes her barefoot escape across the desert as she fled the nomadic life of her family at the age of thirteen in order to avoid marriage to an old man, a deal arranged by her father.[4] Through pure grit and some luck, she made her way to London, where her beauty gave her entrée into the fashion world and later to the high-paying job of an international supermodel. Riding her fame, Waris took the opportunity to speak out about the inequities of life for young girls in Somalia, in particular about female genital mutilation (FGM), performed with blade and thorn, leaving females with chronic urinary, menstrual, and sexual problems.

Somalis practice the most severe form of circumcision, infibulation. The United Nations Children's Fund (UNICEF) estimates that about 95 percent of women in Somalia have been circumcised. In 2000 it brought mosque leaders together to discuss whether Islam sanctioned the practice, because if the Qur'an did not mention it, then, it was thought, there would be no religious motivation for continuing the practice.[5] In "Disarming the Women Who Harm Girls," the *Guardian Weekly* of February 12, 2004, reported that Annalena Tonelli, an Italian health worker in Somaliland, sent out teams of Somali outreach workers to educate women about the dangers of FGM and eventually was able to convince many circumcisers to lay down their tools. She even persuaded religious leader Sheikh Mohammed, who subsequently preached against the practice every week at Friday prayers and defended Annalena's role. Despite his conviction and that of a growing number of men in Somaliland, however, Annalena was murdered at Borama in October 2003 at the hospital where she worked.

Here in the Pacific Northwest, not unexpectedly, most of the women I interview are reluctant to speak about the subject at any personal level. The consensus among them, however, is that circumcision and infibulation are associated with rural, nomadic people and that city people "gave that up a long time ago." I fear they tell me what they believe Americans want to hear. In Seattle, some older Somali women still hang onto the practice despite the community's agreement that it should be ended. A federal law now makes it illegal to circumcise, excise, or infibulate the genitals of girls under the age of eighteen and carries a prison sentence of up to five years. Until the law went into effect in 1997, physicians at Seattle's Harborview Hospital, asked by Somalis to perform the rite on their daughters, offered a symbolic cut instead. The compromise, however, didn't convince those who see the practice as cleansing a girl-child in preparation for marriage and who therefore were prepared to fly their daughters back home to have it done.

Ayaan Hirsi Ali, who carried the struggle for women's rights in politics to The Hague, is the other powerful Somali female voice speaking out on behalf of her sisters. Born into the Darod clan, she, too, underwent infibulation and escaped an arranged marriage, in her case by fleeing to Holland, where she found a job as a cleaning lady and then as a translator for immigration and social service agencies. Her own experience and those of some of her interviewees, women caught in forced marriages, battered wives, and women with AIDS, convinced her that something had to be done to protect Somali and other Muslim women. For Hirsi Ali, the source of their oppression lies in Islam. As a member of the Dutch parliament for the People's Party for Freedom and Democracy, she received numerous death threats and vocal abuse for her public comments as well as for her 2004 book *The Cage of Virgins*, and her controversial short film *Submission*, which explores the treatment of women in Islam. She is indelibly linked with her friend and collaborator on the film, the Dutch director Theo van Gogh, who was murdered on November 2, 2004, by Muhammad Bouyeri. In "Daughter of the Enlightenment," published on April 3, 2005, in the *New York Times*, Christopher Caldwell writes that, after stabbing van Gogh, the killer "left impaled in the corpse a five-page letter addressed to Hirsi Ali."

RECLAIMING WOMEN'S VOICES

Women from the Horn have borne the brunt of violence that they have not initiated, be it rape, looting, starvation, murder of their children, or displacement from their homes. Yet it is they who, quietly, in the background, have tended the wounded, hidden fellow nationals in their homes, or, under cover of night, taken food to guerrillas in the forests. They are heroes of their own stories, women of courage who have pieces of history to add to their country's historical records. Few will publicly ask recognition for their contributions—modesty is too well ingrained in their upbringing. Sonya, for example, says that such contributions "are seen as normal obligations" in the building of Eritrea and points to the greater contributions of the Eritrean *tegadelti*, who fought in the field, the fighters and doctors who contributed directly. They are the ones who "should be mentioned in history," she insists.

Yet, ordinary women sacrificed much for their countries, too. While female fighters in tight shorts make good publicity shots for the cause, the war efforts of all those ordinary Eritrean women also deserve to be noted. Destruction of their homes and fields, injury to their persons, and threats to life and limb should not be mere collateral damage. While

Eritrea certainly recognizes the "mothers of the nation" on Martyrs Day and, in Seattle, Eritrean women celebrate International Women's Day in recognition of female fighters, the heroic stories of ordinary workers and housewives seldom make it into print. Despite that, women in the Pacific Northwest continue to make sacrifices, raising millions of dollars for their home countries and, putting aside their own needs, sending half their salaries to help fill the gaps in what their governments can provide back home.

It's not that the women expect rewards or public praise; they just want their grandchildren and great-grandchildren to know that they, too, have contributed to the whole. Many of the acts of ordinary women who did not carry guns but participated in other ways are being lost to memory. Haddis wishes now that he had recorded some of those long-ago stories about his grandmother in Ethiopia, who, during the war with Italy, "contributed by secretly transporting messages." "If only I could remember the details," he says, "but I was too young when it was shared with me."

Among the Oromo, too, the courage of ordinary women in Ethiopia does not see print. Yet, as Kuwee Kumsa points out, they were the invisible social base on which the Oromo Liberation Front organized and carried out its struggle, in that they provided material and emotional support for the fighting men and looked after the vulnerable. The OLF never officially recognized their assistance and, in fact, never even considered those women who participated in combat as members of the group. Only when the OLF needed their labor did it acknowledge them, and, even then, it pushed them back into the kitchen as soon as the struggle ended. Resistance through literary and cultural productions that promoted Oromo nationalism, such as translations into Oromo or Oromo cultural shows, seemed not to register with the OLF as bravery, even though some resulted in the imprisonment and even death of the women involved. Kuwee Kumsa endured incarceration without charge or trial for ten years, during which time she wrote and smuggled out ten manuscripts.[6]

Though women combatants in Eritrea enjoyed a degree of freedom during the war and, most important for rural women, were provided with literacy classes, the reality of postwar achievement in gender relations has been far more modest than President Afwerki and the rest of the PFDJ leadership promised. Certainly, the revolution had a profound effect on men's perception of women. Initially called "Kalashnikov chicks," the women constantly had to prove themselves to their male counterparts. Their strength and dedication, however, soon won them admiration. In book after book about the Ethiopian-Eritrean war, pictures of strong young Eritrean women shouldering rifles or marching alongside their brothers-in-war impress on readers the liberation movement's gender politics. Women, too, were elected to their village People's Assembly and gained leadership skills that moved them from the private to the public sphere. But once the liberation group became the government, women's concerns moved to the back burner.

Though women today participate in Eritrea's formal party and state institutions, in actuality they have little control over the issues that affect them. When three former women fighters organized the Eritrean Women War Veterans' Association in 1995 to provide financial and technical support for demobilized women, the president's office closed it down a year later. The few women who still benefit from their contributions to the war effort, Tanja R. Müller suggests in *The Making of Elite Women: Revolution and Nation Building in Eritrea*, are those who still believe in the ideological narrative of the Eritrean People's Liberation Front and the People's Front for Democracy and Justice. Those who criticize the government or raise their voices in opposition are soon squeezed out. Astier Feshatsion, one of the G-15 signatories of the "Open Letter to All Members of the PFDJ," which criticized the government's handling of the border war, still languishes in prison after being arrested in 2001. A veteran fighter and postwar regional administrator, she was a powerful voice on behalf of Eritrean women. Amnesty International, which no longer has a presence in Eritrea, reported on its Web site on December 7, 2005, under "Eritrea: Religious Persecution," that three other women have been imprisoned for political reasons and are considered prisoners of conscience: Aster Yohannes, wife of another member of the G-15, former minister Petros Solomon, whom I met in Asmara in 2001; Director of Cinemas Miriam Hagos, who is suspected of having connections with the G-15; and Senait Debessai, a veteran combatant, who is believed to have been picked up at the instigation of her pro-government ambassador husband with whom she was engaged in difficult divorce proceedings and because of her relationship to another prisoner of conscience, her brother, Ermias Debessai, previously ambassador to China. The women all suffer from health problems, and one of the prisoners is said to have died, although it is not known which one, as they are kept incommunicado at an undisclosed detention center. Thus, the societal gains women made during the war have been negated by the government's failure to uphold its democratic ideals in post-1991 Eritrea.

Post-traumatic stress disorder plagues many Eritrean, Somali, and Ethiopian women. "If you kill me, I don't feel nothing," a crying Amina Sheikhuna tells her mother when they are reunited in a refugee camp in Kenya. "If you put a knife in my stomach, I don't feel it," she says about the numbness she experiences after five devastating years of war in Mogadishu. Women were abused or tortured during the years of fighting, and in all three countries, many were raped. Belainesh Araya, director of research and information for the National Union of Eritrean Women, calls rape "the silent pain" because of the women's reluctance to speak out. The shame associated with rape crosses all three communities, and women generally tend to conceal such an experience from even their most intimate acquaintances.

"The Somali word for 'rape' is *yoogid*," Sahra Khalid tells me. We sit in her kitchen, feeding the numerous children she is babysitting for her women friends. She has given me a fictitious name, so I cannot describe her any further other than to say that she is an intelligent, lively woman, a survivor. She talks rapidly in Somali to the kids as she scoops out dollops of food for them and then switches to English to tell me that it is always the women who are victimized, the women who suffer. "Eighty to ninety percent of the women who fled Mogadishu in 1991 were raped," she says. While I'm still trying to register the enormity of what she has just told me, she shouts sharply in Somali at one of her small charges who is smearing his *maraq* over his friend's face. The child stares at her solemnly, his eyes big and scared, but she simply takes a cloth and, while wiping the stew off the other boy's face, explains that the women couldn't tell anyone and that there was no law or court to which they could appeal. "Besides," she adds, "there was so much shame. The torturers came from the countryside and they'd never seen city women, and they were like animals. They forced women to give over their money and gold jewelry and then they gang-raped them, nine or ten at a time. They even raped children as young as seven."

She directs me to a Web site, Hiiraan.com, where a child's face stares out at me below headlines that tell of her gang rape at the age of seven. An American Somali couple brought the now eleven-year-old, diaper-wearing young girl to the States so that she could have her genitals and rectum repaired.

Although male fighters certainly are aware of the rape situation, few want to confront the reality or examine their own actions during the wars. Many of the women who fled Mogadishu were barely teens and "accepted" soldier husbands simply as a way of protecting themselves from gang rape. Now, in Portland and Seattle, they frequently suffer sleep problems, fatigue, or loss of weight or appetite. The Somali language has no word for "depression"; instead, it is described as *qulub, qalbi-jab iyo murugo joogta ah*, with the word *qulub* referring to the feelings of a camel when its mate dies. While poetic and descriptive, the expression, needless to say, inadequately explains depression and gives no idea of symptoms such as flashbacks, nightmares, heightened startle responses, and poor concentration and memory. Most women are too ashamed to seek outside assistance, but within the community, treatment involves a healer reciting verses of the Qur'an or preparing an amulet to protect the person from evil spirits, or *jinns*. There is little understanding of mental health and no conceptual appreciation of the spectrum it covers. In Somali culture, one is just crazy (*waali*) or not crazy. Although the Qur'an forbids suicide as a crime against God, such deaths continue to increase among the Somali community.[7]

Harborview Medical Center in Seattle serves the Horn of Africa communities and has found that AIDS infection is extremely high among recent female arrivals from refugee camps, even among monogamous married women, suggesting either an unacknowledged rape in the camps or perhaps the use of infected needles during health examinations prior to their entry into the United States. The camps have been extremely dangerous places for women, no safer than the countries from which they have fled.

In bringing attention to women's problems, I in no way mean to minimize the problems male ex-fighters experience as they struggle to adjust and incorporate themselves into the economic and social culture of the new postwar era. But women suffer doubly. Caught in the web of traditional family expectations, they must always put their own interests second to those of their husbands, children, and parents.

Some diaspora writers have begun the process of sharing their war narratives with the publication of autobiographical her-stories. Abeba Tesfagiorgis's *A Painful Season and a Stubborn Hope: The Odyssey of an Eritrean Mother*, for example, describes the author's imprisonment by the Derg in 1975 for supposedly supporting the EPLF *tegadelti* during Ethiopia's annexation of Eritrea. The book celebrates the friendships of women in prison and their loyalty in the face of depredation, torture, and rape. In recording their conversations, their depressions, and their songs of defiance, Abeba makes clear that ordinary Eritrean women are no less brave than Eritrean men and deserve recognition. Other books, such as Amrit Wilson's *Challenge Road* and Helena Moussa's *Storm and Sanctuary*, also bring attention to women's history, but all three books were published between 1991 and 1993, at the apex of Eritrean successes and a time of heightened unity and discipline among its supporters. Much has changed since liberation, and women now have more complex and nuanced stories to tell. Some women in the Pacific Northwest have started writing poems or sharing their experiences through skits; some open up about the trauma in their lives only in therapy.

Almaz Bahre lost her family home in Dongolo to Ethiopian fighter planes in 1977 because the house happened to be close to the EPLF camp where soldiers kept a garage for working on their vehicles (as described in chapter 4). Napalm and cluster bombs destroyed the house and all their belongings, and Almaz, just seventeen at the time, eventually fled to Sudan and then to the United States. She arrived on February 8, 1990, only to hear of her mother's death. "She passed away because they bombed our house a second time." Almaz has also lost her brother, her uncles, and an aunt. All of her family. I met one of her uncles, her mother's brother, in Eritrea on my way from Asmara to Massawa in 2003. An educated man who had gone to school in Boston, he spoke to me knowledgeably about Richard Nixon as we sat on the concrete veranda of what was left of Almaz's family home, which looked out over the wide terraced land that led down to the lowlands. Four of us had been traveling tightly packed in a small truck in the 100-degree heat, and kindly people there gave us cold drinks to revive us. The house was close to the main street, close to the camps.

Yosieph says that his wife is a "reflection of the tragedy of Eritrea." She has lost so much. Yet she is always donating to Goodwill and other organizations that help those she considers less fortunate than herself. "That is the kind of woman she is," her husband beams. When Safeway purchased the land at Rainier Beach where she owned a Dollar Store, she was forced to close up shop. She gave away all of the merchandise she had in stock, truckloads of it to the local community and the Union Gospel Mission. The mission, Yosieph says, thought she was one of its clients rather than the donor. I tell this about Almaz to make the point that she is in no way a woman who feels sorry for herself, or who is looking for praise, reward, or compensation. She is modest and self-effacing. Nevertheless, once she started telling me her story, the words just gushed out in a torrent. Even in her broken English, she conveyed the urgency of someone who wanted to get her bit of history on record.

Somali women perhaps have had the worst of it. During the civil war, many of them heroically remained in the cities and were instrumental in saving the lives of neighbors. They opened soup kitchens, operated schools for children, ran the hospital, and helped bring social services to those who needed them, yet their contributions were not noted or acknowledged in Somalia. What is more, in the war's aftermath, despite their best efforts, they were excluded from the reconciliation efforts. No clan would agree to have a woman as a representative. Thus, Somali women were no better off in terms of recognition and rights than they had been after the war of independence against the Italians, when they sold their jewelry to support the war effort, took part in demonstrations, and hid freedom fighters at great personal cost to themselves. Many of them were beaten or landed in jail.

In the nomadic regions of Somalia, women fared even worse. Their often unsupervised lifestyle while their men were away opened them up to the suspicion that they had secretly been in contact with opposition forces. Further, their clan identity, compromised because of their dual membership in their fathers' and brothers' clan as well as that of their husbands, made them susceptible to attacks on their loyalty. When

Amina Sheikhuna, for example, fled Mogadishu to seek refuge in her father's rural village, suddenly his clan was no longer hers and he told her to go back. "Your people are fighting here tomorrow," she recalls him saying, to which she replies to me, "*My* people! I mean, before, it was the people of Mogadishu and the people of the society. But now, it's me and my other tribe!"

The maternal side is not counted in clan lineage, Ubax explains with a cynical smile on her face. "If they took the women's side into the equation, we would all be related!" Bellows of laughter follow. "It's ridiculous! Darod, Isaq, and Hawiye . . . our whole clan system is crazy! And it's not static. For example, me and you, we could have a tenth grandfather in common, but along comes someone else who has a fifth grandfather in common, so they just toss you out." When five years later, in 2010, I speak to Ubax again, she no longer laughs about the clan system. Her involvement in the Somali Rights Network, which seeks to bring to justice Somali war criminals of all clans, including her own, has led to a backlash from the latter. "You know," she hesitates for a moment, "I think Somali women shouldn't have allegiance to any clan because it doesn't benefit them at all. It makes us choose between our sons and our fathers, our brothers and our in-laws." With some bitterness, she says, "Somali men are good at using their wives, daughters, mothers, or sisters to do their dirty work."

Somali men historically have always been a little wary of powerful women with something to say, which is why female heroes are often vilified by men. Take Arraweelo, for example. If you ask a Somali man about the mythical Queen of Somalia, he will say she castrated all her male subjects and ruled with an iron hand. Stories about Arraweelo abound, most of them written by men and ending with her demise. In one version of her life, this Queen of the Habr Toljaale is said to have been outwitted by her daughter, who wanted to save her own son from castration and so hid him in a milk basket, while in another, Arraweelo's life is cut short when her own grandson kills her. Ladan Affi was so fed up with men's treatment of Arraweelo that she chose the queen as a role model for Somali women in an essay she presented at the Somali Peace Conference in Paris in October 1995. Generally, Arraweelo's story is told as an example of why women should not rule, but Ladan's version portrayed a woman of courage and leadership who reigned over most of what is now

Somalia. Having witnessed so many wars and conflicts between Somalis, Arraweelo spoke critically to her husband about some in the council of elders who she thought were not intelligent and capable enough to be in positions of leadership. She thought they should be replaced by competent women, who would make decisions that benefited the community. When her husband disagreed, she organized the women to strike, and while the men were doing housework and caring for children, Arraweelo declared herself queen. From then on, according to Ladan Affi, there was peace and prosperity in the land.[8]

Did Arraweelo really exist? At a small village in the northeast of Somalia, Somali men throw stones at the tomb of the castrating Arraweelo while young women place green branches and fresh flowers on it. And in the Pacific Northwest, when a woman gets too uppity and challenges her husband, Mowliid tells me, it is common for the man to say, "What do you think you're doing? Are you wearing Arraweelo's shoes today?"

Another supposedly mythical woman by the name of Dhegdheer, who gave birth to daughters only, has also been vilified. She is said to have resorted to cannibalism during times of drought. Like Arraweelo, she, too, met an untimely death that put a stop to her dreadful power. In the oral histories, no Somali women are admired and respected by both genders. With men as the formal poets and women's voices restricted mainly to the private spheres of their homes, it is not surprising that men's versions of such women predominate. Only with the rise of a new middle class in the cities, and the subsequent creation of the contemporary Somali popular song, *hees*, did women begin to raise their voices publicly.[9] But even then, though women were intimately involved in the creation of these songs about love and women's rights and sang them on the radio and onstage, officially they could not be the composers. The famines of the 1980s and the crumbling of the state in 1990 brought an end to the songs. In any case, few women or men were literate at that time, and many of the issues regarding women's rights were just shelved. To be fair, the cultural histories of the Ethiopians and Eritreans, unlike that of the Somalis, do credit some of their female rulers. They praise especially those women of royalty who strengthened their husbands' positions. Like Empress Taitu, the wife of Emperor Menelik II. Ethiopians also admire those women who became rulers in their own right.

"Just look at the Ethiopian women in history!" Sofi Mulugeta says proudly, "They have made such an impact on the world. The Queen of Sheba, for instance—it was not only her beauty but her wit that attracted Solomon. And even in our stories, the one they call Yodit Gudit [Queen Judith], she was a pagan, and she was the one who destroyed the Church in order to rule over all Ethiopia." This tenth-century Queen of the Agaw, sometimes known as Queen of the Falashas, led a rebellion against the Axumites who exploited her people and their labor.

Female heroes abound in the Seattle and Portland communities, too. Sofi is herself a role model for other young Ethiopian women. She goes out of her way to help and encourage them and shows them that they, too, can achieve what they want. For her, financial well-being provides empowerment, and she believes that women must be financially independent in order to make their voices heard in the public arena. Born at a time when Ethiopia was undergoing dramatic changes, Sofi believes in speaking out and letting people know your views.

Not all Somali men are of the opinion that women's voices are irrelevant. Somalia's internationally known novelist and essayist Nuruddin Farah describes his Somali sisters and their lives with great understanding. In fact, he is sometimes called a feminist because of his supposed empathy for Somali women. During a book tour stop in Seattle when his novel *Secrets* was released in 1998, he told my students that after the 1970 publication of his first book, *From a Crooked Rib*, which describes a Somali woman struggling with the restraints of traditional Somali society, he received a letter addressed to *Mrs.* Nuruddin Farah! Nuruddin grew up in the Ogaden under Ethiopian rule, with a famous poet for a mother, Faduma Aleeli.

Today, the Somali Academy of Sciences and Art lays the foundations for women's studies in Somalia. Although there is no academic freedom and open discussion is impossible, women researchers struggle to collect and document oral literature told by women.[10] Here in Seattle, local poet Susan Rich bears witness to their stories by creating poems about their lives. An award-winning poet, she weaves their journeys from Somalia into verse that she both performs and publishes. Local Somali women themselves, however, are not writing, or, if they are, they do not show their work. In Somalia, where for so many centuries women have symbolized the other and been denied the status of speaking subjects in the public arena, such conditioning is internalized, and women take their time finding their poetic tongues. Every Somali woman I interviewed readily expressed her love of poetry. Ubax, for example, spoke fondly of Elmi Bodheri, the Somaliland poet of the 1940s who is said to have died of unrequited love for the young woman Hodan, whose family married her off to a rich man. Women's lives in the United States do not leave much time for writing poetry, yet more than ever, female bards are called upon to make their testimonies part of the history that will enrich the culture of future Somali generations in this country.

No doubt, this will eventually happen. Both male and female Somalis testify to the amazing strength of these women and also to their oratorical skills. Asia has even stronger words to describe the verbal prowess of her mother. "She was like Mussolini," she says, describing a particular incident in 1989 when her mother used her powerful oratory to recruit war-weary Somali men to action. The meeting took place in her grandmother's house, and about three hundred men, "really dark, malnourished, skinny all of them, with red teeth, and red eyes," were transfixed by her mother's voice, she explains. "It's really weird. I could really see Mussolini in my mother. I mean, there's this room full of men, and she's the only woman."

"She must have been very powerful."

"She was. She was!" Asia laughs, then describes how her mother got up in front of all the men and said, "This is our time. We tried with bullets, now we're going to try with this." She continues, "I mean, she's trembling with power. But I was so-o-o-o frightened and so-o-o-o just, just . . . you know . . . And everything that was coming out of her mouth was 'kill' and 'destruction' and 'here's the money,' you know, 'this is our time,' 'we need to show . . .'"

"This is right at the end, just before Barre was overthrown?" I ask.

"Exactly, exactly. The Somali government had already bombed Burao and Hargeisa, but now, what they were looking for were actual people to go in and get killed. That's what they were recruited for. And I just remember I was so frightened. Somebody tell me, you know, explain what it is that I'm seeing. So I went to my grandmother. This is the first person you trust, your grandmother, this is your nana, you know? And I said," she assumes a childlike voice, incredulous, "Mom is like the Mafia! Mom is like Mussolini!"

Perhaps one day, Asia's mother's story will make it into the Somali history books. She came from a poor family and at the age of fifteen joined the Somali military in order to earn some money, then quickly rose through the ranks, trained in the Soviet Union, and became especially close to Siyad Barre. At this point in time, however, leaders like lineages are defined in masculine terms. Even with her mother, Asia tells me, people implied that she acquired her power from her husband's family's clout and did not acknowledge her own efforts and skill. Yet Asia is adamant that her mother was hungry for acknowledgment for herself. It's very common in Somalia, she says, for women to hunger after power for themselves. But, as she informs me, "it is never said, it is never said, it is never said!" She explains, "If you really want to see who moves the Somalis, it's the women. It's really the women. But they do it in such a malignant way!" She bursts out laughing before backtracking and explaining, "No, if they try to do something good, they really do a good job. But when it comes to love or wars," she opens her eyes wide, "it's all or nothing!"

Women here and at home in the Horn are finding their public voices and speaking out on behalf of themselves and their families. In 2003 sixty women peace activists in Mogadishu tried to persuade the various factions to agree on a common regional administration. "This city has suffered more than anywhere else in Somalia, and it is the women who bear the brunt of the problems. We are the mothers, sisters, and the wives who have to care for the family after our men are killed and maimed," Sharifo Adow said at a women's forum held in Mogadishu that June. The women have different clan affiliations and formerly had supported different factions in the struggle, but they were determined to leave the past behind and move forward for the common good. They continue to pressure the leaders and denounce those who prove to be obstacles to peace. Like the community of Somali women in Tigard, near Portland, who also are of diverse clans, they cooperate and support one another in the realization that what is good for women and families must be good for the country as a whole.

Somalinimo may still be uncertain, but *Somalināgnimo* (Somali womanhood) looks to be on the march.

NEW AMERICAN
NARRATIVES

I don't have any illusion that we're going to be living happily
ever after, at least in my generation. We're more likely to
continue to see people who are entrenched in their beliefs and
their own interpretations of the way it should be. However,
I am also optimistically clear that harmony will occur through
more and more interyouth, interfaith, interculture relationships
that provide opportunities for looking beyond our past pains
and finding ways to deal collectively with shared problems.

—DAVID MAKONNEN, SEATTLE, 2005

W HEN DAVID Makonnen expressed the above views to me,
we were sitting in a Renton coffee shop speculating about the
future relationships of the three East African communities in
Seattle and Portland. At this point, although it was clear that
some Somalis, Ethiopians, and Eritreans still flailed within the past's
haunting cobwebs, it was equally obvious that many more were valiantly
striving to push aside its sticky threads. Not that they wanted to forget
what had happened to their countrymen and countrywomen, but they
were ready to move forward and create new and more inclusive stories for
the future. They reasoned that if their communities wanted to attain the
American Dream, they needed to let go of past hatreds, work together,
and embrace their lives here in the Pacific Northwest. Cooperation, unity,
and teamwork were their keywords, and they not only employed them

within their own communities but projected them outward to incorporate relations between the various Horn groups and even beyond that, in some cases, to include the African American community as a whole.

These voices of the future come from all walks of life, but they share a common empathy. Because the speakers interact out of the security of their own national, ethnic, or religious convictions, they can afford to "hear" what an erstwhile "enemy" has to say without losing their own certitudes. Sofi, an Ethiopian, opens her mind to the other's story. "Teach me," she says to an Eritrean freedom fighter she meets in Seattle and "feels for the first time" what his story means to him and now what it means to her. If people like Sofi and the Eritrean People's Liberation Front vet are able to mentally change places and perceive through the other's story how the whole fits together, they hold out hope that others may yet do the same.

Such voices as Sofi's and David's grow louder with time. They are fortunate perhaps in that schools and colleges or socioeconomic positions provide them with the platforms that enable them to be heard. These help them lead their communities forward by example and in so doing to create the beginnings of new cooperative American narratives, which in turn begin to shape communal identity in yet other developing configurations.

DREAMS OF RETURN

At the Yatana Music Shop, a couple of middle-aged Eritrean men flip through the CDs. You can find all kinds of music at Yatana's, but the men gravitate to those with pictures showing *tegadelti* on the covers. On some, the fighters carry machine guns and move in single file along mountainous paths, while on others, they relax in their mountain strongholds smoking cigarettes or listening with eyes closed to a *krar*-playing member of their group.

"No one can sing like this anymore," says one of Yatana's elderly customers, who holds up a CD by the legendary vocalist Haile Ghebru. He passes his finger down the list of cuts at the back. "Here's 'Alewuna.'" His friend hums a couple of bars, and they both close their eyes. Farther down the aisle, another man listens to "Shigey Habuni" (Give Me My Freedom), a well-loved independence song written by Tewolde Redda.

The man stands erect as he listens and stares into the distance across the miles of ocean to a place called home. What's in his head, nobody knows, but it is clear that all three men feel great longing and nostalgia for this little country on the Red Sea that has endured so much bloodshed.

Most Eritreans living in the Pacific Northwest out of necessity feel that longing, too, as do Ethiopians for Addis and Somalis for Mogadishu. Almost everyone I spoke to nursed nostalgia for the nation and had long dreamed about going home. "It is such a beautiful country," Desta Wondwassen reminisces about Ethiopia; "we had every intention of going back," Ezra Teshome recalls. In the seventeenth century, German doctors considered homesickness, or *heimweh* (literally, "home ache"), a medical condition. Even so, few of the exiles have any immediate plans for going home, and most of those committed to nurturing a cooperative Horn coalition here invest themselves fully in their new country. This refocusing of energy from the homeland to communities in the Pacific Northwest is perhaps the most crucial point of departure for those who seek to build bridges of cooperation to the future. While maintaining their cultural identity and continuing to support their extended families and friends in their mother countries, they avoid meddling in government affairs back home as well as its divisive fallout in the diaspora. For some, the steps toward such decisions have been set in motion by the realization that the governments in their home countries have deteriorated beyond the point that they consider morally acceptable and that therefore they would not be returning home, that, in fact, home was America: they were becoming American.

While the imagined community remains a static, nostalgic utopia in the minds of some of the older members, reality on the ground has created disillusion among others whose histories have been constructed around a loss of innocence and who find the corruption, violence, conscription, censorship, and imprisonment back home offensive and embarrassing. It is they who slowly but surely dissociate themselves from their governments and warlords, although never from their people.

Even Abraha now speaks with sadness of what has happened in his country. The People's Front for Democracy and Justice in Eritrea continues to react in knee-jerk fashion to any criticism and tries to control all speech, including that of religious institutions. It persecutes members of the evangelical churches and has even excommunicated members and jailed leaders of the Mekane Hiwet Medhane Alem, an internal Orthodox movement that draws thousands of young followers to weekly Sunday school classes and Bible study. The Holy Synod itself has been put under government control, and Patriarch Abune Antonios was fired in January 2007. As for other government critics, the eleven senior PFDJ and National Assembly members arrested in 2001 for questioning the government's handling of the border war with Ethiopia are believed to be held at Eiraeiro, a desert prison in the Red Sea region. These prisoners of conscience as well as many of the journalists and students arrested with them remain incommunicado. One of them is believed dead. Indefinite conscription continues to drain the country, which has been completely militarized. In December 2009 the entire national Eritrean soccer team defected in Kenya. Youths trying to evade further military service flee into the countryside or escape to Sudan in search of asylum. Those who make it to Yemen have been returned and/or tortured. The government, convinced that parents facilitate the escape of their children, has begun a policy of arresting them, too, shutting down the parents' businesses as punishment or sentencing them to stand in for their missing children. Alternately, they are obliged to pay huge fines of approximately $1,200. A sense of sadness and despair pervades Asmara, and people feel manipulated as the laws keep shifting and they don't know where they stand. Their sentiments reach Pacific Northwest Eritreans, who wonder when it's all going to stop. How much longer can they send money to a government that insists on using up its young males rather than educating them and providing them with better opportunities for advancement?

The situation in Ethiopia hardly differs. In both countries, freedoms of speech, assembly, movement, and the press have been severely restricted. In Ethiopia, government forces shot dead eighty demonstrators and detained thousands of others during the June and November 2005 public demonstrations that followed the alleged fraud of the May 15 elections. Of those detained, 129 were opposition leaders, journalists, and aid workers who had been arrested and accused of treason and even genocide, a claim that in this context Amnesty International considers absurd.[1] Whether absurd or not, nearly all the charges carry the death penalty. Landownership, too, continues to create tension and violence in

Ethiopia. Private land confiscated by Mengistu Haile Mariam's regime still belongs to the government, and those Ethiopians who want to work have to lease the hectares from the government. Those who cannot afford to lease become sharecroppers on their own land. "There's no reason why the government should own and control the land," Ezra insists. The government appropriated his father's dairy farm, he explains, so if his dad wants to improve the land and expand the farm, he cannot use the land as equity. With the land tethered to the government in this way, the economy cannot grow.

Beyond landownership problems, Ethiopia's military ventures set local refugees and exiles here on edge. In 2006, for example, in preparation for Ethiopia's military support of the Transitional Federal Government against the Islamic Courts Union in Somalia, the army forcibly conscripted men in the Ogaden. On the economic front, the Heritage Foundation's 2009 Index of Economic Freedom reports widespread corruption and the government's distortion of prices through its regulation of state-owned enterprises. Thousands of people have no chance of supporting themselves even in the informal sector, and many flee to Somalia in the hope of being smuggled from there to Saudi Arabia, where they might work illegally. More often than not, the lawlessness of Somalia leaves them robbed and stranded before they ever reach the Gulf of Aden.

The Somalis themselves try to escape the same way. In the aftermath of the ICU's defeat in December 2006, more than 320,000 men, women, and children had fled by April 2007.[2] The figures continue to climb. The Ethiopian rout of the ICU, instead of bringing about stability in the region, has left an even more complicated mess, with hostile clans and returned warlords plus foreign militias and jihadis back on the scene. Al-Shabaab, which grew out of the ICU and which the United States has designated a terrorist organization with links to al-Qaeda, continues to fan the flames of insurgency along with Hizbul Islam, another rebel group. Both refuse to negotiate with the UN-backed TFG, which they consider a pawn of the West. Even though most Somalis decry al-Shabaab's violence and its harsh interpretations of Islam, almost half the population consists of uneducated teenagers who are easy recruits for extremists. Al-Shabaab's forces now control southern and central Somalia, while the TFG barely holds onto parts of

Mogadishu—the presidential palace (Villa Somalia) and the seaport. In such an environment, aspirations to normal life have little chance of realization. In November 2009 a suicide bomber killed nineteen people at a graduation ceremony for young medical and engineering students in Mogadishu. Also killed were three cabinet members: the ministers for education, culture and higher education, and health.

"Islam has taken over from the clans," Ubax affirms. People fear the power of the extremists, and even children now cover their entire bodies when going to school. On a visit to Somalia, says Ubax, she was stoned in a Bosaso supermarket for wearing only a head covering and jeans.

Such developments and the lack of progress toward political and economic stability in these three countries have shattered dreams of return for many Horn locals. When the debris from the homeland's continuing violence overwhelms nostalgic memories, it takes some mental contortions to protect them from contamination. Most Somalis don't even try. In any case, "We have no homes to return to," Abdhakim tells me. "You can't go to Mogadishu and meet the people you used to know because the neighborhood doesn't exist any longer. Perhaps if I go to London, or other places with high-density Somali residents, I will meet lots of my high school mates and all of my neighbors." He sighs. "So it's like that," he says.

Thus, although some of the refugees I interviewed spoke of rebuilding their lives back home once order was restored in Mogadishu, Addis, or Asmara, in actuality few expect that kind of normality to occur anytime soon, at least not in their lifetimes. Besides, in the meanwhile, their children receive good educations, more skilled jobs become available to them, and, as the younger generation learns to negotiate the system, American Dream–type goals appear to be within reach. "At first," Abraha explains, "everybody was thinking, as soon as Eritrea becomes independent, we're all going to go back home. Because of that, we didn't buy houses, and some of us didn't marry or have families. Then the reality came. Eritrea became independent in 1991, and we couldn't go."

"What were the reasons?" I ask.

"First, it was blaming somebody else. If the government was more accommodating, then we'd all go back. People had different reasons, and it took us ten years of hesitation before we realized we couldn't go back. So, where are we? Where do we go? Well, you know, we have kids now, and we're getting old ourselves. So what should we do? OK, let's settle down."

For many now, "going home" refers simply to a brief vacation to visit families and bring them material support. When Rahel returned to Eritrea for a visit in 2002 and worked at a Microsoft office job teaching professionals, she had "the best experience of [her] life." "It made me aware of how much I loved being an Eritrean," she tells me, "and how much we still need to do to help our people." Such a brief vacationer, however, is known locally as a fig cactus, after the plant that blooms there every couple of years and then is gone. Those who have returned for visits, while thrilled with being among extended family, frequently find themselves foreigners in their own land. Few who immigrated or fled to the States as children speak their mother tongue fluently and thus often find themselves sidelined as "Americans" in their home countries and excluded from intimate political conversations. Not many of them wish to live there, at least permanently, admitting they have become too American to fit in.

"As soon as I found someone who spoke English, I lost my mind," Senait remembers. "It was like, 'OK, OK, let's talk!' And when I did finally get home, all I wanted was teriyaki!" For young people like these, home is the transnational community here in the Pacific Northwest, with its teriyaki, sushi, tacos, and pad Thai. It is not the country of their parents, and while cultural ties may bind the young in loyalty to a utopian ideal conceptualized through the narratives of their parents, their interests are grounded in the here and now, in making life better for those of similar background. For them, "the community" perhaps represents a kind of cultural club in which members have similar interests and feel at home, but when they leave the club to follow their other interests, they return to their everyday American lives.

"We have to focus on what's happening here," Abraha says emphatically. "Our primary goal is to succeed in our lives here and to help our kids and ourselves."

Not all the kids are doing well. At the gym at my local YMCA, I notice a young Ethiopian woman, probably in her twenties, making her way toward the weights. Besides the fact that she is bejeweled, extravagantly braided, and outfitted in a bright blue and maroon sweat suit, she is to my American eyes also extremely overweight, even obese. And that is what catches my attention. I suspect that the older Ethiopians may admire her plumpness and perhaps understand it as a reflection of how well her family must be doing here in the American economy, but it pulls me up short. In fact, it makes me wonder about our American economy too, especially our emphasis on consumer indulgence that encourages immediate gratification. Not only do our gangs and racists kill off Horn immigrants, but our diets are leading them to the same end.

"It's a real problem in our community," Yosieph tells me as we dig into a dinner of traditional Eritrean stews. "You see, when Eritreans come here, the mothers are often busy working and don't have time to prepare traditional stuff, so the children, instead of eating what their bodies are used to, buy hamburgers and doughnuts and French fries . . . So their diet changes. And then also we all become sedentary. In Eritrea, people walk everywhere, but here, we come home from work by car and we want to lie on the couch with a bag of Cheetos." He pats his own small belly.

"Well, it happens to most immigrant groups who come here," I say. "The Eritreans are not alone."

"But now they have high blood pressure, too, and also diabetes. *That* is not good."

He is right. It is not good. Those Eritreans who have been here longest understand the problem and point to the causes they see as responsible for it. Abraha puts it down to the self-indulgence high-tech society offers at the press of a button. He explains:

> In Eritrea, when you eat a meal, you sit down and you eat it with the community, your family, and you digest it and you get up, and that's the last time you're going to see food again until the next meal in the house. Here, though, we're eating at McDonald's, and we're eating twenty-four hours a day! We indulge and create this monster . . . and then it's a big fix because we cannot work it. And so now we have first-generation Eritrean kids who are becoming obese. In Eritrea, you can walk throughout the entire country and never see an obese person. Do you know that the food you eat in one day in the United States feeds an Eritrean for a week?

Horn parents must contend with even more than their children's eating habits. A huge chasm of a generation gap separates them from their children. The kids are often more adept at fitting into American culture and eagerly adopt new values at odds with those of their parents. Since many of the older generation have limited educations and English-language skills, and some still suffer from post-traumatic stress disorder, they often feel adrift in a sea of values they don't understand. Most work long hours, leaving them little time for counseling their kids. Then, when the kids get into trouble, American child protection laws deprive parents of their usual control mechanism, corporal punishment, and they struggle to find new ways of stopping their children's more egregious behavior. In February 2006 sixteen young East Africans in Seattle—Ethiopians, Eritreans, and Somalis—were indicted on federal drug crimes charges, sending their communities into a tailspin of pain and disbelief. The gang, which the police refer to as the "East African posse," had been under surveillance for a year, following the drug-related murder of a twenty-one-year-old Eritrean man in the University District in May 2005 and the November death of an Ethiopian man of the same age who was struck by a car as the driver tried to elude police. The communities' shame about these incidents is palpable. Although every immigrant group loses children to crime, East Africans pride themselves on their morality and do not understand where they have gone wrong. They cannot conceive of their young people acting this way outside of a war context, especially given how the older generation suffered to bring them here. As unwelcome as is this new narrative of crime, it cannot be ignored and adds its own painful force to the changing identities of the three groups. Ironically, the "posse" has contributed to communal identities a narrative not only of crime but also of intergroup cooperation.

UNIFIERS AND UNITERS

The real unifiers and uniters, however, cooperate for the *good* of their communities. A few well-intentioned individuals have banded together in formal service organizations to lend a hand to those within their communities, irrespective of ethnic or clan identity, who need help in their new country. They offer access to assistance in obtaining housing and preparing visa applications and advise applicants on finding medical treatment, schooling for their children, and paying their bills. They point them toward jobs and prepare them for the American workplace. Such service providers exist in each of the three communities, and they play an important role in the resettlement of their people. While most start out intending to be ethnicity- or clan-free, they are frequently thwarted in their ideals by less tolerant segments of the community who cannot bring themselves to accept help from the other.

Mowliid, explaining why some Somali men find it so difficult to accept help, quotes a Somali proverb—"The hand that receives is lower than the hand that gives"—and tells me that one never wants to be the lower hand, because it suggests a position that is demeaning. "You want always to be the hand that gives," he says, "the one at the top." The power dynamics of Somali culture permeate all levels of the society even though they derive traditionally from the independent nomad who never needed to accept assistance from anyone. Those were earlier days, however, and a changing economy has altered patterns of status, while droughts and violence have brought even the proudest hands level with the ground. I would like to think that at least some of the Somali service organizations that provide such valuable aid to their communities function as much out of a sense of responsibility toward others as from the appeal of having the upper hand.

The organization that Mowliid directs, Northwest Somaliland Society, he tells me, offers young people cultural classes that teach them respect for their own culture and religion and answers the following questions:

What are good habits? How can you assimilate with others? How can you give the image of a good person? How can you view others who are of different color, religion, etc.? How can you integrate? How can you be independent? How can you give them the good image that your religion and your culture give you? How can you give them a good picture of your religion, because today it is synonymous with terrorism? How can you choose that, how can you pacify and say, "No, I'm against all that"? What are the obligations on you from your host country? What are your rights?

Although service centers don't always succeed in transcending the ancient barriers of clan and ethnicity, their very aspirations familiarize their countrymen and countrywomen with the concept and bring about a new way of being. It is a story that slowly emerges from each of the three communities, one filled with the hope of a more inclusive togetherness that will strengthen each community and provide it with the unity needed to make itself felt in the broader context of Washington and Oregon. ·

When Ubax helped establish the Somali Rights Network to bring to justice clan warlords accused of crimes against humanity, she also tried to make it inclusive of everybody. "This kind of human rights violation has touched every person, irrespective of his clan," she explained, talking about the deaths and suffering experienced by Darods, Isaqs, and Hawiyes alike. The absence of a recognized nation-state in Somalia, however, complicated SRN's program, and the group planned to campaign in Washington, D.C., for a mandate that deals with cell-states, making Somalia a case study for other cells in the world. SRN lobbied Congressman Adam Smith, and on July 21, 2005, he introduced bill H.R. 3396 to Congress. The bill, which aimed "to facilitate lasting peace, democracy, and economic recovery in Somalia," included a section titled "Investigation of War Crimes and Crimes against Humanity in Somalia." Those individuals responsible for such crimes were to be held accountable for their actions as a matter of U.S. policy.

For Ubax, the appearance of the bill should have been a time of celebration. Her hard work had moved matters into the public arena. Instead, she was at the receiving end of a backlash from her own clan, the very same subclan to which the president of the Transitional Federal Government, Abdullahi Yusuf, belonged. The bill's introduction and the president's election, she says, took place the same week, and people wrongly assumed that she was out to get Abdullahi Yusuf.

Ultimately, only Islam provides the common denominator that brings Somalis from different clans together to rub shoulders with one another. At Portland's Bilal Masjid, the members of different clans clear their minds of past rivalries and, if only for the duration of the service, worship together and afterward speak as one people about the problems facing all Muslims in the Pacific Northwest. The worshippers also include Ethiopian and Eritrean Muslims, Tigre, Ogadeni, Oromo, Bilen, and Beni-Amir. At Bilal, leaders have stayed faithful to the founders' decision not to have a designated imam, so as to avoid sectarian discussions and verbal attacks. Instead, they invite different leaders from both within and outside the community to lead the congregation in prayer, in English. The mosque serves as a liaison between the Portland Muslim community and local government agencies and carries the potential for achieving status for the Somali community in the Pacific Northwest.

Sports, too, bring the various segments of each community together. Soccer may be the great equalizer within each diaspora East African community here, as it cuts across ethnic, religious, and class boundaries to unite players and their supporters in urban American chauvinism. Ethiopians, for example, sponsor a huge soccer tournament every year on July 4, "a big get-together," Desta Wondwassen tells me, "with players from about twenty-three to twenty-four cities in the United States assembling in one place to compete." His voice reveals excitement as he paints a picture for me of families congregating, friends who haven't seen each other for years making contact, and everyone eating Ethiopian food and buying Ethiopian goods.

Somalis also sponsor numerous local soccer teams and congregate in Seattle once a year to compete. "Soccer is very important to us," Abdihakim confirms, "and just the other day I went to watch the Portugal-Germany game at a café around the corner, and it was packed with Somalis watching." Somalia hasn't competed in international sports since 1991, and sadly, only two months after I interviewed Abdihakim in 2006, extremist factions of the ICU in central Somalia shot and killed two people for watching a banned World Cup soccer broadcast.

Another interest which draws Ethiopians together in enthusiastic and nationalistic fervor that ignores ethnic politics in favor of Ethiopian identity is athletics. Whether the athletes profess Christianity or Islam, or identify themselves as Amhara or Tigray, they are first and foremost Ethiopian. "Everyone loves sports, and we love our athletes," Haddis confirms, explaining how their athletes' successes bring people together regardless of their differences. He proudly fills me in on their records, citing Abebe Bikila, a two-time Olympic marathon champion who achieved his first win in 1960 in Rome, where he ran barefoot. But "the tradition didn't stop there," he says. "Ethiopia's dominance in long-distance races continues with Haile Gebreselassie, Kenenisa Bekele, women runners such as Derartu Tulu and Meseret Defar, and many others who have been a source of pride for the country."

Although uniting the different ethnic groups within each community remains of major importance for that community's future well-being, the greater challenge confronting the groups in Seattle and Portland is the bridging of differences *among* Ethiopians, Eritreans, and Somalis. Many Horn refugees and exiles see the benefits of working together for mutual benefit, but some distrust their neighbors and fear financial or political betrayal at their hands. War is hardly ever a straightforward us/them, good/evil dichotomy, and the emotions it engenders can be even more complicated as people try to come together for the common good in its aftermath. To the credit of human nature, such emotions often pleasantly exceed expectations. Ezra Teshome recalls an incident from a few years back when the U.S. State Department asked the Rotary Club in Seattle to set up a land mine conference, and he was part of the committee charged with the job. "What we did," he remembers, "was to invite people from those areas that have land mines to come here and sit down and work out solutions." He invited an Ethiopian doctor and an Eritrean, prompting concern that the two men would create tension at the conference.

> So, the night before the conference, we went to a reception and took the fellow from Ethiopia. The Eritrean was already there, and as we started walking inside, we saw the Eritrean standing in the distance. And this doctor saw him as well. And they both looked at each other, and the other guy came to him, and they just started crying. They knew each other. The other guy was deported from Ethiopia, he had lived in Ethiopia, and he started crying. And he said, "Gosh, you know, how's so-and-so, and how's so-and so?" And the state department was shouting, "Ezra, Ezra, take a picture!"

This dual relationship—enemies yet friends—is perhaps what makes it easier for those in the diaspora to reach out to others across the chasm. The story is not uncommon.

Mixed Ethnicity and Nationality

In Seattle and Portland, the unifiers are often people of mixed ethnicity who have intimate understanding of both sides and refuse to choose one over the other, deciding instead to leave hatred behind, work together, and move on. David Makonnen, for example, is of Tigray-Eritrean heritage and took it upon himself to slowly edge forward a new narrative of identity, one of an interactive East African group bent on securing its rightful position in the American cultural marketplace. He initially spearheaded the effort to get the three groups working together as a project for a 1994 Seattle seminar in self-expression and leadership. Required by his instructor to come up with a project he thought beyond the realm of possibility but which he'd like to see materialize, he chose to bring together the polarized East African communities and persuade them to pool their energy and resources for their common good. He elaborates:

> The issues they face are the same, for poverty and unemployment do not discriminate between Ethiopian and Eritrean. Each group struggles alone with unemployment, identity, assimilation . . . and the lack of dialogue perpetuates the polarization and ineffectiveness. So, I asked myself, "What would it take for them to put aside their differences so that they could get together and agree on a common platform that would allow them to play the same 'numbers' game that other mature communities can to work the political system and make a difference?" The more I started thinking about it, the more I started sweating. The ideal didn't seem to be within the realm of possibility. I thought I could be physically beaten up.

His fears were realistic. At first, when he spoke of a social service agency that would serve all three groups, community leaders eyed him suspiciously. Only when they had satisfied themselves he had no vested financial or political interests in pushing cooperation, and they could see the benefits of working together on common problems, did they steer David toward Horn of Africa Services (HOAS), which was then being run by a white Lutheran minister out of a Lutheran church. David explains that with "50 percent of the community here being of Muslim faith, the HOAS leadership failed to attract East Africans to the services it offered and was shutting down." He adds that some East Africans even thought the HOAS staff were working for the CIA. So David recruited members for an East African board that represented each of the communities, moved the social service organization out of the church, and started writing grants. Most important, he initiated a dialogue and kept it going, even during the border war. "Although the Tigrayan and Eritrean community leaders at the time each participated in rallies supporting opposing causes," he says, "as a result of the trust built through a healthy and open dialogue at HOAS, they continued to meet privately and work on issues that improved the lives of Ethiopians and Eritreans in the Pacific Northwest." Horn of Africa Services soon became an umbrella organization, a coalition that helped smaller organizations in Seattle with their legal structures, and with fund-raising, and impressed on them the importance of being accountable to their donors.

The dialogue David started continues today. The organization offers computer classes for young people, instruction in English as a second language, and job training and also provides services for single mothers and older women and men who are here on their own because their relatives have been killed or left behind. It helps residents living in housing projects when they have disputes with management or with other residents and generally involves itself in conflict management. It has had uneven success. Nevertheless, the communities have come a long way.

Others of mixed ethnicity have also been forerunners in bringing the communities together for the common good. Dawit Nerayo, for example, has an Ethiopian mother and an Eritrean father, the latter a medical doctor and Eritrean People's Liberation Front fighter who fled Ethiopia for Seattle when the Derg attempted to kill him. Since Dawit's arrival in Seattle, he has renewed acquaintance with his father and speaks positively of his mixed heritage. "I'm actually blessed because I'm half Ethiopian and half Eritrean," he says. "I can hold both sides responsible. I can say what I like to both sides, and nobody can accuse me of bias and that I'm saying this because I'm Ethiopian or I'm saying that because I'm Eritrean."

It wasn't only marriage that produced mixed identity. The very fact that Eritrea was a province of Ethiopia between 1962 and 1991 meant that many Eritreans moved to Addis in pursuit of jobs and brought up their families in an Ethiopian environment where their children spoke Amhara and identified as Ethiopian. To be Eritrean in Addis at that time invited abusive reactions, so many young people sided with the Amhara rulers who held power over their lives. Others spoke Tigrinya only in private. David, whose Eritrean father and half-Tigrayan mother moved to Addis after the Second World War, grew up not knowing the difference between Ethiopians and Eritreans. Eritrea was just the fourteenth province at the time, so he considered himself Ethiopian, but he had cousins and uncles and aunts who were Eritrean and supported Eritrean independence during the struggle, some who supported the Eritrean Liberation Front, others the Eritrean People's Liberation Front. "From my perspective," he says, "I think each one of them had a specific cause they were fighting for that made sense at some stage. But in the bigger scheme of things, they're missing the point in terms of living in harmony and what the long-term humanitarian goal is, which is improving the life of the people."

Not everyone, however, sees things the same way, nor does everyone have a war hero for a father, like Dawit, who acquires Eritrean credibility from his father's status. For most young people of mixed heritage, the situation feels less secure. Sometimes, they are viewed with suspicion by political diehards and trusted by neither side. In Seattle, Abraha expresses concern for them. "Most of the kids in that situation don't feel very comfortable in their own world because of the zones. I feel so sorry for them." Yet when I talked to some of these young people, I found that having links to both sides, far from being a burden, liberated them from the divisive politics of their elders and enabled them to create new all-encompassing narratives of tolerance and compassion.

The Younger Generation Leads the Way

Where the elders fear to tread, the young have no trepidation. They cross the bridges of nationality with open arms, agents of goodwill and reconciliation, refusing to listen to parents who forbid them to play soccer with children of other groups. Dressed in their American baggy pants and high-top Nikes, speaking fluent English and dropping American slang with the familiarity of natives, these East African youngsters look beyond nation and religion for their friendships. Of more interest to them is how "fly" their student friends can be, what computer games they play, which hip-hop artists they admire. Seattle or Portland is their home, not Addis or Mogadishu or Asmara, and as their confidence as young Americans increases, these children act as interpreters between the adult groups, putting the youths in positions of authority and often unsettling family dynamics. Lidwien Kapteijns calls the actions of this younger generation "selected acculturation."[3] Supported by their peers, they count co-ethnics as their friends and accumulate relational resources, social capital, which they bring to their ethnic communities. In this way, they oblige the older members of the community to rub shoulders with the sons and daughters of those who seem both different and the same. Each treads on sensitive ground.

Older diaspora members could not have imagined children who played soccer with "the enemy" or engaged them in other competitive games. Most certainly, they never foresaw their daughters dating young men from the other ethnic group or clan. Parents often forbid interethnic dating, but, as different immigrant groups before them have discovered, such intolerance simply heightens attraction and leads young Romeos and Juliets into each others' arms. "Still," Abdihakim says of Somali-Ethiopian dating, "it is done mostly behind the scenes. There's a lot of it happening, but the community doesn't like it if you hold hands or kiss in public. Like on the campus."

"And what about interethnic dating within the community?" I ask.

"Somali Bantus and other clan Somalis also are starting to date. They are few in number still, and I haven't seen many married families yet, but it is happening. Even though many people don't like it, they see that in American culture it doesn't matter any longer."

As with most other immigrants before them, for the East African newcomers, dating and marriage outside the community represents a crossing of the Rubicon, one that can damage family relations. Adaptation and assimilation can go only so far before some parents call a halt. For many young Ethiopians, Somalis, and Eritreans, dating becomes the final power struggle in which they assert their identity and alienate themselves from their own people. Senait was luckier than most. When she attended high school and lived in a predominantly black neighborhood in Seattle, her mother liked her Jamaican boyfriend of five years and welcomed him into their home. But now, as she comes to the end of her university education, even her more tolerant parent has made it quite clear that she expects her daughter to marry an Eritrean. Still, tolerance has its own rewards, and Senait, unlike many of her Eritrean peers, identifies totally with her people. She understands where her mom's coming from, she explains to me, and sees her demands not so much as a "parental barrage" but as an expression of her "community's expectations." For her personally, Eritrean identity "tops Horn of Africa," but even so, she despairs of the rifts within the community itself and is determined that her generation will fight it.

> We don't want to be like our parents. We see our parents celebrating the same holidays with two different groups. "You can't hang out with these people because they might not be of your political affiliation . . . , you can't go to that party, because those people might not be of your parents' political affiliation." We don't want that for our community. We're already a small community as it is, and to divide us even more is to make us even smaller and our voice even dimmer. Every time you split, every time you make another sect, it's very difficult. Now I think our community is learning. I think now is the time. My generation is going to take the reins, and we're going to try to do things. We are watching our parents, and we don't want to become that. That's not to say our parents are wrong. That's their beliefs and that's fine, but they cannot expect us to be pro-Eritrean and do all these things and yet ignore Eritreans who are different from us. I think a lot of what we're doing now . . . a lot of kids in our generation, what we're trying to do . . . there's a big push to unify. Even if it's not along political lines, that's fine. Have your own political beliefs. We're all Eritreans first, and Eritreans in the diaspora.

Thus, a more modern, open-minded generation emerges in the Pacific Northwest, a generation of young women and men who, once they get beyond measuring their worth with the materialistic yardstick used by teenagers, begin to recognize the beauty and richness of their cultures. Since most have not been personally involved in the trauma of war and violence in the Horn, their emotional attachment to their ancestral countries is often forged through witnessing their parents' stories. Some have never even seen their families' country of origin, but reared on its stories, they have absorbed the emotional knowledge of long-ago events and carry within them a core of affection for and commitment to their imagined community. Any cultural bitterness implanted by parents, however, they try to bury in secret compartments of their identities in accord with their more personal desires for cultural acceptance and identity in the United States. Girded by these desires, they reach out across ethnic divisions and begin to construct an all-American story by which they can interact with the children of "the enemy" and move forward.

In the universities and colleges of Seattle and Portland, the optimism of youth encourages risk and leads many to take a chance on forming relationships. "I have a number of friends from Ethiopia," Ubax informs me, "and my best friend is from Eritrea. She was my roommate in school, and I was surprised once I got to know her how much we had in common. Despite our different allegiances, we connect at a human level. In fact, it was she who was there for me during hard times."

Exposure to the Internet also facilitates such discoveries of sameness, and MySpace or YouTube, for example, allows for exploratory and anonymous interactions. The young have grown up online, and this electronic medium creates a third space that can blur, as well as emphasize, the delineating consciousness between "them" and "us." In this space, young people can create other narratives; in it, they can create new ways of being Americans. Their course does not always run smoothly. It hasn't in the past either. Historically, events back home have subverted the best of diaspora intentions. In the 1970s, for example, after the fall of Haile Selassie, Oromo students in Seattle and Portland broke away from the Ethiopian student unions, and at the University of Washington, between 1998 and 2000, animosities aroused by the border war led Eritrean and Ethiopian students to gradually dissolve their Horn of Africa Students Association. The Somalis, who are relative newcomers to the area, have their own Somali Students Association. On the positive side, some students from all three communities now belong to the much broader African Students Association, which aims to unify the African student body within the university. At Portland State, the African Students Association counts Eritreans, Somalis, and Ethiopians among its members and cosponsors Africa-related events at the university's multicultural center. These are the new leaders of tomorrow, the young people who will make a difference. In April 2007 Ethiopian University of Washington student Alula Asfew became a Harry S. Truman Scholarship recipient for his exceptional leadership potential. One of sixty-five winners out of 585 candidates nominated from 280 universities nationwide, Alula Asfew was chosen not only for his intellectual ability but for the likelihood that he would make a difference in the world. He wants to serve his people.

For these young people, the question of identity is all-consuming. As acculturation takes place, the initial "Who are we?" develops into a more considered "Who do we want to be?" Success in the academic and social environments of the university builds confidence, and students examine their choices, trying on different identities for fit: Are they still Ethiopian, Somali, or Eritrean, despite their American accents? Or are they American? Or simply Africans? East African is yet another option, or else Ethiopian American, Eritrean American, or Somali American. Like other Africans before them, these students increasingly identify with "black" or the cultural designation "African American," and not always by choice. Previously, few Eritreans, Ethiopians, or Somalis thought much about race. Having grown up in black communities, they had never needed to define themselves by the color of their skins, but upon entering the Pacific Northwest, they entered an ethnic marketplace that, despite local claims to the contrary, bases itself on race. Americans here seldom, for example, make distinctions between Japanese, Korean, and Chinese, referring to them all indiscriminately as Asians. How much easier it is then to categorize everyone with a black skin as African American. For example, when Senait first started school in Spokane, she was the only black student. Since most Americans hadn't heard of Eritrea, she thought of herself as the only African American. "A lot of my life I identified as an African American because, as much as I want to be Eritrean," she says, "people don't see me as that. First they see me as a black person."

"I'm not going to die if somebody calls me black or African; it makes me complete as a person," explains Redi Mehanzel. He sees his color and race as simply further designations of his multifaceted identity, like ethnicity, nationality, and religion. His sister Mehret goes further. "As soon as one becomes American, one inherits the problems and issues of African Americans, but at the same time one benefits from the sacrifices they have made over the last one hundred years." She goes on to say, "I'm proud to identify as an African American."

That young Eritrean Americans assume they will eventually become African Americans, with all the complexities that involves, suggests that race remains a factor in how we perceive people in Seattle and Portland. Skin color adds yet another category of separation to the many divisions with which East Africans contend, although not an entirely new one. Degrees of lightness have long denoted status in each of these communities, and claims to Arab or Jewish descent have led some Somalis and Ethiopians to consider themselves of Semitic lineage and therefore not quite African. In all three places, darker-skinned rural peoples have been the victims of discrimination at the hands of their lighter-skinned compatriots. Besides the Somali Bantu, other black groups, like the Anuak in the fertile area of Gambella in southwest Ethiopia and the Kunama of Eritrea, have also suffered persecution. In all three cases, the lighter-skinned community correlates black with inferior. In addition, many Bantu were brought to Somalia as slaves and, historically, the Kunama and Anuak were captured by slave traders and sold to the wealthier highlanders as workers and concubines. This has created a black-slave connection in the mind that resonates with the history of African Americans and prevents some older members of Horn communities from identifying with African Americans in the Pacific Northwest.

The young, however, do not make that connection, and, despite their parents' disapproval, many of them aspire to the African American nomenclature. In the final analysis, of course, racists often do not distinguish between East Africans and African Americans. Whether Ethiopians, Eritreans, and Somalis desire it or not, the African American narrative of race may be imposed on them, their complex characteristics of nationality, ethnicity, and clanship condensed into a single symbolic identity: black.

Whether African Americans welcome them into their community is a complex question. Some African Americans perceive the newcomers as unsophisticated and "from the bush." To them, they are other, different in many ways, and yet strangely the same. Many African Americans still carry historical chips on their shoulders and deride those Africans whose ancestors might have known about, if not actively participated in, the sale of their own ancestors into slavery. Yet others, particularly unskilled and manual laborers, simply count them as more competition in a scarce job market. And then there are African Americans like George Valery, a local Seattle business consultant; Erik Evans, president of Urur Livestock Company; and Frank Procella, a Microsoft alumnus. Together, they have gone into business with Somali immigrant Ahmed (Rashid) Mohamed to buy and sell cattle just outside Mogadishu. Urur (a word related to the Somali verb "to organize") employs forty people and exports about one hundred cattle every two to three weeks. Once the business begins to thrive, benefits will accrue to the local population as well. According to an October 1, 2006, article by Jerry Large in the *Seattle Post-Intelligencer*, "These guys are bullish on business—and on Somalia." Urur plans "to build a mosque, help fund schools and teach modern agricultural practices."

Women Reach Out

Among young people, young women in particular lead the way, joining hands in sisterhood across clan, ethnic, and national lines. In the Somali community in Tigard, near Portland, women representing numerous clans live together and care for one another's children, one another's sick. "We are all family," they tell me. Some of them hail from Mogadishu, others from the countryside, others from the south and the east, but they "like each other" and "support each other," they say. Five of them crowd around me as we talk, while what seems like hundreds of children run around us, all of them happy and secure, shrieking with laughter, banging drums, or sucking frozen ices. It is a swelteringly hot day. Outside, other Somali kids repeatedly set off my car alarm, and their mothers scream at them to stop.

In many ways, the women interact with one another much as they would in Somalia, where it is not unusual for married women to come from different clans. There, however, they are absorbed into their husbands' clans, which provide the unifying structures and demand their loyalty even if it means they must take sides against their own familial clans. In Tigard, however, many of the women are single, having escaped alone from the destruction of the civil war. Some used to have husbands but are no longer sure of the men's whereabouts, or even whether they are still alive. For themselves, having made it out and being aware of what women have suffered back home, they consider the clan membership of their women friends irrelevant.

Solidarity has always existed among East African women, but with the addition of feminist support, the women feel empowered to make their own decisions about how they want to live their lives and with whom they want to be friends. Their embrace of feminism may also be seen as a means of fitting in, of becoming American. In part, it is this accommodation to the mores and values of their host country that brings young women to the multicultural table. After experiencing the hell of war, the loss of husbands and brothers, they are perhaps readier for overtures of peace that will allow them to move on with their lives. Sonya attributes their greater receptivity to communicating across old barriers to their greater happiness because they've been empowered and may have found themselves in America. That's what enables them to set past politics aside and reach out, she says. In many instances, their reach extends even beyond East African women to the broader African community, whose members they embrace as sisters. In Portland, Lutheran Community Services Northwest has created a community-based organization, the African Women's Coalition, which helps improve the economic conditions of refugee families and facilitate their integration into the wider community. At their meetings, members dress in their traditional clothing and share the food and music of their home countries with other Africans. They learn to understand one another's cultures and appreciate them in spite of past antagonisms. Haddis, who claims to practice equality with his wife at home, "where it all starts," has great confidence in the "ability and resilience" of young women. "They may not have power today, and their voices may be suppressed," he says, "but look out. There is incredible talent coming up, and we will be a lot better off when women have more control."

Successful women who have made it in Seattle and Portland assume heroic status in the eyes of their younger sisters, inspiring them to grasp opportunities for self-enhancement. Mehret, for example, enthuses about Lette Hadgu, at the time director of the Seattle Early Scholars Outreach program GEAR UP (Gaining Early Awareness and Readiness for Undergraduate Programs) at the University of Washington. "Lette's a role model for us younger women," she says. "You can go to her for help, and she's always ready to listen. She's a leader, very professional, and connects with young and old alike and understands both cultures." Women like Lette become mentors to the younger women and help them negotiate the complexities of their new, emancipated lives, the conflict between their more assertive behavior at work and the demure demeanor considered appropriate for women by traditional men.

Lidwien Kapteijns claims in "Educating Immigrant Youth in the US" that Somali women have "excelled" in the diaspora because they collaborate, but young men have a harder time of it because they are less able to work together for the common good. With *Somalinimo* damaged in the civil war and having a low priority within the cultural marketplace of the new host country, a sense of crisis exists. Most definitely, Somali men have had the most difficult challenge of all East African arrivals in the Pacific Northwest. Leadership is lacking, and even Seattle's Koshin Mohamed appears humble about his own. "I'm a lousy leader, myself," he claims, "but I'm the best they've got." He continues:

> Somalis don't have leaders—they haven't had an honest leader since 1969! Anyone who is a minister and controls an office is corrupt; he takes everything that comes out of it. So that's the mentality. How can you show them what a leader is? I used to get mad about it, but I'm learning what my people went through, and now I'm sympathetic. When they talk about corruption, I understand why they're corrupted. When they excuse their leaders' lies, I understand. It's because they've never had an honest leader leading them. I understand now and I say, "Please give me a chance, and I will show you that I can be someone you can trust. I can show you that I want for you what I want for myself."

ACCULTURATION AND CULTURAL INTEGRITY

A conceptual adjustment gradually plays out. Like immigrants before them, Eritreans, Ethiopians, and Somalis adapt to the changing contexts of their lives. They widen their centers of personal identity in order to benefit from the combined force of partnering with their East African brothers and sisters or joining hands with the well-established African

American lobby. In the process, these new leaders slowly but surely drag the rest of their communities into the future. Their hearts may remain ineluctably linked to the countries of their ancestors, but in the framework of their new American lives, they know they must accommodate in order to move forward on both material and emotional levels. So they reposition themselves in relation to the stories of their past, compartmentalizing their histories and at the same time formulating their own American myths in partnership with their historical enemies. Pragmatism, ambition, and acceptance of the other's story create a new space for their special versions of the American Dream.

The more they mix socially and professionally, the easier it becomes to separate the person from the politics of his country. At City Center Parking in Portland, where staff includes Eritreans, Ethiopians, and Somalis, Desta says that good relationships prevail and everybody socializes. "We practice what President Clinton proposed: Don't ask, don't tell!" We both laugh, but sadness tinges the sound. Nobody really wants to hide his identity. Ethiopians, Somalis, and Eritreans all take pride in who they are, and although becoming American is part and parcel of their dream, not everything about American culture thrills them. It's not that they see life in the Pacific Northwest as utopian. In fact, much disturbs East Africans, particularly in the American value system that permeates all tiers of society and frequently clashes with the values of home. Mehret points to the individualism that she believes displaces family values and destroys community, while Abraha notes American society's emphasis on self-indulgence, which Horn children now emulate. Immigrant parents deplore American kids' lack of respect for adults, their low-slung pants with underwear showing, their unwillingness to take responsibility for themselves and others. "The way they walk, the way they talk," Almaz complains, "I see no respect. They throw things in the street, their Kleenex, and when they come into my shop, they don't line up and they will go on talking to one another and keep you waiting so that you can't serve another customer."

Of course, Americans, too, dislike this behavior and try to guide their children to more respectful and responsible attitudes. Still, the Horn parents worry about their kids. And they worry about their safety. Amina Sheikhuna in Portland fears that her kids will be kidnapped if she lets them out on the street. Although terrible things happen to children in Mogadishu now, children traditionally were always safe in Somali culture and in Eritrean and Ethiopian cultures, too. Children in the United States, however, are murdered and abused, according to Abraha, and "this despite the fact that we have social workers, psychologists, and historians all trying to explain how such things happen. If I did anything wrong in my hometown," he says, "the entire town knows who I am and where I come from. And so the shame is borne not only by me but extends to my family as well. People there have pride; they have ethical and moral codes."

Yet for every criticism, there was also enthusiastic admiration for what America offers the newcomers: the opportunity to go to school, the diversity of people with whom to make communities, freedom of expression and movement, and the chance to excel to the full extent of their abilities. The list went on and on, but even among those with positive opinions, some expressed hesitation. Yodit, for example, agrees that the opportunity to challenge yourself based on your own dreams is the greatest thing about America, but she also cautions about the selling of false dreams. "It's hypocrisy," she says, "to make people believe they can be whatever they want to be and that race doesn't play a part. Yes, you can go to the best university and be the best you want to be, but in terms of mainstream America, you are never treated equally."

The dilemma facing these young people, the same one that has confronted generations of other immigrants before them, is to find a way of being that allows them to retain their cultural integrity and yet at the same time take advantage of what America has to offer so that they can move into the mainstream and have a chance at living the American Dream. Everyone welcomes acculturation into American ways. Nobody I spoke to wants to stay outside of American cultural life; nobody relishes the isolation and chronic marginality that nativism inevitably spawns. Nevertheless, the boundaries where the two cultures meet—Ethiopian and American, Somali and American, Eritrean and American—create doubt and insecurity about what exactly such a mixed identity will mean. From the perspective of both an individual and the community, which are the values to adopt and which are the ones to disregard? Which values will contribute to success in the United States, their new home, and on what terms will that success be negotiated? Will the *hijab* have to go? The kisses of greeting? The punches of friendship? In Islam, where usury is forbidden, Horn Muslims refuse to take loans, thus excluding them from home ownership and preventing them from accumulating wealth in their new country. How are they to get around the imperatives of the Qur'an and still attain the American Dream?

The answers, needless to say, vary from person to person, and examples of eclecticism, syncretism, hybridism, and pragmatism abound in all three communities. No one situation ever signifies the same for all exiles, but all methods inevitably link to the blending of cultures to some degree. Ahmed Samatar addresses himself specifically to Somali Muslims and offers "critical adaptation" as his approach to the problem of identity in the United States. It is, he says, an organic process by which Muslims can hold onto their Islamic identity while accepting heterogeneity. He argues that it is possible to have a stake in the American system, to create a worthwhile life for oneself and one's family, and to make contributions to the shaping of the new homeland "without giving in to right-wing racists or left-wing liberal-paternalists." All that is needed is "a reasoning Islam," which Samatar defines as "an Islamic identity that abides by the law of the land, is at ease with disputatious heterogeneity and consequently, is confident enough to enter into an open and respectful dialogue with others who share a civic identity but follow a different set of religious beliefs."[4] Somalis hold numerous allegiances—clan, region, *diya*-paying group, *tariq*, for example—so adding the United States to their list would seem unproblematic were it not for the fact that so many Somalis have been conditioned by anti-American rhetoric from extremists in their home countries and so many Americans still refuse to see Somali Muslims as Americans.

Ethiopian Mawi Asgedom, author of the memoir *Of Beetles and Angels*, also offers advice about survival in the United States. Drawing on his own experiences as a bullied welfare student who struggled with the English language in junior high school but ultimately rose from refugee status to Harvard graduate, he passes on to his teenage readers what he learned about holding onto Ethiopian values and assuming new American ones. He considers teenagers the movers and shakers of the future and speaks to them of finding their own comfort zone, setting their own goals, and being the people they've always wanted to be. He has written a number of inspirational books for teenagers and has devised a code for teen success that may help them negotiate the hazards of life in America.

Slowly, the three communities find their comfort level. They change and combine, adapt and adjust according to the limits of their needs. Thus, for example, when Senait's sister married a Jamaican, she struck a deal with her parents to hold both an American wedding and a traditional Eritrean ceremony. "Saturday's event was on the lakefront, with crystal, fine china, and all that," Senait remembers, "and Sunday was beautiful, too, but in its own traditional way, with traditional seating arrangements, where you eat at benches and all the men eat from one plate of *zanzetta*." She continues:

> My sister's hair was braided for the day, and she wore a *zurriya*. Her husband had on the traditional all-white *stable kiramba*, and all her bridesmaids had *zurriyas* made for them. On the Saturday night, although the choice of music started off as a bone of contention, everyone eventually agreed that it should be half Jamaican reggae and half Eritrean *krar* music. It was beautiful. It was a coming together of two different cultures.

The coming together of cultures is what America is all about: the creation of new combined narratives. "The way we dance, too, has changed," Senait adds. In the traditional Tigrinya dance, women mainly move their shoulders, but "we have made the dance our own," she says. "We kind of adapt it, move our hips, mix it up a bit, and give it an Americanized flavor."

MAKING A DIFFERENCE

Listening to Senait and other young people like her, it becomes clear that tolerance and openness to change does not alienate one from one's own community but rather brings with it a wider perspective that allows one to see the community's needs in context. Young people like her, educated in the United States and exposed to the stories of other communities in the Pacific Northwest, find it easier to focus on events in their diaspora community than on what happened in the homeland that is so distant in time and space. They are the new Americans, Americans of Somali,

Eritrean, and Ethiopian descent, who by broadening their own identities enlarge those of their communities and ultimately transform society.

Transforming the Community

Many among the older generation and those who were personally involved in their countries' violence react negatively to words like "cooperation," "joining together," or "uniting" because their experience does not allow them to conceive of such interaction without a primary actor who dominates the others. Certainly, they have every right to be fearful. There are indeed people in communities here who even now are working hard to effect change in the Horn of Africa that will favor their particular national, ethnic, or clan interests over those of others and derive benefit from the outcome. The United States' increasingly close association with Ethiopia and the possibility that it aims to empower Ethiopia in the region by making it one of its regional bases in Africa, has Eritreans and Somalis as well as Ethiopian Muslims nervous. Some Amhara organizations raise funds in Seattle to throw out the Tigray government and regain power for the Amhara, while among the Somalis, some Darods maneuver for advantages at home. Such intrigue and transnational machinations relating to the home countries are not unexpected. But something else also bubbles beneath the surface, the aspiration to better things right here and to bring about the kind of economic and social cooperation that would allow locals to improve their situation and fulfill their individual and communal dreams. I am convinced that most of those I interviewed desire peaceful relations with their neighbors. The alternative is just too destructive.

"I remember this one time," Ezra recounts a conversation he had with an Oromo man. "We were having this discussion and couldn't see eye to eye," he explains, continuing:

> He was telling me stories about this thing that happened, which in my opinion had never happened. So finally, after it had gone on and on, a heated discussion, I said to him, "OK. Let me just for a moment agree to whatever you say. OK? But I want you to help me"—he has a son and I have four kids—"I want you to tell me what I should tell my kids, how

they should look at your son. Should they look at him and feel guilt and shame? I tell them that my tribe killed his grandparents. So now they don't get along. Help me. How should I explain it to my kids?" That stopped it. He said, "You're right. You're right." We need to look at the message, so that *they* can get along, because our generation is pretty much lost. There's no way his position and mine can come together, but do we have to pass down our differences for another generation? We must unite, respect our differences, and strive to create a better Ethiopia for our children.

During interviews, parents expressed immense pride in their ethnicity and culture and said that they tried their best to tell their children about their inheritance, while younger parents felt keenly that animosity should not be perpetuated. Even if they stopped short of approving interethnic dating and marriage, they wanted their children to be open-minded. After all, intolerance and discrimination most often were the reasons their children were growing up in the United States and not in their parents' homeland. "The most important thing is to take care of the next generation," Yosieph, the father of a young son and two older daughters, explains. "The other you cannot change." Speaking of the Eritrean government and the "strong personalities" in the Eritrean community here who have agendas, he says, "I see them putting all their energy into this trivial stuff, and I tell them, 'This is awful, stay away from this stuff.' But unless they're in corporate America, they don't understand these things, and they make issues."

Like Yosieph, David, too, tries to impress on his daughter the need for tolerance. As the child of an Ethiopian father and an Eritrean mother, she has been taken to visit both countries and when asked about her heritage says she's both Ethiopian and Eritrean. He says she knows the difference and appreciates both.

I think we've made sure she knows that there is no right or wrong in this instance. The two countries have wars, but both are part of her heritage. And America, too. She's as American as can be, because she was born and raised here, but she also goes to Amharic school to learn the language and has asked to go to the Eritrean Community Center to learn Tigrinya as well. She goes to events at both places and celebrates both cultures.

Most parents make it a priority to keep their language alive, knowing the cultural codes will be absorbed along with the mother tongue. But they push English harder, aware that being articulate in the language of the United States opens more doors in business, education, and politics.

In Minnesota, Obi Sium became the first Eritrean ever to be nominated by the Republican Party. A sixty-five-year-old retired water resources engineer and the Republican nominee for the Fourth Congressional District in Minnesota, Obi (Ogbazghi) received 30 percent of the vote in the 2006 midterm elections. In Seattle and Portland, Eritreans and Ethiopians, too, begin to find their political feet. Their members develop political savvy and learn to use the resources of the two cities in order to make their voices heard. Even the Somalis, latecomers to Western ways of negotiating influence, now flex their political muscles. Abdihakim has been working with the office of U.S. Senator Maria Cantwell, encouraging her to involve herself in Somali affairs, while Ubax and her group at Somali Rights Network have on their side U.S. Representative Adam Smith, who serves Washington's Ninth District. While lip service to immigrant issues is the norm much of the time, Seattle's own Congressman Jim McDermott has always been responsive to African concerns. McDermott, often referred to as the father of the African Growth and Opportunity Act, which facilitates trade between the United States and countries in Africa, attends East African functions in Seattle and promotes community economic development wherever he can. The new Americans learn to reach out, persevere, and persist.

Enriching the Pacific Northwest

A number of East Africans have already built successful lives in the Pacific Northwest. Muslim Microsoft workers, known as Muppies (Muslim yuppies), as well as Christian Ethiopians and Eritreans who work at the Redmond campus contribute their expertise and energy to the software giant, whose success in turn enriches the economy of the Pacific Northwest. These professionals also buy homes and cars, send their children to private or parochial schools, and donate money to community projects in Seattle.

Achieving the American Dream, however, involves more than money. "That is not the only path to success," Yosieph points out. "Success could be being able to sit down and talk about philosophy, about Plato and Nietzsche, literature, and stuff like that." It is what he wants for his son, Abraham—to be "a critical thinker." "It's time for us to be part of the greater society in the higher areas of the mind," he continues, "because that's what the future is about." Nevertheless, a certain degree of economic stability can provide the leverage to gain involvement in American affairs, and certainly the Eritrean community wants that, too. Yosieph concurs. "I'd like to see an Eritrean Bill Gates," he muses, "or an Eritrean who is a vice president or executive in corporate America, a Boeing executive." The idea thrills him, but he admits that "the voice of leadership in the community hasn't yet emerged. Still," he adds, "slowly and surely, we are building our network."

Ethiopian, Eritrean, and Somali scholars who speak for these communities are slowly emerging in the Pacific Northwest. Other professionals already have. Young doctors and engineers, bankers, and entrepreneurs build careers here and find their places in the larger American community. Here, they interact with others in their fields and bring their influence to bear on the medical, technical, and economic development of the region and the United States as a whole. Secure in their identity as well as in their position in the American economy, they reach out to their Horn neighbors, creating new bridges of understanding. Banker Sofi Mulugeta, for example, regularly hikes, camps, and eats out with a bunch of professionals of Ethiopian, Eritrean, and Somali descent, while Haddis, who "loves it here in Seattle" and says, "This place has been good to me," tries to place not just young Ethiopians but other Africans in different political campaigns. "I want young people to see democracy in action and draw best practices so they can help Africa in the future."

And so, progressive individuals in the Pacific Northwest create change through speaking it and lead their institutions forward cautiously into their American future. Each new voice adds its own particular influence to the mix and reconfigures the old balance of forces that shape the communities. The story playing out in the Pacific Northwest is an old one. The area has seen other new American narratives being forged by the Vietnamese, Cambodians, Laotians, and, more recently, the

Russians. But no two versions of new community acculturation are ever the same. Each is unique and adds its own cultural particularities to the ever-changing identity of the Pacific Northwest. What is more, it does so in a continuing two-way process. Seattle and Portland will never be the same; neither will any of the three communities. Communal identity remains an ongoing story of becoming.

TIME LINE (1890–2010)

1890   Eritrea becomes a colony of Italy.

1895-96   First Italo-Ethiopian War. Ethiopians defeat Italians at Battle of Adwa.

1930   Haile Selassie is crowned emperor of Ethiopia.

1935-36   Second Italo-Ethiopian War. Italy invades Ethiopia. Somali-speaking parts of Ethiopia combine with Italian Somaliland to form the province of Italian East Africa. Selassie flees to England.

1941   Ethiopians defeat Italians with help from Allied troops. Selassie returns from exile. Eritrea comes under British administration.

1943-44   Weyane rebellion. Tigrayans revolt against Selassie's abuse of Tigray province and people.

1948-54   Britain cedes Ogaden, including the Haud, to Ethiopia.

1950   Italian Somaliland becomes a United Nations trust territory.

1956   Italian Somaliland is renamed Somalia and granted internal autonomy.

1960   British Somaliland gains independence from Britain and merges with southern Somalia to form the Somali Republic.

            Eritrean Liberation Front (ELF) formed in Cairo.

1961   ELF guerrillas fire the first shots of the Eritrean thirty-year war against Ethiopia.

1963-70   Oromo peasant uprisings break out in Ethiopia.

1962   Haile Selassie officially annexes Eritrea as Ethiopia's fourteenth province.

1964   Border hostilities erupt between Ethiopia and Somalia.

1969   Mohammad Siyad Barre becomes president of Somalia after a military coup following the assassination of the former president, Abdirashid Ali Shermarke.

1970   Siyad Barre declares Somalia a socialist state and nationalizes most of the economy.

1970–72   ELF splits, and the core of the Eritrean People's Liberation Front (EPLF) is established.
ELF declares war on the EPLF.

1972–74   Severe drought and famine in Ethiopia, largely ignored by the government, lead to attacks by dissident groups.

1974   Revolution in Ethiopia. Haile Selassie is overthrown by committee of junior army officers, the Derg.

Somalia joins the Arab League.

ELF and EPLF declare a truce and work together for Eritrean self-determination.

Oromos form the Oromo Liberation Front.

1975   The Tigray People's Liberation Front (TPLF), a rebel group, emerges in Ethiopia.

1977   ELF and EPLF succeed in capturing the majority of Eritrean towns.

1977–78   Lieutenant Colonel Mengistu Haile Mariam becomes chairman of the Derg and aligns Ethiopia with the Soviet Union. The Derg unleashes the campaign of bloody violence known as the Red Terror.

Ogaden War between Ethiopia and Somalia. Ethiopian forces aided by Cuban troops and Soviet advisers push Somali fighters out of the Ogaden.

1978–79   Ethiopia, with Soviet backing, reoccupies Eritrea's major towns and cities. EPLF withdraws to its mountain base around Nakfa.

1981   Renewed civil war between EPLF and ELF. ELF units driven into Sudan, where they splinter into competing factions. Some ELF members reconcile with EPLF and rejoin the war against Ethiopia.

Somali opposition group, the Somali National Movement (SNM), forms in London and then moves to Ethiopia.

1982   EPLF repulses Ethiopia's Red Star campaign.

1984-85   Famine in the Horn, caused by war and drought.

1986   Mengistu adopts a Marxist-Leninist constitution and renames the country the People's Democratic Republic of Ethiopia.

1988   EPLF victory over Ethiopia at Afabet.

Ethiopia and Somalia sign agreement to respect one another's borders.

SNM attacks Somali government troops in northern Somalia. In reprisal for the attacks, Siyad Barre's forces massacre Isaqs.

1989   The TPLF drive Mengistu's government from Tigray and together with other rebel groups forms the Ethiopian People's Revolutionary Democratic Front (EPRDF).

1990   Somali opposition groups challenge Siyad Barre, and the violence spreads throughout Somalia, disrupting food supplies and causing widespread starvation.

1991   Siyad Barre flees Somalia, and civil war breaks out. Competing clan factions take over the country.

Somaliland declares unilateral independence.

Mengistu flees Ethiopia, and EPRDF enter Addis Ababa; EPLF march into Asmara and establish a provisional government.

1993   Eritrea becomes independent from Ethiopia after 98 percent of the population vote in favor.

Battle in Mogadishu between U.S. forces and those of Somali warlord Mohamed Farah Aideed.

1994   EPLF becomes the new government, the People's Front for Democracy and Justice (PFDJ), and establishes an independent constitution.

1998-2000   Border incidents escalate and become the Ethiopian-Eritrean border war.

2000   Ethiopia and Eritrea sign a peace agreement in Algiers.

2002   Eritrea-Ethiopia Boundary Commission awards Badme to Eritrea.

2004   Somalia's Transitional Federal Government (TFG) set up in Kenya under the presidency of Abdullahi Yusuf Ahmed.

2005-6   Tensions continue to plague both Eritrea and Ethiopia.

2006   Somalia's TFG, with help from Ethiopia and the United States, regains control of Mogadishu from the Islamic Courts Union (ICU).

2006-9   Ethiopian and U.S. forces battle terrorist ICU splinter groups in Somalia, among them the Alliance for the Re-liberation of Somalia (ARS).

2009   ARS leader Sheikh Sharif Sheikh Ahmed and his faction break with the more extreme wing of that group and agree to cooperate with the TFG. Ethiopian troops leave Somalia, and a restructured TFG is set up under Sharif's presidency.

2009-10   Violence continues between the TFG and al-Shabaab (Youth), an ICU extremist wing with ties to al-Qaeda.

PARTICIPANTS

Listed alphabetically by first name

Abdi Madey Ali

Abdihakim Hassan

Abraham (Abe) Demisse

Aklilu (Tefono) Debesay Foto

Almaz Bahre

Amina Sharif

Amina Sheikhuna

Asia Mohamed Egal

Bereketab Gebrehiwet

David Makonnen

Dawit Nerayo

Desta Wondwassen

Esayas Mehanzel

Ezra Teshome

Haddis Tadesse

Haji Shongolo

Hamadi Hassan

Jamal Gabobe

Koshin Mohamed

Lette Hadgu

Makonnen (Michael) Damtew

Mehret Mehanzel

Mohamed Omer

Mowliid Abdullahi

Mursal Abdullah

Nuria Agraw

Omar Eno

Rahel Gebreab

Redi Mehanzel

Senait (Sonya) Damtew

Senait Habte

Sofanit (Sofi) Mulugeta

Ubax Gardheere

Yegizaw Michael

Yodit Tekle

Yosieph Tekie

....

Interviewees who requested that I not identify them
for reasons of security were given fictional names or had
their words absorbed into general or anonymous contexts.

FICTIONAL NAMES

Abraha Alemseged

Tesfaya Kumera

Shigut Kumera

Gelete Gemechu

Sahra Khalid

NOTES

ONE: AT "HOME" IN THE PACIFIC NORTHWEST

1   The English spelling of Eritrean and Ethiopian words varies, but unless I am quoting, I use the most common forms found in academic texts. Where politics defines spelling, I apply the spelling of the people quoted, as is the case for the use of "Tigre," "Tigrinya," and "Tigray." Although the speech of all three groups derives from the same language—Tigrinya means "the language of the Tigre"—Eritreans understand "Tigrayans" as those living in the Tigray province of Ethiopia, "Tigrinyas" as Semitic people from the highlands of Eritrea, and "Tigres" as related speakers in Eritrea who are mostly Muslim. To Ethiopians, however, "Tigrayans" refers to those in Tigray and anywhere else where the language is spoken.

2   Nuruddin Farah, *Maps* (New York: Penguin, 2000), 258.

3   Ibid., 174.

4   Catherine Besteman, *Unraveling Somalia: Race, Violence, and the Legacy of Slavery* (Philadelphia: University of Pennsylvania Press, 1999), 123.

5   Mawi Asgedom, *Of Beetles and Angels: A Boy's Remarkable Journey from a Refugee Camp to Harvard* (New York: Little, Brown, 2001), 17.

6   Atsuko Karin Matsuoka and John Sorenson, *Ghosts and Shadows: Construction of Identity and Community in an African Diaspora* (Toronto: University of Toronto Press, 2001).

7   Nuruddin Farah, *Yesterday, Tomorrow: Voices from the Somali Diaspora* (New York: Cassell, 2000).

8   Ibid., 188.

9   Rima Berns McGown, *Muslims in the Diaspora: The Somali Communities of London and Toronto* (Toronto: University of Toronto Press, 1999).

10 Andrew Rice, "The Long Interrogation," *New York Times*, June 4, 2006, magazine section, 50–57.

11 Robin Cohen, *Global Diasporas: An Introduction* (Seattle: University of Washington Press, 1997).

12 Ahmed I. Samatar, "Beginning Again: From Refugee to Citizen," *Bildhaan* 4 (2004): 1–17.

TWO: WITHIN THE AMERICAN GAZE

1 Half a million people, including children, died during the Red Terror massacre, which lasted until 1978. In 2007, the Ethiopian Supreme Court tried Mengistu in absentia for genocide, and when Zimbabwe, to which he'd fled, refused to extradite him, he was sentenced to death in 2008.

2 Okbazghi Yohannes, *Eritrea, a Pawn in World Politics* (Gainesville: University of Florida Press, 1991), 234.

3 Nicholas Clapp, *Sheba: Through the Desert in Search of the Legendary Queen* (New York: Houghton Mifflin, 2001), 221.

4 Alemseged Abbay, *Identity Jilted or Re-Imagining Identity? The Divergent Paths of the Eritrean and Tigrayan Nationalist Struggle* (Lawrenceville, N.J.: Red Sea Press, 1998) 223–25, 163.

5 Joseph E. Harris, *African-American Reactions to War in Ethiopia, 1936–1941* (Baton Rouge: Louisiana State University Press, 1994), 1–2.

6 Some of the most oft-quoted references are Genesis 2:13 (relationship of the Garden of Eden to Ethiopia); Numbers 12 (marriage of Moses to an Ethiopian woman); Psalms 68:31 (Ethiopia would soon stretch out her hands unto God); Amos 9:7 (children of Israel likened by God to the children of Ethiopia); and Acts 8 (the Apostle Philip baptized the Ethiopian Jew on his way to worship in Jerusalem).

7 For a detailed account of this period and a discussion of the reasons for Ethiopia's failure, see Bahru Zewde, *History of Modern Ethiopia, 1855–1991*, Eastern African Studies, 2d ed. (Athens: Ohio University Press, 2001), 153–58.

8 Chinweizu, *Decolonizing the African Mind* (Lagos, Nigeria: Pero, 1987).

9 Michela Wrong, *"I Didn't Do It for You": How the World Betrayed a Small Nation* (New York: HarperCollins, 2005), 99, 131–36.

10 "Somali Merchants Finally Receive Compensation for Government Raid," ACLU Washington, July 22, 2004, www.aclu-wa.org/Issues/otherissues/News-SomaliSettlement.html (accessed August 30, 2005).

11 Roland Marchal, "Islamic Political Dynamics in the Somali Civil War," *Islamism and Its Enemies in the Horn of Africa,* ed. Alex de Waal (Bloomington: Indiana University Press, 2004) 125.

12 Ioan M. Lewis, *Blood and Bone: The Call of Kinship in Somali Society* (Lawrenceville, N.J.: Red Sea Press, 1994), 20.

THREE: WITH EYES OPEN

1   Bartamaha, "Seattle Somali Community Response to Terrorism," http://www.bartamaha.com (accessed November 2, 2009).

FOUR: HAVING THE LAST WORD

1   Alan Parry and Robert E. Doan, *Story Re-Visions: Narrative Therapy in the Postmodern World* (New York: Guildford Press, 1994), 27.

2   Jacobo Timerman, *Prisoner without a Name, Cell without a Number*, trans. Toby Talbot (Madison: University of Wisconsin Press, 2002).

3   Matsuoka and Sorenson, *Ghosts and Shadows*, 29–30.

4   Harold G. Marcus, *A History of Ethiopia*. Updated ed. (Berkeley: University of California Press, 1994), 227.

5   Bahru Zewde, *A History of Modern Ethiopia, 1855–1991* (Athens: Ohio University Press, 2001), 261.

6   Among his alleged victims were noncombatants such as prominent businessman Garag Mohammed Said Gom'ad and Sultan Ahmed Mohammed Hurre, a British citizen who opposed the extension of Abdullahi's presidency in Puntland. Abdullahi's militia has also been implicated in the murder of Colonel Farah Dheere and the traditional leader Malaaq Seemow Abdi Garuunin.

7   Maxamed D. Afrax, "The Mirror of Culture: Somali Dissolution Seen through Oral Expression," in *The Somali Challenge: From Catastrophe to Renewal*, ed. Ahmed I. Samatar (London: Lynn Rienner, 1994), 248.

8   Dominique Jacquin-Berdal and Martin Plaut, eds., *Unfinished Business: Ethiopia and Eritrea at War* (Trenton, N.J.: Red Sea Press, 2004).

9   Ibid., 17.

10   See articles criticizing the United States and the United Nations for not stepping in and settling things before war breaks out once again: Dan Connell, "Eritrea/Ethiopia War Looms as Washington Watches and Waits," *Foreign Policy in Focus*, January 21, 2004; and Yohannes Woldemariam, "UN's Double Standard vis-à-vis Eritrea, Ethiopia Border War," Global Policy Forum, *Sudan Tribune*, December, 16, 2005.

11   Nega Mezlekia, *Notes from the Hyena's Belly* (New York: Picador, 2000), 131.

12   Ayaan Hirsi Ali, *Infidel* (New York: Free Press, 2007), 58.

13   Abdurahman Mahdi, "The Ogaden People: Past and Present," *Sidamo Concern* 5, no. 1 (2000), http://sidamaconcern.com/articles/ (accessed January 19, 2010).

14 Marcus, *A History of Ethiopia*, 240.

15 Ibid., 254–55.

16 Wrong, *"I Didn't Do It for You,"* 371.

17 Marcus, *A History of Ethiopia*, 255; Jacquin-Berdal and Plaut, *Unfinished Business*, 118.

18 Jacquin-Berdal and Plaut, *Unfinished Business*, 118.

19 Ibid., 116–17.

20 Hirsi Ali, *Infidel*, 157.

FIVE: CULTURAL AND ECONOMIC RIVALS

1 Alemseged Abbay, *Identity Jilted or Re-Imagining Identity? The Divergent Paths of the Eritrean and Tigrayan Nationalist Struggles* (Lawrenceville, N.J.: Red Sea Press, 1998), 77–78.

2 Marcus, *History of Ethiopia*, 225–27.

3 Abbay, *Identity Jilted*, 87–94, 5.

4 Lidwien Kapteijns, "Women and the Crisis of Communal Identity: The Cultural Construction of Gender in Somali History," in *The Somali Challenge: From Catastrophe to Renewal?* ed. Ahmed I. Samatar (London: Lynne Rienner, 1994), 227.

5 Africa Watch Committee, *Somalia: A Government at War with Its Own People: Testimonies about the Killings and the Conflict in the North* (New York: Africa Watch Committee, 1990), 89–94, 69.

6 Ibid., 207.

7 Jamal Gabobe, *Love & Memory: Reflections of an Exile from Somaliland* (Seattle: Cune Press, 1996).

8 Nuruddin Farah, *Yesterday, Tomorrow*, 5.

9 U.S. State Department, "Ethiopian Human Rights Practices 1993," January 31, 1994, http://dosfan.lib.uic.edu/ERC/democracy/1993_hrp_report/93hrp_report_africa/Ethiopia.html (accessed November 13, 2009).

10 Ibid.

11 David Dickson, "Political Islam in Sub-Saharan Africa: The Need for a New Research and Diplomatic Agenda," U.S. Institute of Peace, May 2005 Special Report No. 140, http://www.usip.org.

12 Nuruddin Farah, "America, Spare Somalia for God's Sake," *The Monitor* (Kampala), January 2, 2002

13 Kay Kaufman Shelemay, who studied the music of the Falasha, claims that they are not Jewish at all. See *A Song of Longing: An Ethiopian Journey* (Chicago: University of Illinois Press, 1991), in which she describes them as

an Ethiopian people of indigenous Agan stock who "came into contact with fringe Ethiopian monastic groups in the late Middle Ages and adopted the eclectic Judaic religious traditions that the monks brought with them" (144).

14   Marcus, *History of Ethiopia*, 214.

15   Ben Parker with Abraham Woldegiorgis, *Ethiopia: Breaking New Ground* (Oxford: Oxfam, 2003), 61.

16   For more on the economic conflict, see David Styan, "Twisting Ethio-Eritrean Economic Ties: Misperceptions of War and the Misplaced Priorities of Peace, 1997–2002," in *Unfinished Business: Ethiopia and Eritrea at War*, ed. Dominique Jacquin-Berdal and Martin Plaut (Trenton, N.J.: Red Sea Press, 2004), 177–200.

17   Parker, *Ethiopia*, 61.

18   Tekeste Negash and Kjetil Tronvoll, *Brothers at War: Making Sense of the Eritrean-Ethiopian War* (Athens: Ohio University Press, 2000), 44.

19   Alex de Waal, *Islamism*, 205, 213.

20   "Ogaden Rebels Challenge Ethiopia Oil Deal," Afrol News, March 12, 2007, http://www.afrol.com/articles/22623 (accessed May 20, 2007).

21   Alex de Waal, "Class and Power in a Stateless Somalia," Social Science Research Council, February 20, 2007, http://hornofafrica.ssrc.org/dewaal (accessed April 13, 2007).

SIX: THE CHALLENGERS WITHIN

1   Francesco Declich, "Fostering Ethnic Reinvention: Gender Impact of Forced Migration on Bantu Somali Refugees in Kenya," *Cahiers d études africaines* 157 (2000), 25–54, quoting E. Cerulli, "Somalia: Scritti editi e inediti 1," Rome (1957), 161–63, http://etudesafricaines.revues.org/index2.html (accessed November 17, 2009).

2   Besteman, *Unraveling Somalia*, 236.

3   See the exchange between Catherine Besteman and I. M. Lewis about the causes of the civil war, in *Cultural Anthropology* 13, no. 1 (1998), 109–20.

4   See, for example, E. Ullendorf, *The Ethiopians* (London: Oxford University Press, 1960). Also the U.S. Library of Congress Country Study, "Oromo Migrations and their Impact," http://countrystudies.us/ethiopia/11.htm (accessed November 23, 2009).

5   Lemmu Baissa, "Contending Nationalisms in the Ethiopian Empire State and the Oromo Struggle for Self-Determination," in *Oromo Nationalism and the Ethiopian Discourse: The Search for Freedom and Democracy*, ed. Asafa Jalata (Lawrenceville, N.J.: Red Sea Press, 1998), 83.

6   John Sorenson, "Ethiopian Discourse and Oromo Nationalism," in Jalata, *Oromo Nationalism*, 229.

7   See *Gada: Three Approaches to the Study of an African Society* by Asmerom Legesse, who received an honorary award from the OLF in 2009 for his work on the *gada* system and on Oromo history.

8   Asafa Jalata, "The Struggle for Knowledge: The Case of Emergent Oromo Studies," in *Oromo Nationalism*, 258–59, quoting Donald N. Levine, *Greater Ethiopia: The Evolution of a Multi-ethnic Society* (Chicago: University of Chicago Press, 1974), 26, and "Meles Zenawi and the Politics of Identity," *The Ethiopian Review* (1992): 16, and Ullendorff, *The Ethiopians*, 76.

9   Tesfaye claims Oromo identity for Menelik's mother. Menelik's father, Haile Malekot, at the age of eighteen impregnated a palace servant girl named Egigayahu whom he later married (Marcus, *History of Ethiopia*, 66). Although historical accounts claim there is controversy over Menelik's birth, they do not confirm his half-Oromo heritage. Tesfaye also claims that Selassie was of Oromo extraction, his mother having come from Wollo, which was Oromo, but became Amhara when people there lost their language. See also Henze, *Layers of Time*, 189, who notes, too, that Selassie's mother was Muslim.

10 Jalata, "The Struggle," 270.

11 For further information on Oromo religion, see Lambert Bartels, *Oromo Religion: Myth and Rites of the Western Oromo of Ethiopia, an Attempt to Understand* (Berlin: Dietrich Reimer Verlag, 1983).

12 Jalata, *Oromo Nationalism*, 8.

13 For further information on Oromo history and politics, see Mohammed Hassen; Asaf Jalata; and Bonnie Holcomb and Sissai Ibssa. *Oromia: An Introduction* is also interesting, but its authors are a group of Oromo nationalists who write under the pseudonym Gadaa Melbaa.

SEVEN: WOMEN SPEAK OUT

1   Maria H. Brons, *Society, Security, Sovereignty and the State in Somalia: From Statelessness to Statelessness?* (Utrecht: International Books, 2001), 198–99; Lidwien Kapteijns, "Women and the Crisis of Communal Identity," 229.

2   Francesca Declich, "Fostering Ethnic Reinvention," 28.

3   Virginia Lee Barnes, *Aman*, 196.

4   Waris Dirie and Cathleen Miller, *Desert Flower: The Extraordinary Journey of a Desert Nomad* (New York: Perennial, 2001).

5   "Female genital mutilation," http://www.unicef.org/somalia/cpp_136.html
    (accessed December, 3, 2009).

6   Martha Kuwee Kumsa, "Oromo Women and the Oromo National Move-
    ment: Dilemmas, Problems, and Prospects for True Liberation," in *Oromo
    Nationalism and the Ethiopian Discourse*, ed. Asafa Jalata (Lawrenceville, N.J.:
    Red Sea Press, 1998), 164, 158.

7   David McGraw Schuchman and Colleen McDonald, "Somali Mental
    Health," *Bildhaan* 4 (2004): 67–71.

8   http://www.mbali.info/doc384.htm (accessed November 26, 2010).

9   Lidwien Kapteijns with Maryan Omar Ali, *Women's Voices in a Man's
    World: Women and the Pastoral Tradition in Northern Somali Orature,
    c. 1899–1980* (Portsmouth, N.H.: Heinemann, 1999), 104–55.

10 Brons, *Society, Security, Sovereignty*, 199–200.

CONCLUSION: NEW AMERICAN NARRATIVES

1   Amnesty International USA, press release, "Ethiopia: Treason Trial of
    Prisoners of Conscience Opens in Addis Ababa," May 2, 2006, http://
    www.amnestyusa.org/news/document.do?id=ENGAFR25015
    2006 (accessed November 22, 2006).

2   Ginny Hill, "Somali Refugees Brave Sea Passage to Escape Insurgency,"
    Christian Science Monitor, April, 23, 2007, http://www.ginnyhill.
    co.uk/?p=161 (accessed December 15, 2009).

3   Lidwien Kapteijns, "Educating Immigrant Youth in the United States:
    An Exploration of the Somali Case," *Bildhaan* 4 (2004): 24.

4   Samatar, "Beginning Again."

BIBLIOGRAPHY

Abbay, Alemseged. *Identity Jilted or Re-Imagining Identity? The Divergent Paths of the Eritrean and Tigrayan Nationalist Struggles.* Lawrenceville, N.J.: Red Sea Press, 1998.

Adera, Tadesse, and Ali Jimale Ahmed, eds. *Silence Is Not Golden: A Critical Anthology of Ethiopian Literature.* Lawrenceville, N.J.: Red Sea Press, 1995.

Afrax, Maxamed D. "The Mirror of Culture: Somali Dissolution Seen through Oral Expression." In *The Somali Challenge: From Catastrophe to Renewal,* edited by Ahmed I. Samatar, 233–51. London: Lynne Rienner, 1994.

Africa Watch Committee. *Somalia: A Government at War with Its Own People: Testimonies about the Killings and the Conflict in the North.* New York: Africa Watch Committee, 1990.

Ahmed, Ali Jimale, ed. *The Invention of Somalia.* Lawrenceville, N.J.: Red Sea Press, 1995.

Ahmed, Christine Choi. "Finely Etched Chattel: The Invention of a Somali Woman." In *The Invention of Somalia,* edited by Ali Jimale Ahmed, 157–90. Lawrenceville, N.J.: Red Sea Press, 1995.

Ali, Mohammed Hassen. "Some Aspects of Oromo History That Have Been Misunderstood." *The Oromo Commentary: Bulletin for Critical Analysis of Current Affairs in the Horn of Africa* III, no. 2 (1993): 24–31.

Anderson, Benedict. *Imagined Communities.* New York: Verso, 1991.

Arthur, John A. *Invisible Sojourner: African Immigrant Diaspora in the United States.* Westport, Conn.: Praeger, 2000.

Asgedom, Mawi. *The Code: The 5 Secrets of Teen Success.* New York: Little, Brown, 2003.

———. *Of Beetles and Angels: A Boy's Remarkable Journey from a Refugee Camp to Harvard.* New York: Little, Brown, 2001.

Atkinson, Robert. *The Life Story Interview: Qualitative Research Methods.* Qualitative Research Series 44. Thousand Oaks, Calif.: Sage Publications, 1998.

Baissa, Lemmu. "Contending Nationalisms in the Ethiopian Empire State and the Oromo Struggle for Self-Determination." In *Oromo Nationalism and the Ethiopian Discourse: The Search for Freedom and Democracy*, 79–108. Lawrenceville, N.J.: Red Sea Press, 1998.

Bakhtin, M. M. *Art and Answerability*. Edited by Michael Holquist and Vadim Liapunov. Translated by Vadim Liapunov. Austin: University of Texas Press, 1990.

———. *The Dialogic Imagination*. Edited by Michael Holquist. Translated by Caryl Emerson and Michael Holquist. Austin: University of Texas Press, 1981.

Barnes, Virginia Lee. *Aman: The Story of a Somali Girl, as told to Virginia Lee Barnes and Janice Boddy*. New York: Vintage, 1995.

Bartels, Lambert. *Oromo Religion: Myths and Rites of the Western Oromo of Ethiopia, an Attempt to Understand*. Berlin: Dietrich Reimer Verlag, 1983.

Battuta, Ibn. *The Travels of Ibn Battuta, ad 1325–1354, translated with revisions and notes from the Arabic text edited by C. Defrémery and B. R. Sanguinetti, by H. A. R. Gibb*. Vol. 2. Second Series, no. 117. Cambridge: Cambridge University Press, 1962.

Bhabha, Homi K., ed. *Nation and Narration*. New York: Routledge, 1990.

Besteman, Catherine. "The Invention of Gosha: Slavery, Colonialism, and Stigma in Somali History." In *The Invention of Somalia*, edited by Ali Jimale Ahmed, 43–62. Lawrenceville, N.J.: Red Sea Press, 1995.

———. *Unraveling Somalia: Race, Violence, and the Legacy of Slavery*. Philadelpia: University of Pennsylvania Press, 1999.

Besteman, Catherine, and Lee Cassanelli, eds. *The Struggle for Land in Southern Somalia: The War behind the War*. Boulder, Colo.: Westview Press, 1996.

Boness, Stefan. *Asmara: The Frozen City*. Berlin: Jovis Verlag, 2006.

Breasted, James Henry. *Ancient Records of Egypt: Historical Documents*. Vol. 2. Chicago: University of Chicago Press, 1906.

Brison, Susan J. "Trauma Narratives and the Remaking of the Self." In *Acts of Memory: Cultural Recall in the Present*, edited by Mieke Bal, Jonathan Crewe, and Leo Spitzer, 39–54. Hanover, N.H.: University Press of New England, 1999.

Brons, Maria H. *Society, Security, Sovereignty and the State in Somalia: From Statelessness to Statelessness?* Utrecht: International Books, 2001.

Brooks, Miguel F., ed. and trans. *Kebra Nagast (The Glory of Kings): The True Ark of the Covenant*. Lawrenceville, N.J.: Red Sea Press, 1996.

Bulcha, Mekuria. *The Making of the Oromo Diaspora: A Historical Sociology of Forced Migration*. Minneapolis: Kirk House, 2002.

———. "Onesimos Nasib's Pioneering Contributions to Oromo Writing."
   Nordic Journal of African Studies 4, no. 1 (1995): 36–59.
Burton, Richard F. *First Footsteps in Africa: or, An Exploration of Harar.* Edited
   by Isabel Burton. New York: Dover, 1987.
Chait, Sandra, and Ghirmai Negash. "Teaching Multicultural Life-History
   Writing Texts through Technology's Third Space: Reflections on a
   University of Washington–University of Asmara Collaboration." In
   Teaching Life Writing Texts, edited by Miriam Fuchs and Craig Howes,
   239–51. Options for Teaching series. New York: Modern Language
   Association, 2007.
Chinweizu. *Decolonizing the African Mind.* Lagos, Nigeria: Pero, 1987.
Clapp, Nicholas. *Sheba: Through the Desert in Search of the Legendary Queen.*
   New York: Houghton Mifflin, 2001.
Cliffe, Lionel. "Regional Implications of the Ethiopia-Eritrea War." In
   Unfinished Business: Ethiopia and Eritrea at War, edited by Dominique
   Jacquin-Berdal and Martin Plaut, 151–68. Trenton, N.J.: Red Sea
   Press, 2004.
Coffey, Amanda. *The Ethnographic Self: Fieldwork and the Representation of
   Identity.* London: Sage Publications, 1999.
Cohen, Robin. *Global Diasporas: An Introduction.* Seattle: University of
   Washington Press, 1997.
Connell, Dan. *Against All Odds: A Chronicle of the Eritrean Revolution.* Trenton,
   N.J.: Red Sea Press, 1993.
———. *Conversations with Eritrean Political Prisoners.* Trenton, N.J.: Red Sea
   Press, 2005.
———, ed. *Eritrea: A Country Handbook.* Asmara, Eritrea: Ministry of
   Information, 2002.
Courlander, Harold, and Wolf Leslau. *The Fire on the Mountain and Other
   Stories from Ethiopia and Eritrea.* New York: Henry Holt, 1950.
Crewe, Jonathan. "Recalling Adamastor: Literature as Cultural Memory in a
   'White' South Africa." In *Acts of Memory: Cultural Recall in the Present*,
   edited by Mieke Bal, Jonathan Crewe, and Leo Spitzer, 75–86. Hanover,
   N.H.: University Press of New England, 1999.
Currie, Mark. *Postmodern Narrative Theory.* New York: Palgrave, 1998.
D'Alisera, JoAnn. *An Imagined Geography: Sierra Leonean Muslims in America.*
   Philadelphia: University of Pennsylvania Press, 2004.
de Waal, Alex. "Class and Power in a Stateless Somalia." Social Science
   Research Council. February 20, 2007. http://hornofafrica.ssrc.org/dewaal
   (accessed April 13, 2007).

————, ed. *Islamism and Its Enemies in the Horn of Africa*. Bloomington: Indiana University Press, 2004.

Declich, Francesca. "Fostering Ethnic Reinvention: Gender Impact of Forced Migration on Bantu Somali Refugees in Kenya." *Cahiers d études africaines* 157 (2000): 25–54. Quoting E. Cerulli, "Somalia: Scritti editi e inediti 1," Rome (1957): 161–63. http://etudesafricaines.revues.org/index2.html (accessed November 18, 2009).

————. "Identity, Dance and Islam among People with Bantu Origins in Riverine Areas of Somalia." In *The Invention of Somalia*, edited by Ali Jimale Ahmed, 191–222. Lawrenceville, N.J.: Red Sea Press, 1995.

Demoz, Abraham. "State Policy and the Medium of Expression." In *Silence Is Not Golden: A Critical Anthology of Ethiopian Literature*, edited by Taddesse Adera and Ali Jimale Ahmed, 15–38. Lawrenceville, N.J.: Red Sea Press, 1995.

Derrida, Jacques. *Of Grammatology*. Translated by Gayatri Chakravorty Spivak. Baltimore, Md.: Johns Hopkins University Press, 1976.

D'Haem, Jeanne. *The Last Camel: True Stories of Somalia*. Lawrenceville, N.J.: Red Sea Press, 1997.

Dirie, Waris, and Cathleen Miller. *Desert Flower: The Extraordinary Journey of a Desert Nomad*. New York: Perennial, 2001.

Donham, Donald L. *Marxist Modern: An Ethnographic History of the Ethiopian Revolution*. Berkeley: University of California Press, 1999.

Eno, Omar. "Slavery, Stigma, and Legacy: The Case of the Wazigwa Diaspora and the Indigenous Bantu/Jareer People in Southern Somalia (1850–2000)." PhD diss., York University, Toronto.

Farah, Nuruddin. "America, Spare Somalia for God's Sake." *Monitor* (Kampala), January 2, 2002.

————. *Maps*. New York: Penguin, 2000.

————. *Yesterday, Tomorrow: Voices from the Somali Diaspora*. New York: Cassell, 2000.

Gabobe, Jamal. *Love & Memory: Reflections of an Exile from Somaliland*. Seattle: Cune Press, 1996.

Haile, Rebecca. *Held at a Distance: My Rediscovery of Ethiopia*. Chicago: Academy Chicago Publishers, 2007.

Hanghe, Ahmed Artan. *Folk Tales from Somalia*. Uppsala, Sweden: Nordic Africa Institute, 1988.

Harris, Joseph E. *African-American Reactions to War in Ethiopia, 1936–1941*. Baton Rouge: Louisiana State University Press, 1994.

Hassan, Ahmed I. "Them Southerners and Us Northeners Are Not the Same People. Period." *Somaliland Times*, October 12, 2002. http://www. somalilandtimes.net/Archive/Archive/00003800.htm (accessed November 9, 2006).

Hendrix, H. "Historiographical Anecdotes as Depositories and Vehicles of Cultural Memory." In *Genres as Repositories of Cultural Memory*, edited by Hendrik van Gorp and Ulla Musarra-Schroeder, 17–26. Atlanta, Ga.: Radopi, 2000.

Henze, Paul B. *Layers of Time: A History of Ethiopia*. New York: Palgrave, 2000.

———. *The United States and the Horn of Africa: History and Current Challenge.* Santa Monica, Calif.: Rand, 1990.

Hirsch, Marianne. "Projected Memory: Holocaust Photographs in Personal and Public Fantasy." In *Acts of Memory: Cultural Recall in the Present*, edited by Mieke Bal, Jonathan Crewe, and Leo Spitzer, 3–23. Hanover, N.H.: University Press of New England, 1999.

Hirsi Ali, Ayaan. *Infidel.* New York: Free Press, 2007.

Hofmann, Steven R. "The Divergent Paths of Somalia and Somaliland: The Effects of Centralization on Indigenous Institutions of Self-Governance and Post-Collapse Reconciliation and State-Building." Paper presented at the Institutional Analysis and Development Mini-Conference, April 27 and 29, 2002.

Holcomb, Bonnie K., and Sisai Ibssa. *The Invention of Ethiopia: The Making of a Dependent Colonial State in Northeast Africa.* Trenton, N.J.:Red Sea Press, 1990.

Holstein, James A., and Jaber F. Gubrium. *The Self We Live By: Narrative Identity in a Postmodern World.* Oxford: Oxford University Press, 2000.

Hussein, Ikram. *Teenage Refugees from Somalia Speak Out.* In Their Own Voices Series. New York: Rosen, 1997.

Jacquin-Berdal, Dominique, and Martin Plaut, eds. *Unfinished Business: Ethiopia and Eritrea at War.* Trenton, N.J: Red Sea Press, 2004.

Jalata, Asafa. "The Emergence of Oromo Nationalism and the Ethiopian Reaction." In *Oromo Nationalism and the Ethiopian Discourse: The Search for Freedom and Democracy*, edited by Asafa Jalata, 1–26. Lawrenceville, N.J.: Red Sea Press, 1998.

———. *Oromia and Ethiopia: State Formation and Ethnonational Conflict, 1868– 1992.* Trenton, N.J.: Red Sea Press, 2005.

———. "The Struggle for Knowledge: The Case of Emergent Oromo Studies." *Oromo Nationalism and the Ethiopian Discourse: The Search for Freedom and*

Democracy, edited by Asafa Jalata, 253–90. Lawrenceville, N.J.: Red Sea Press, 1998.

Johnson, John William. *"heelloy": Modern Poetry and Songs of the Somali*. London: Haan Publishing, 1996.

———. "Power, Marginality and Somali Oral Poetry: Case Studies in the Dynamics of Tradition." In *Power, Marginality and African Oral Literature*, edited by Graham Furniss and Liz Gunner, 111–21. New York: Cambridge University Press, 1995.

Johnson, Robert. International Rescue Committee. Interview by author. IRC office, Seattle, April 4, 2006.

Kacandes, Irene. "Narrative Witnessing as Memory Work: Reading Getrude Kolmar's 'A Jewish Mother.'" In *Acts of Memory: Cultural Recall in the Present*, edited by Mieke Bal, Jonathan Crewe, and Leo Spitzer, 55–71. Hanover, N.H.: University Press of New England, 1999.

Kapteijns, Lidwien. "Women and the Crisis of Communal Identity: The Cultural Construction of Gender in Somali History." In *The Somali Challenge: From Catastrophe to Renewal?* edited by Ahmed I. Samatar, 211–32. Boulder, Colo.: Lynne Rienner, 1994.

Kapteijns, Lidwien, with Abukar Arman. "Educating Immigrant Youth in the US: An Exploration of the Somali Case." *Bildhaan V4* (2004): 18–43.

Kapteijns, Lidwien, with Maryan Omar Ali. *Women's Voices in a Man's World: Women and the Pastoral Tradition in Northern Somali Orature, c. 1899–1980*. Portsmouth, N.H.: Heinemann, 1999.

Kastoryano, Riva. *Negotiating Identities: States and Immigrants in France and Germany*. Translated by Barbara Harshav. Princeton, N.J.: Princeton University Press, 2002.

Keneally, Thomas. *To Asmara*. New York: Warner, 1990.

Kumsa, Kuwee. "Oromo Women and the Oromo National Movement: Dilemmas, Problems and Prospects for True Liberation." In *Oromo Nationalism and the Ethiopian Discourse*, edited by Asafa Jalata, 153–82. Lawrenceville, N.J.: Red Sea Press, 1998.

Kusow, Abdi M. "The Somali Origin: Myth or Reality." In *The Invention of Somalia*, edited by Ali Jamale Ahmed, 81–106. Trenton, N.J.: Red Sea Press, 1995.

Lacan, Jacques. *Écrits: A Selection*. Translated by Alan Sheridan. New York: W. W. Norton, 1977.

Laitin, David D., and Said S. Samatar. *Oral Poetry and Somali Nationalism: The Case of Sayyid Mahammad Abdille Hasan*. Cambridge: Cambridge University Press, 1982.

————. *Somalia: Nation in Search of a State.* Boulder, Colo.: Westview Press, 1987.

Langer, Elinor. *A Hundred Little Hitlers.* New York: Metropolitan, 2003.

Lata, Leenco. *The Horn of Africa as Common Homeland: The State and Self-determination in the Era of Heightened Globalization.* Waterloo, Calif.: Wilfred Laurier University Press, 2004.

Legesse, Asmerom. *Gada: Three Approaches to the Study of African Society.* New York: Free Press, 1973.

Lewis, Herbert S. *A Galla Monarchy: Jimma Abba Jifar, Ethiopia, 1830–1932.* Madison: University of Wisconsin Press, 1965.

Lewis, Ioan M. *Blood and Bone: The Call of Kinship in Somali Society.* Lawrenceville, N.J.: Red Sea Press, 1994.

————. *Modern History of Somalia: Nation and State in the Horn of Africa.* Athens: Ohio University Press, 2002.

————. *The Modern History of Somaliland.* London: Weidenfeld and Nicolson, 1965.

————. *A Pastoral Democracy: A Study of Pastoralism and Politics amongst the Northern Somali of the Horn of Africa.* New York: Oxford University Press for the International African Institute, 1961.

Linde, Charlotte. *Life Stories: The Creation of Coherence.* New York: Oxford University Press, 1993.

Malkki, Liisa H. *Purity and Exile: Violence, Memory, and National Cosmology among Hutu Refugees in Tanzania.* Chicago: University of Chicago Press, 1995.

Marcus, Harold G. "Does the Past Have Any Authority in Ethiopia?" *Ethiopian Review* (1992): 18–21.

————. *A History of Ethiopia.* Updated ed. Berkeley: University of California Press, 2002 (originally published in 1994).

Matsuoka, Atsuko Karin, and John Sorenson. *Ghosts and Shadows: Construction of Identity and Community in an African Diaspora.* Toronto: University of Toronto Press, 2001.

McAdams, Dan P., Ruthellen Josselson, and Amia Lieblich, eds. *Identity and Story: Creating Self in Narrative.* Washington, D.C.: American Psychological Association, 2006.

McGown, Rima Berns. *Muslims in the Diaspora: The Somali Communities of London and Toronto.* Toronto: University of Toronto Press, 1999.

McGraw Schuchman, David, and Colleen McDonald. "Somali Mental Health." *Bildhaan V4* (2004): 65–77.

Medhanie, Tesfatsion. *Eritrea and Neighbours in the "New World Order":*

Geopolitics, Democracy and "Islamic Fundamentalism." Hamburg, Germany: Lit Verlag, 1994.

Melbaa, Gadaa. *Oromia: An Introduction to the History of the Oromo People.* Khartoum, Sudan: Gadaa Melbaa, 1988.

Mezlekia, Nega. *The God Who Begat a Jackal.* New York: Picador, 2002.

———. *Notes from the Hyena's Belly.* New York: Picador, 2000.

Miran, Jonathan. *Red Sea Citizens: Cosmopolitan Society and Cultural Change in Massawa.* Bloomington: Indiana University Press, 2009.

Mitchell, W. J. T., ed. *On Narrative.* Chicago: University of Chicago Press, 1981.

Molvaer, Reidulf Knut. *Tradition and Change in Ethiopia: Social and Cultural Life as Reflected in Amharic Fictional Literature, ca.1930–1974.* Leiden: Brill, 1980.

Morson, Gary Saul, ed. *Bakhtin: Essays and Dialogues on His Work.* Chicago: University of Chicago Press, 1986.

Morson, Gary Saul, and Caryl Emerson. *Mikhail Bakhtin: Creation of a Prosaics.* Stanford, Calif.: Stanford University Press, 1990.

Moussa, Helene. *Storm and Sanctuary: The Journey of Ethiopian and Eritrean Women Refugees.* Dundas, ON: Artemis Enterprises, 1993.

Mukhtar, Mohamed Haji. "Islam in Somali History: Fact and Fiction." In *The Invention of Somalia,* edited by Ali Jimale Ahmed, 1–28. Lawrenceville, N.J.: Red Sea Press, 1995.

Müller, Tanja R. *The Making of Elite Women: Revolution and Nation Building in Eritrea.* Afrika-Studiecentrum Series. Boston: Brill, 2005.

Negash, Ghirmai. *A History of Tigrinya Literature in Eritrea: The Oral and the Written, 1890–1991.* Research School of Asian, African and Amerindian Studies 75. Leiden, Netherlands: University of Leiden, 1999.

———. "Tradition of Tigrinya Oral Poetry in Eritrea." *Journal of Eritrean Studies* 11, nos. 1–2 (May–December 2003): 9–38.

Negash, Tekeste, and Kjetil Tronvoll. *Brothers at War: Making Sense of the Eritrean-Ethiopian War.* Athens: Ohio University Press, 2000.

Norrick, Neal R. *Conversational Narrative: Storytelling in Everyday Talk.* Current Issues in Linguistic Theory. Philadelphia: John Benjamins Publishing, 2000.

Parker, Ben, with Abraham Woldegiorgis. *Ethiopia: Breaking New Ground.* Revised ed. Oxford: Oxfam, 2003.

Parry, Alan, and Robert E. Doan. *Story Re-Visions: Narrative Therapy in the Postmodern World.* New York: Guildford Press, 1994.

Pateman, Roy. *Eritrea: Even the Stones Are Burning.* Lawrenceville, N.J.: Red Sea Press, 1990.

Patterson, Orlando. *The Ordeal of Integration.* Washington, D.C.: Counterpoint, 1998.

Pool, David. *From Guerrillas to Government: The Eritrean People's Liberation Front.* Athens: Ohio University Press, 2001.

Rice, Andrew. "The Long Interrogation." *New York Times Magazine,* June 4, 2006.

Riessman, Catherine Kohler. *Narrative Analysis:Qualitative Research Methods Series 30.* Newbury Park, Calif.: Sage Publications, 1993.

Rubin, Herbert J., and Irene S. Rubin. *Qualitative Interviewing: The Art of Hearing Data.* Thousand Oaks, Calif.: Sage Publications, 1995.

Samatar, Ahmed I. "Beginning Again: From Refugee to Citizen." *Bildhaan V4* (2004): 1–17.

————. "The Contours of Contemporary Somali Politics." In *The Horn of Africa and Arabia: Conference Papers,* edited by David A. Korn, Steven R. Dorr, and L. T. Neysa M. Slater, 27–39. Washington: Defense Academic Research Support Program, December 1990.

Schaffer, Kay, and Sidonie Smith. *Human Rights and Narrated Lives: The Ethics of Recognition.* New York: Palgrave Macmillan, 2004.

Shack, William A. *The Central Ethiopians: Amhara, Tigrina and Related Peoples.* Ethnographic survey of Africa. Northeastern Africa. London: International African Institute, 1974.

Shelemay, Kay Kaufman. *A Song of Longing: An Ethiopian Journey.* Chicago: University of Illinois Press, 1991.

Sorenson, John. "Ethiopian Discourse and Oromo Nationalism." In *Oromo Nationalism and the Ethiopian Discourse: The Search for Freedom and Democracy,* edited by Asafa Jalata, 223–52. Lawrenceville, N.J.: Red Sea Press, 1998.

————. *Imagining Ethiopia: Struggles for History and Identity in the Horn of Africa.* New Brunswick, N.J.: Rutgers University Press, 1993.

Stoller, Paul. *Money Has No Smell: The Africanization of New York City.* Chicago: University of Chicago Press, 2002.

Tesfagiorgis, Abeba. *A Painful Season & a Stubborn Hope: The Odyssey of an Eritrean Mother.* Lawrenceville, N.J.: Red Sea Press, 1992.

Timerman, Jacobo. *Prisoner without a Name, Cell without a Number.* Translated by Toby Talbot. Madison: University of Wisconsin Press, 2002.

Todorov, Tzvetan. *Mikhail Bakhtin: The Dialogic Principle.* Theory and History of Literature 13. Translated by Wlad Godzich. Minneapolis: University of Minnesota Press, 1984.

Ullendorf, E. *The Ethiopians: An Introduction to Country and People.* London: Oxford University Press, 1960.

Van Gorp, Hendrik, and Ulla Musarra-Schroeder, eds. *Genres as Repositories of Cultural Memory.* Atlanta, Ga.: Rodopi, 2000.

Van Lehman, Daniel J. Interview by author. Portland State University, April 7, 2005.

Van Lehman, Daniel, and Omar Eno. "The Somali Bantu: Their History and Culture." Cultural Profile 16. Washington D.C.: Center for Applied Linguistics, Cultural Orientation Resource Center, 2003. www.cal.org/co/bantu/somali_bantu.pdf (accessed November 11, 2010).

Wilson, Amrit. *Women and the Eritrean Revolution: The Challenge Road.* Trenton, N.J.: Red Sea Press, 1991.

Wrong, Michela. *"I Didn't Do It for You": How the World Betrayed a Small Nation.* New York: HarperCollins, 2005.

Yohannes, Okbazghi. *Eritrea, a Pawn in World Politics.* Gainesville: University of Florida Press, 1991.

Zewde, Bahru. *A History of Modern Ethiopia, 1855–1991.* Eastern African Studies. 2d ed. Athens: Ohio University Press, 2001.

Zunes, Stephen. "Somalia as a Military Target." *Foreign Policy in Focus,* January 11, 2002. http://www.fpif.org/articles/Somalia_as_a_military_target (accessed July 3, 2007).

INDEX